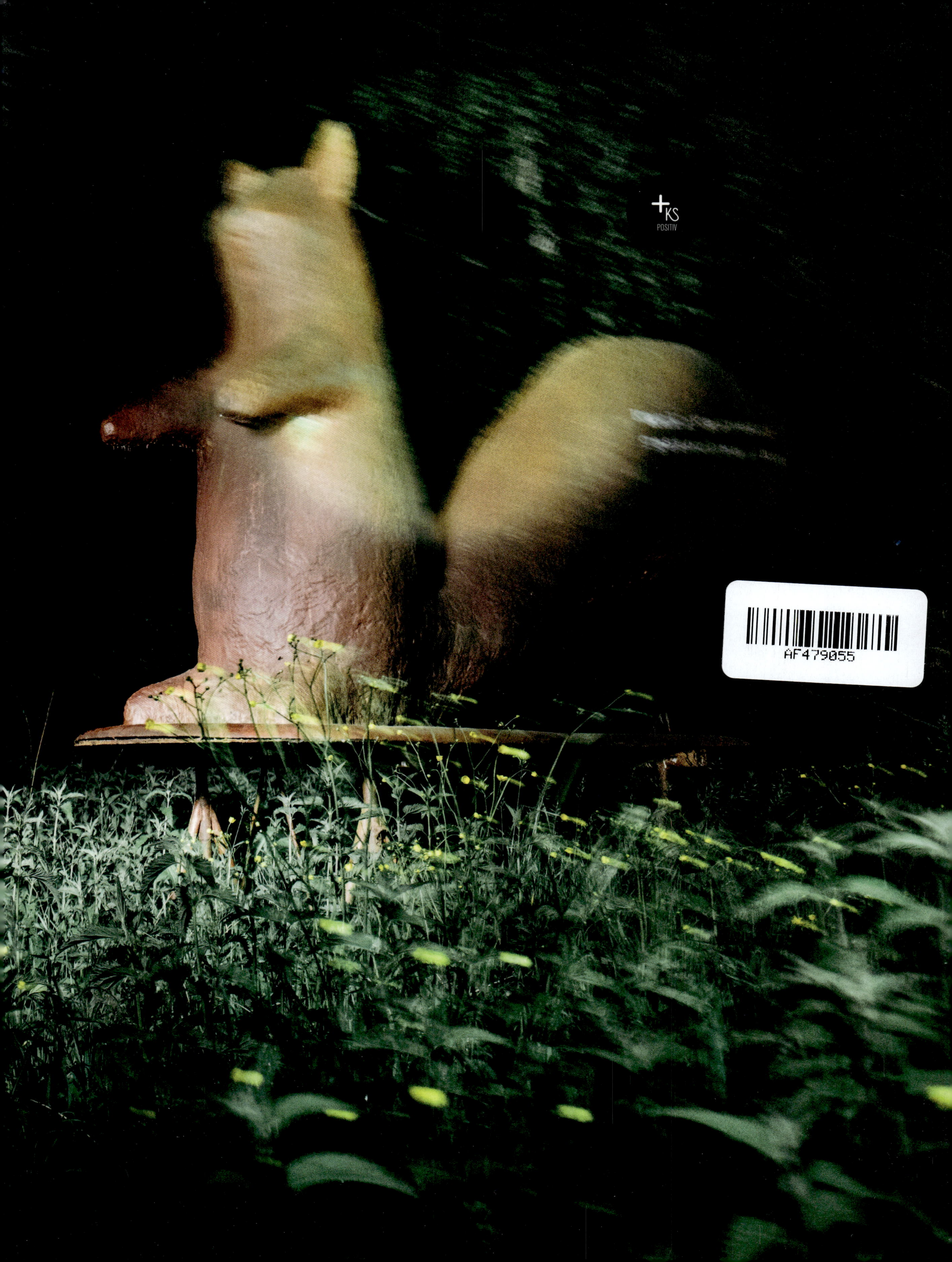
+KS
POSITIV

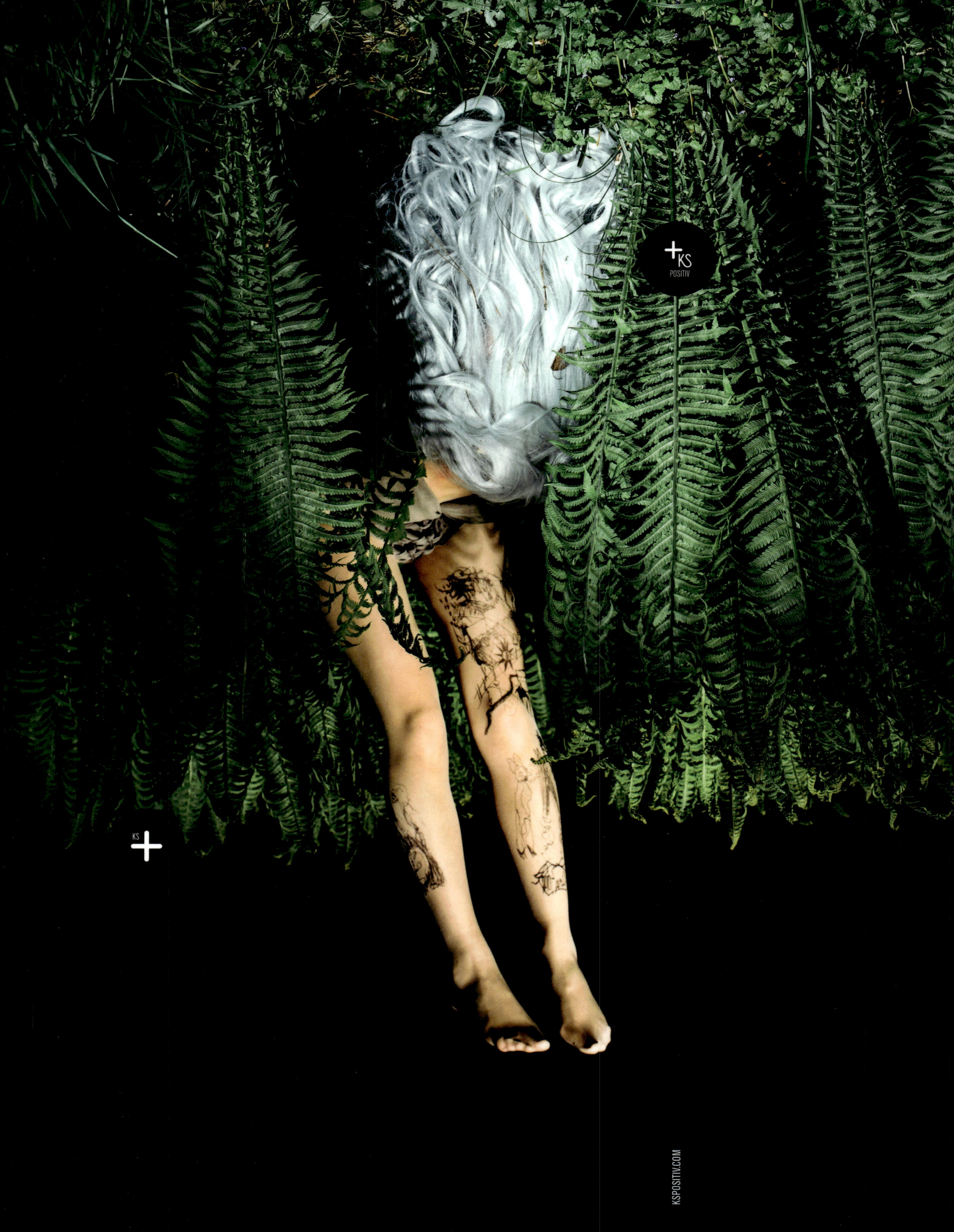

KS
POSITIV
KS
KSPOSITIV.COM

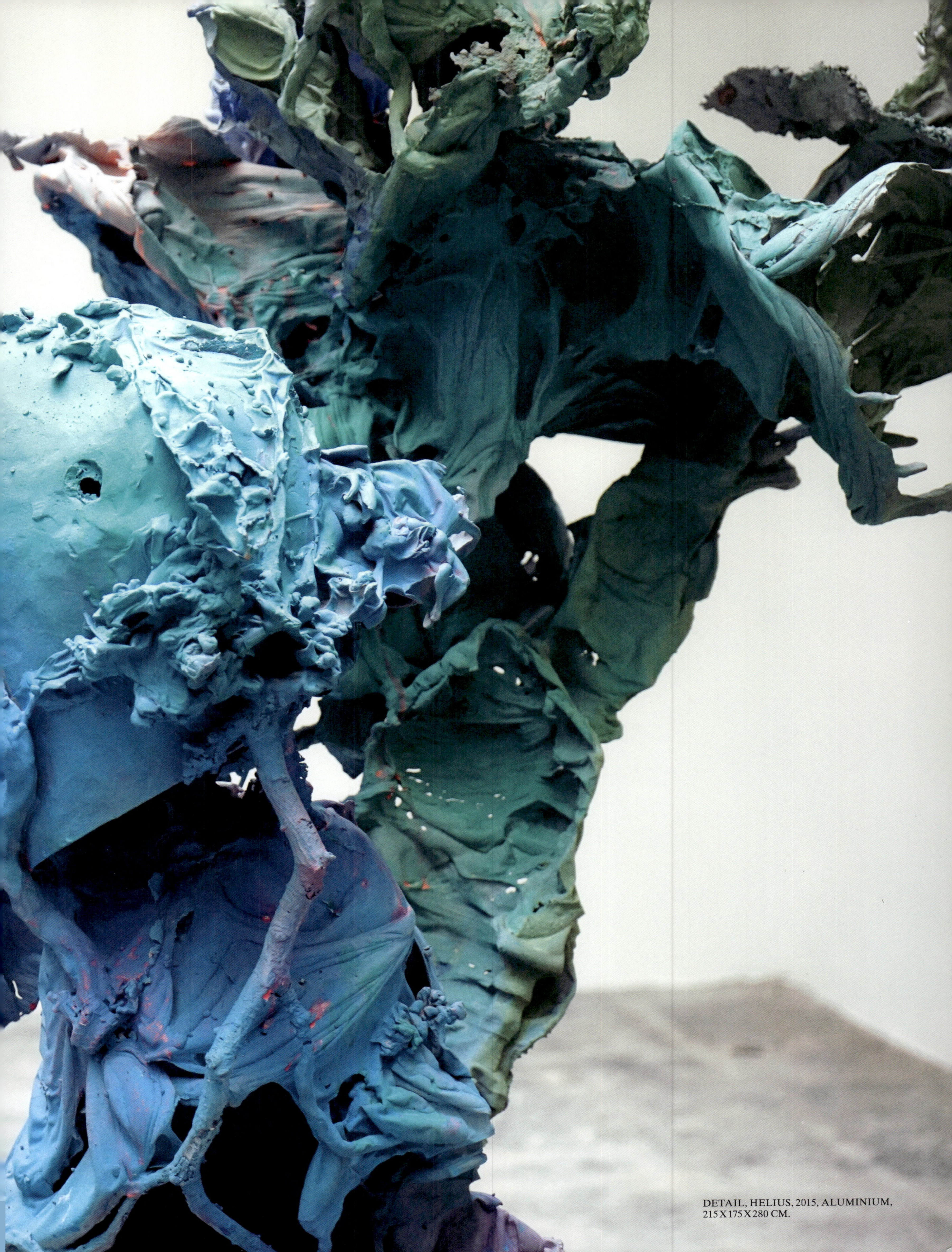

DETAIL, HELIUS, 2015, ALUMINIUM,
215 X 175 X 280 CM.

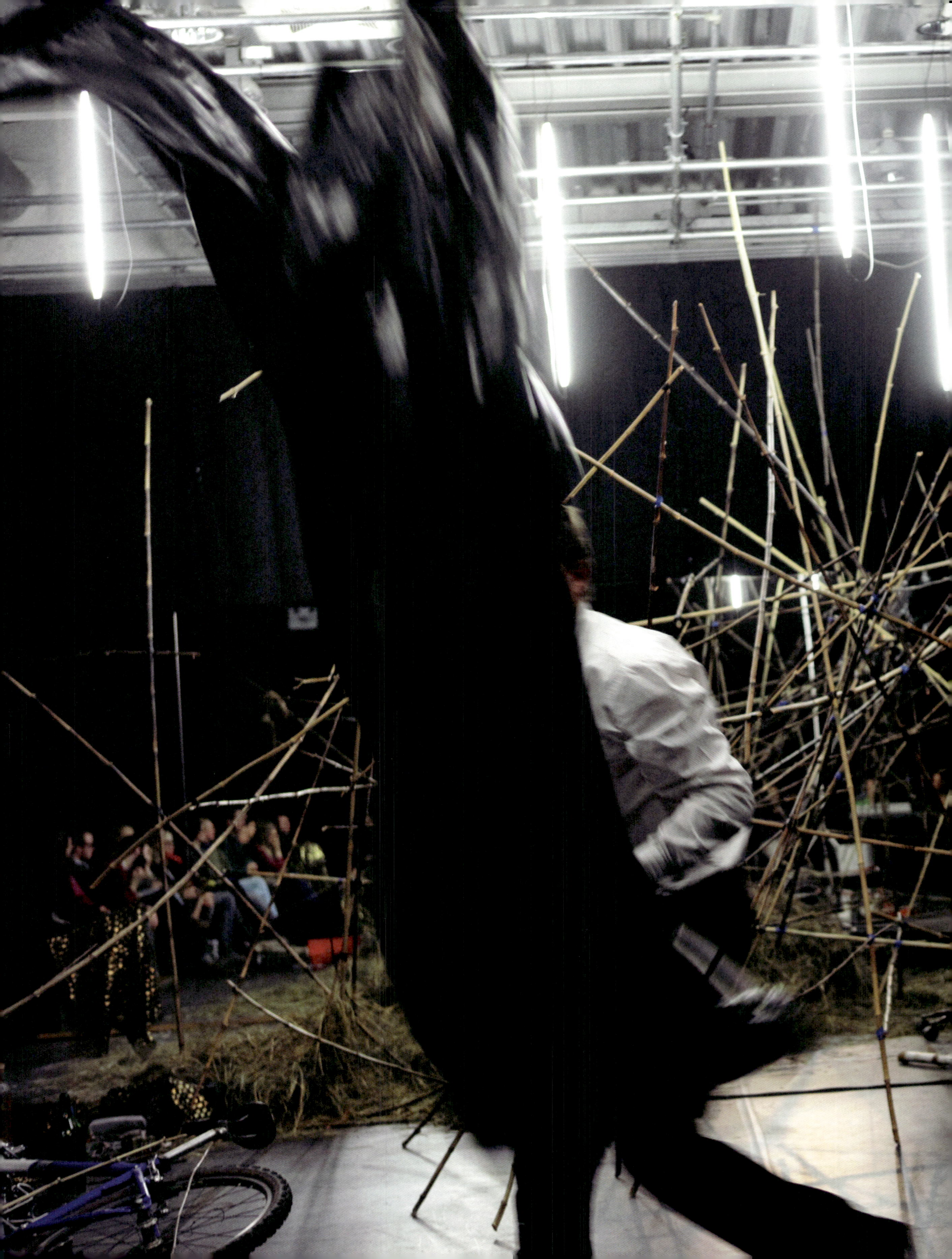

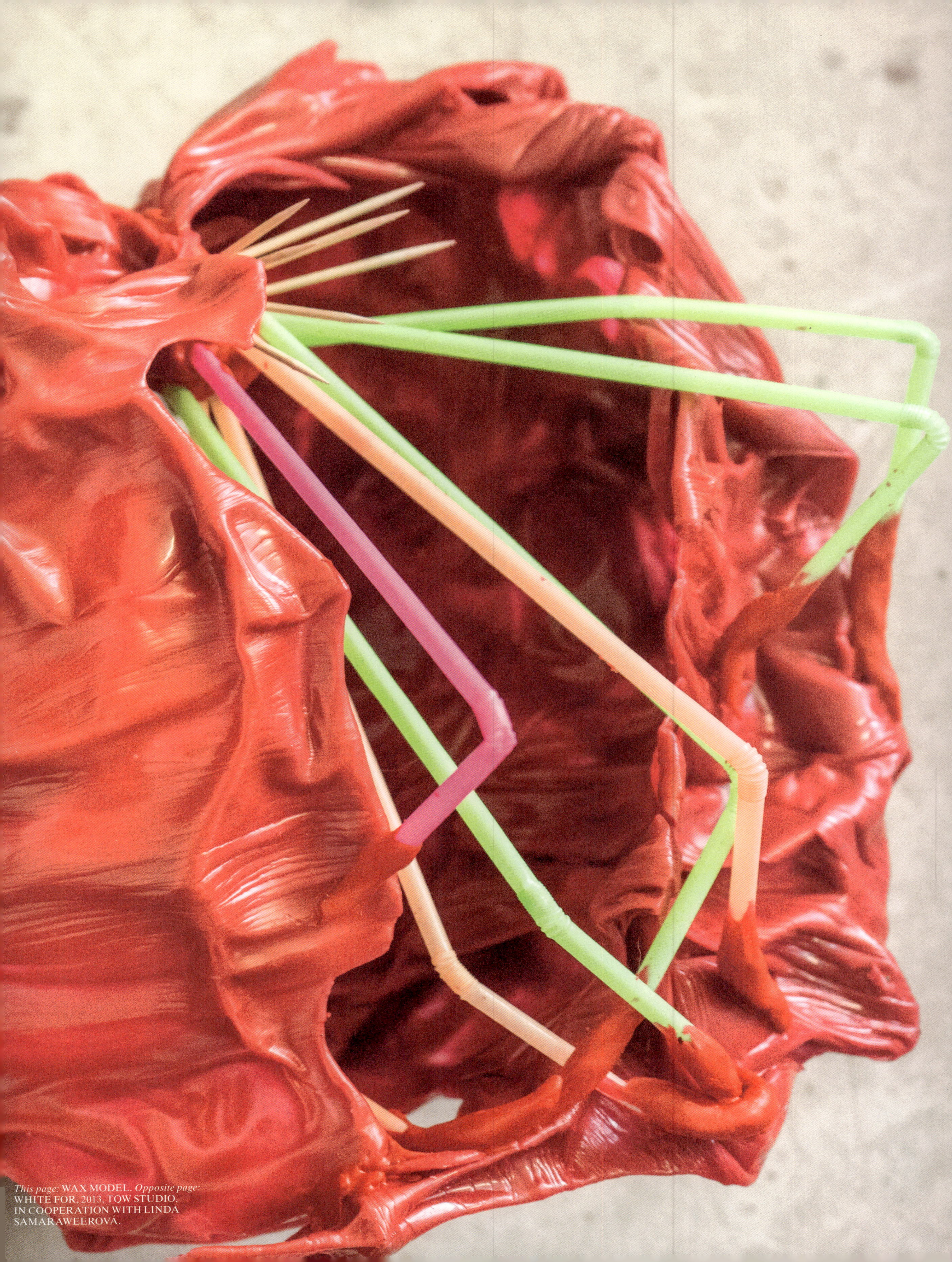

*This page:* WAX MODEL. *Opposite page:* WHITE FOR, 2013, TOW STUDIO, IN COOPERATION WITH LINDA SAMARAWEEROVÁ.

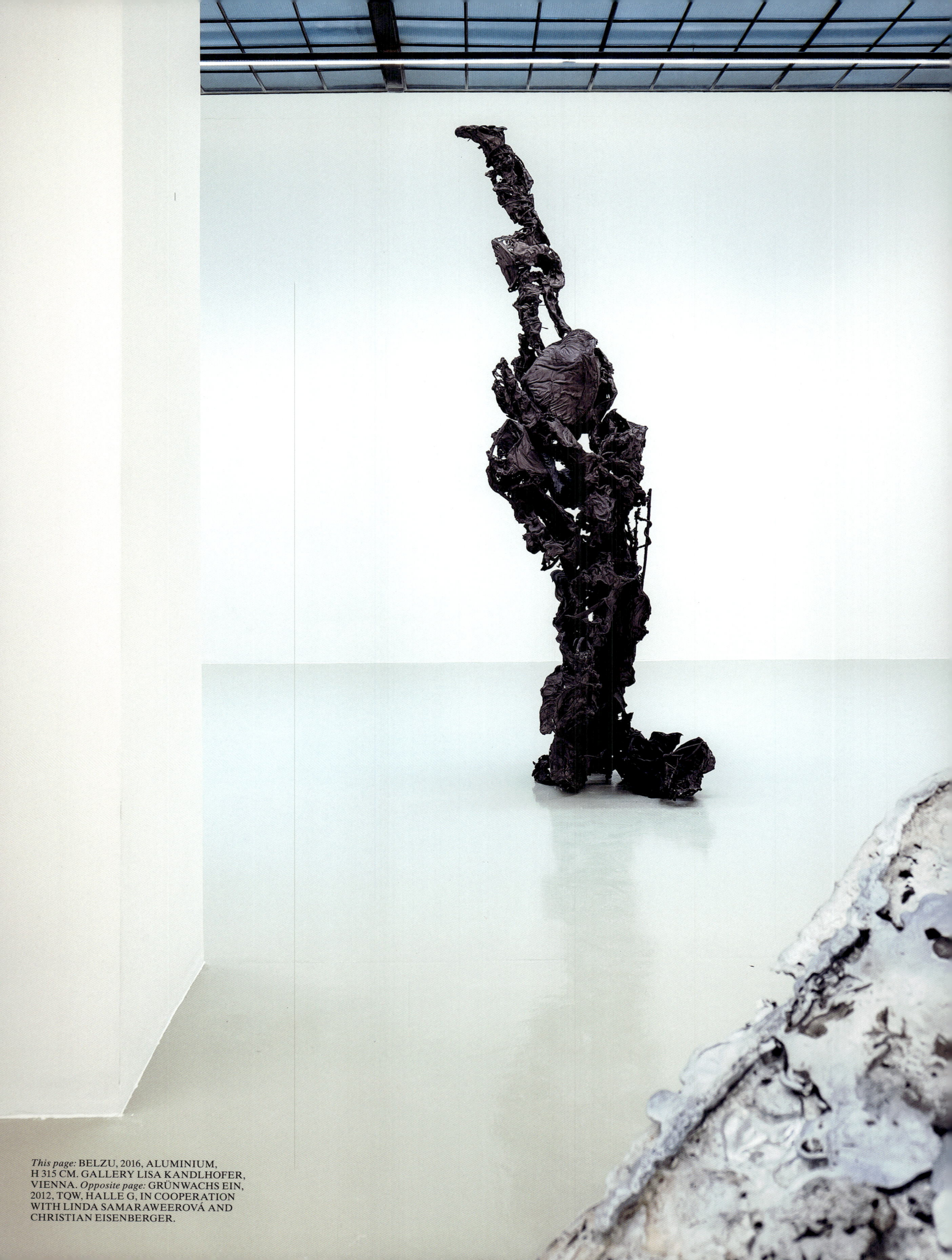

*This page:* BELZU, 2016, ALUMINIUM, H 315 CM. GALLERY LISA KANDLHOFER, VIENNA. *Opposite page:* GRÜNWACHS EIN, 2012, TQW, HALLE G, IN COOPERATION WITH LINDA SAMARAWEEROVÁ AND CHRISTIAN EISENBERGER.

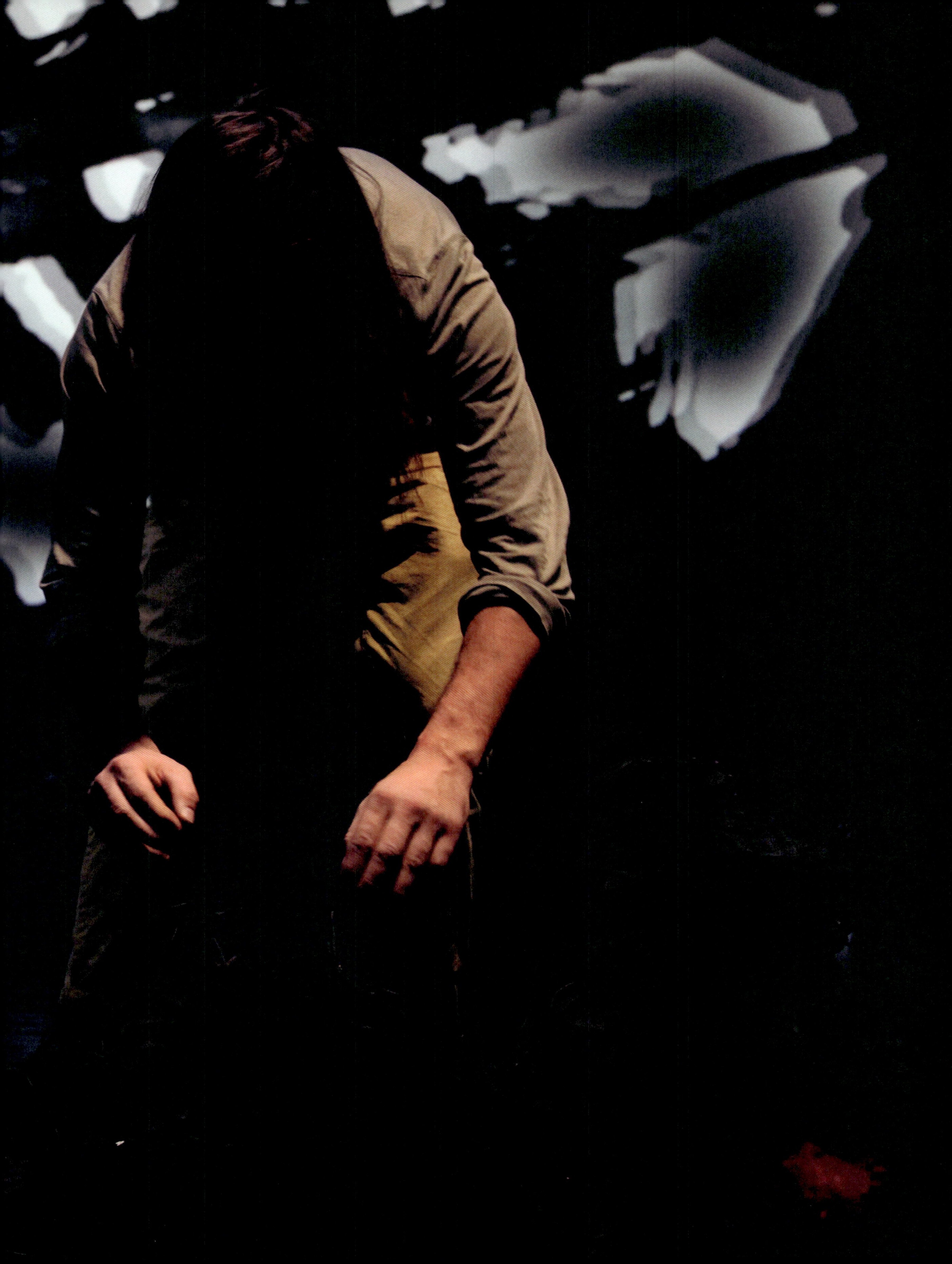

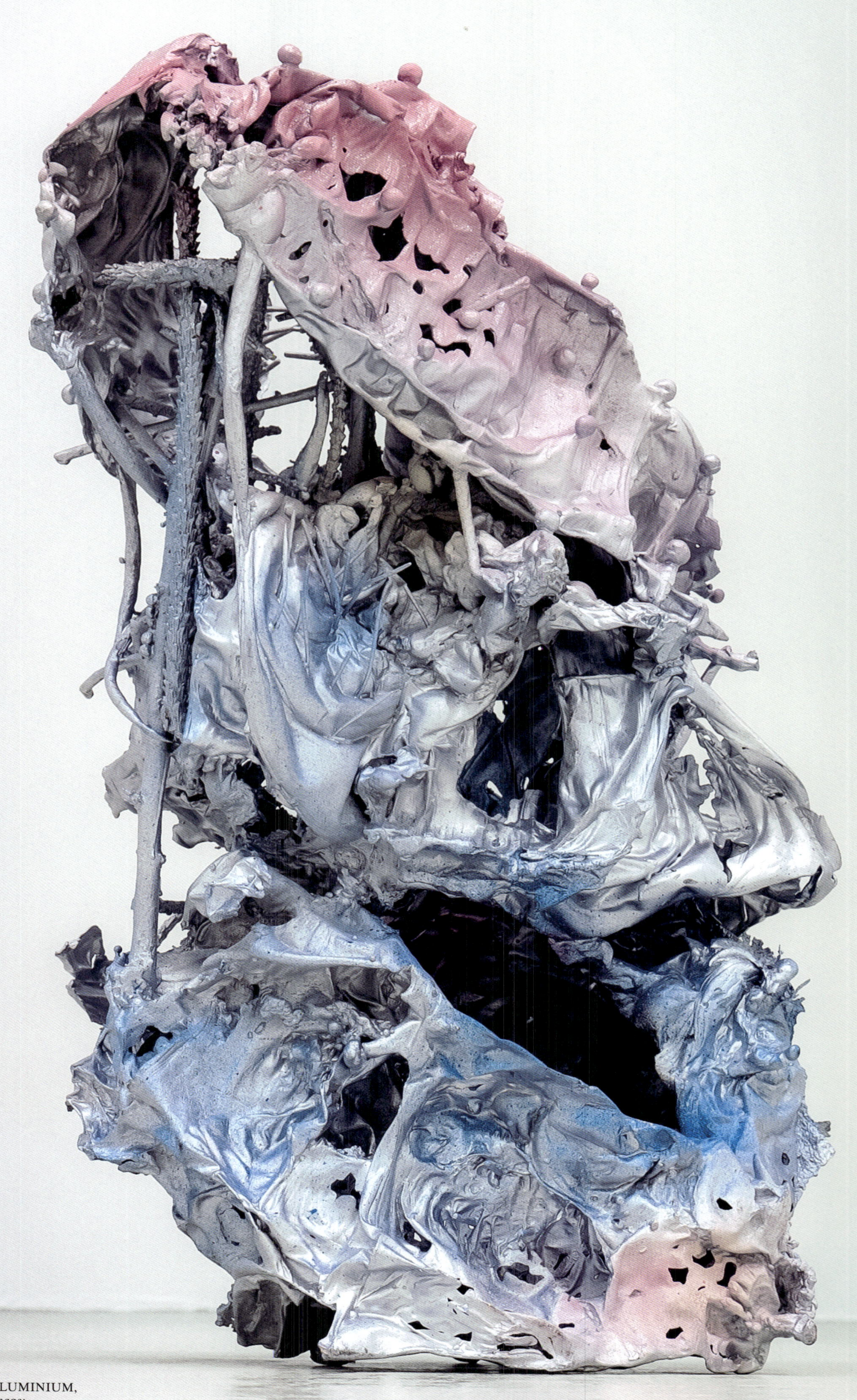

*This page:* MALU, 2016, ALUMINIUM, 30 X 40 X 65 CM. *Opposite page:* WÜRFELN FELL MIT BALL, 2016, KM-KÜNSTLERHAUS, GRAZ, IN COOPERATION WITH LINDA SAMARAWEEROVÁ.

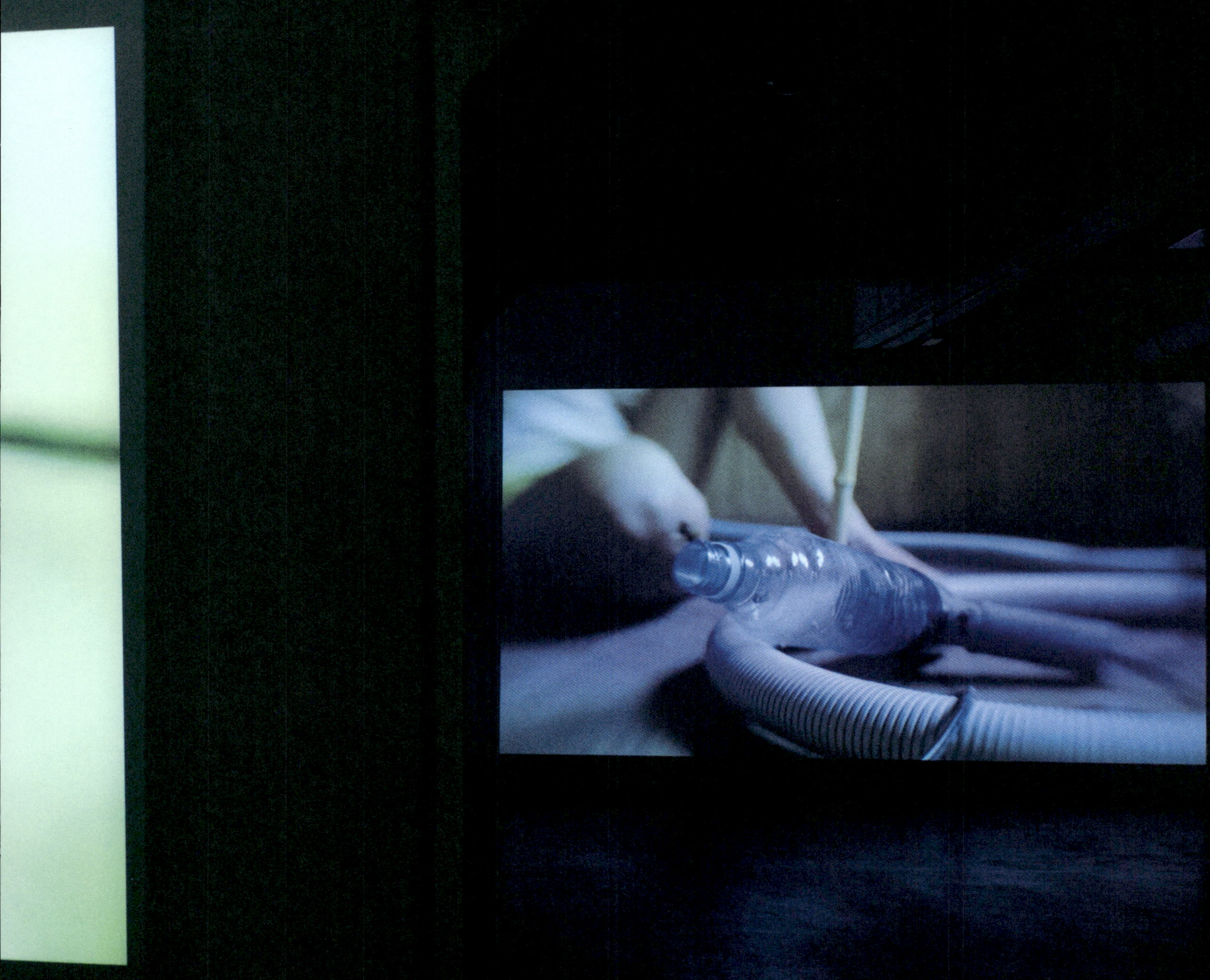

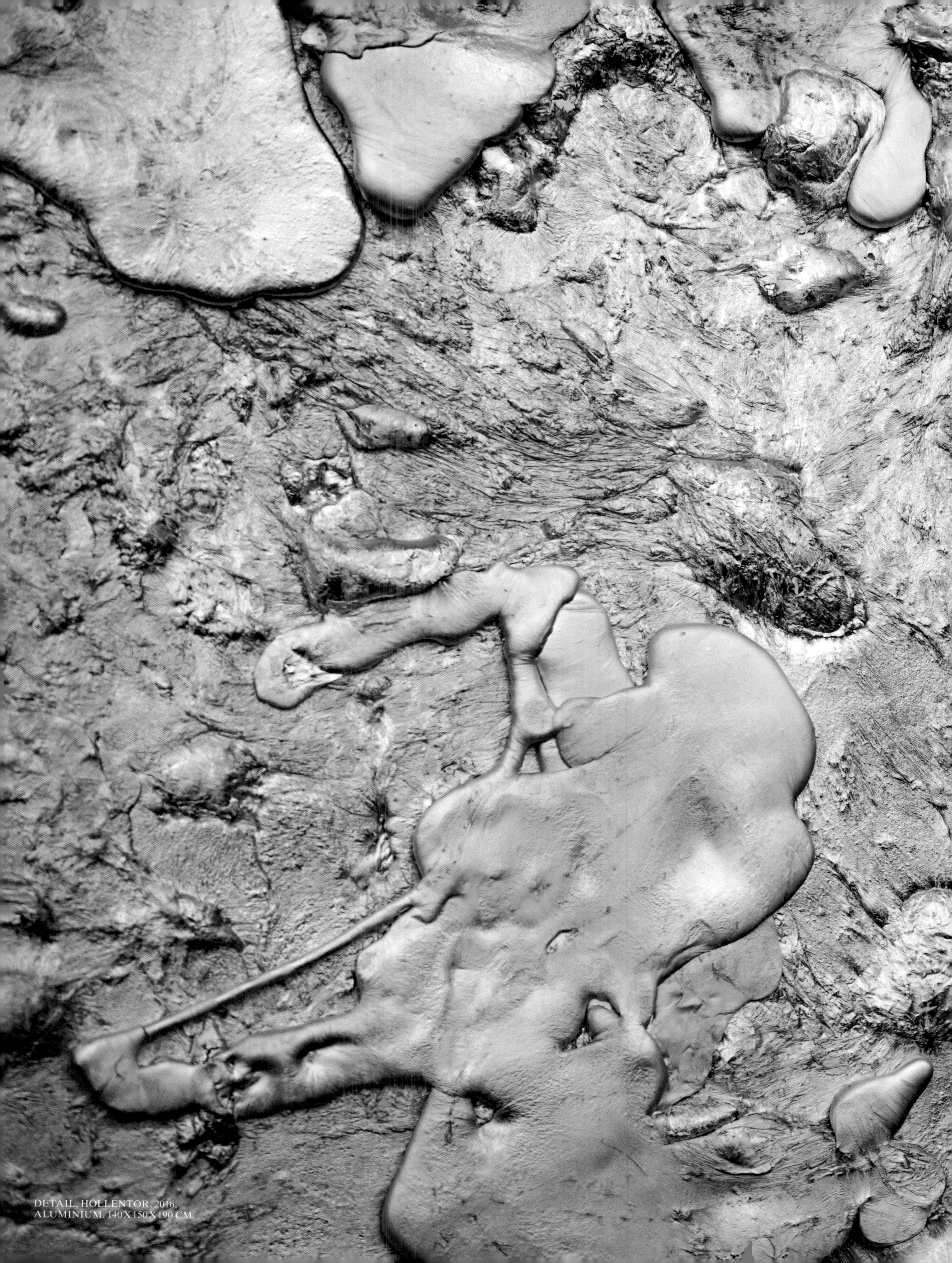

DETAIL, HÖLLENTOR, 2016,
ALUMINIUM, 140 X 150 X 190 CM.

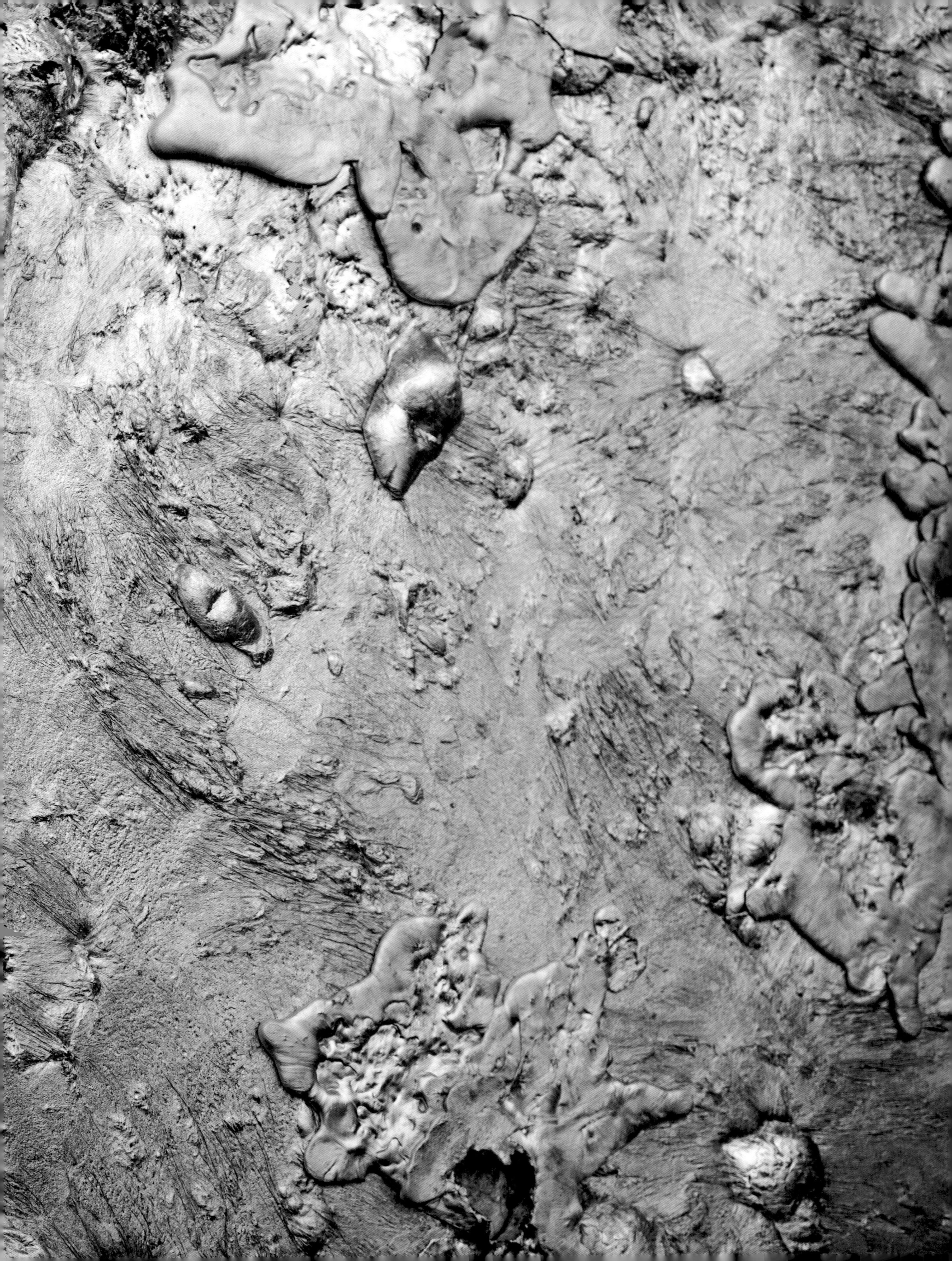

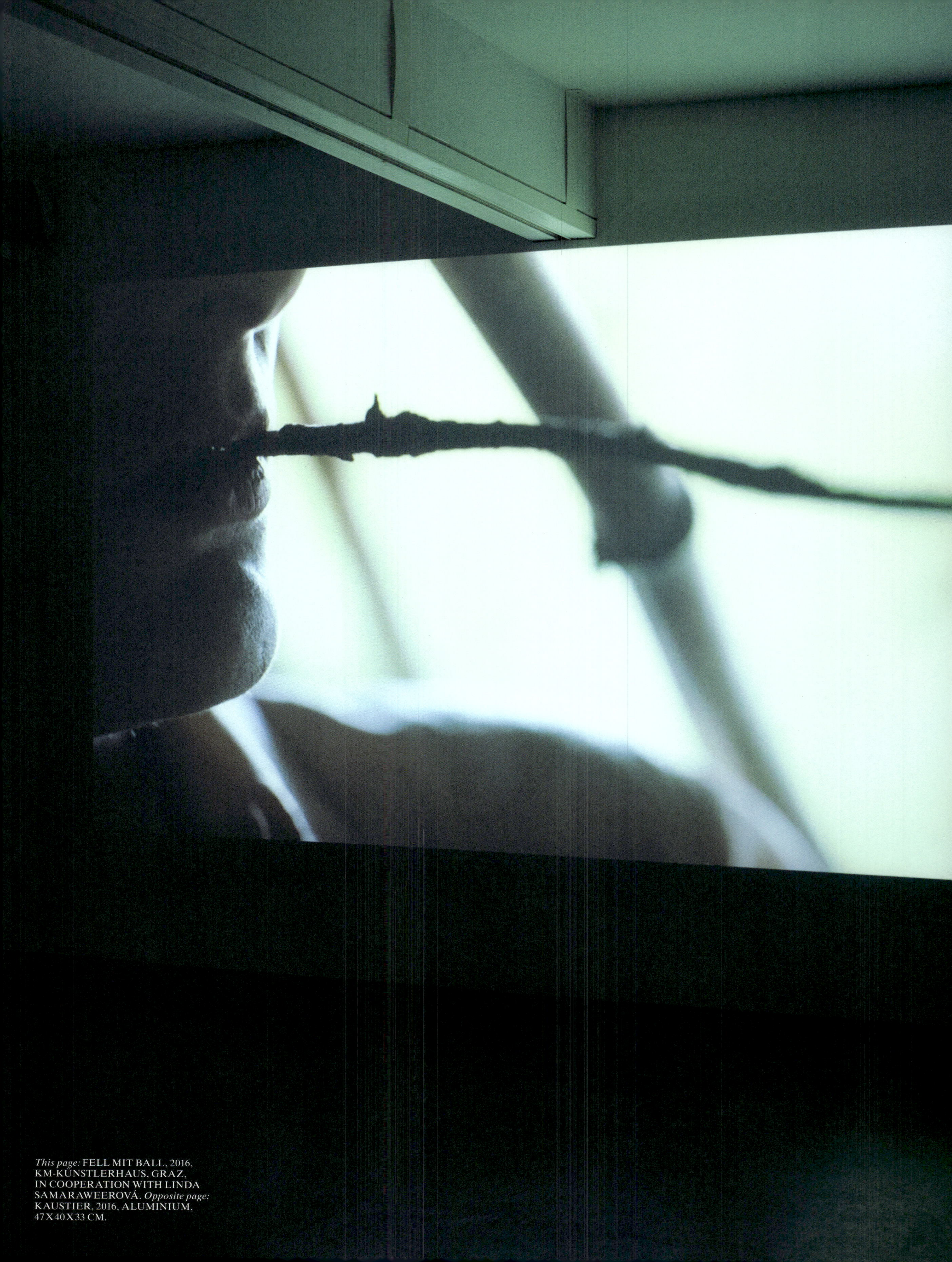

*This page:* FELL MIT BALL, 2016, KM-KÜNSTLERHAUS, GRAZ, IN COOPERATION WITH LINDA SAMARAWEEROVÁ. *Opposite page:* KAUSTIER, 2016, ALUMINIUM, 47 X 40 X 33 CM.

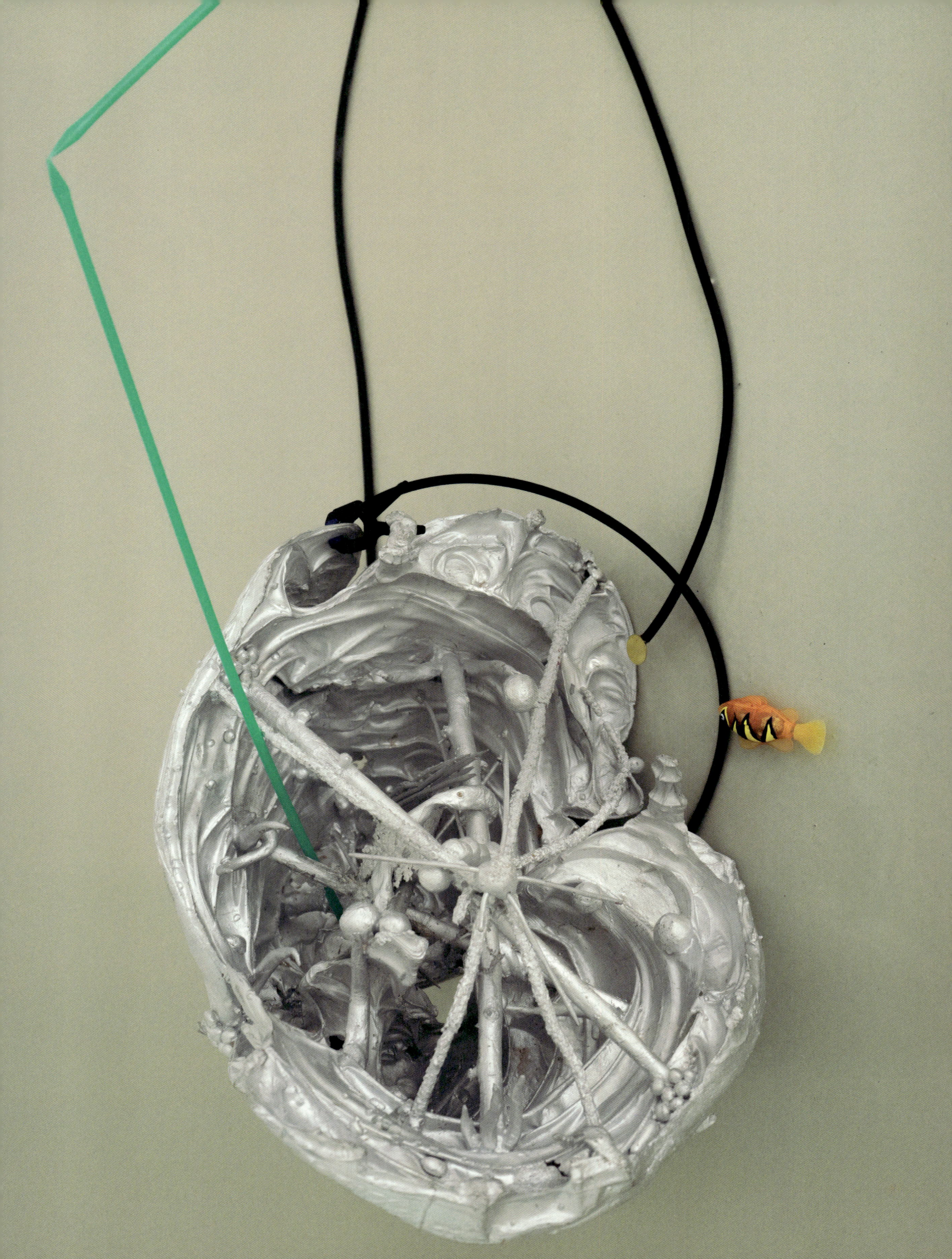

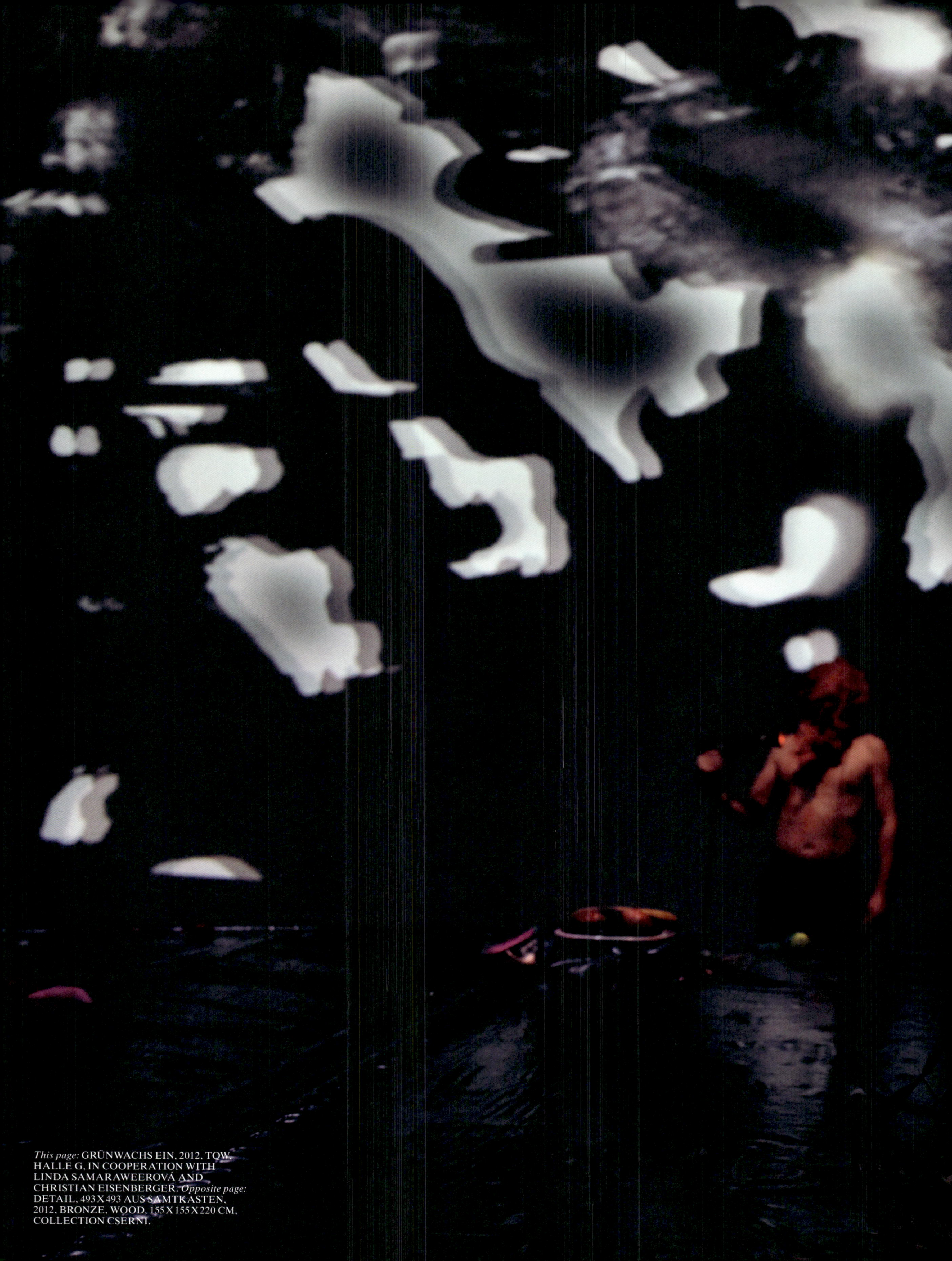

*This page:* GRÜNWACHS EIN, 2012, TQW, HALLE G, IN COOPERATION WITH LINDA SAMARAWEEROVÁ AND CHRISTIAN EISENBERGER. *Opposite page:* DETAIL, 493 X 493 AUS SAMTKASTEN, 2012, BRONZE, WOOD, 155 X 155 X 220 CM, COLLECTION CSERNI.

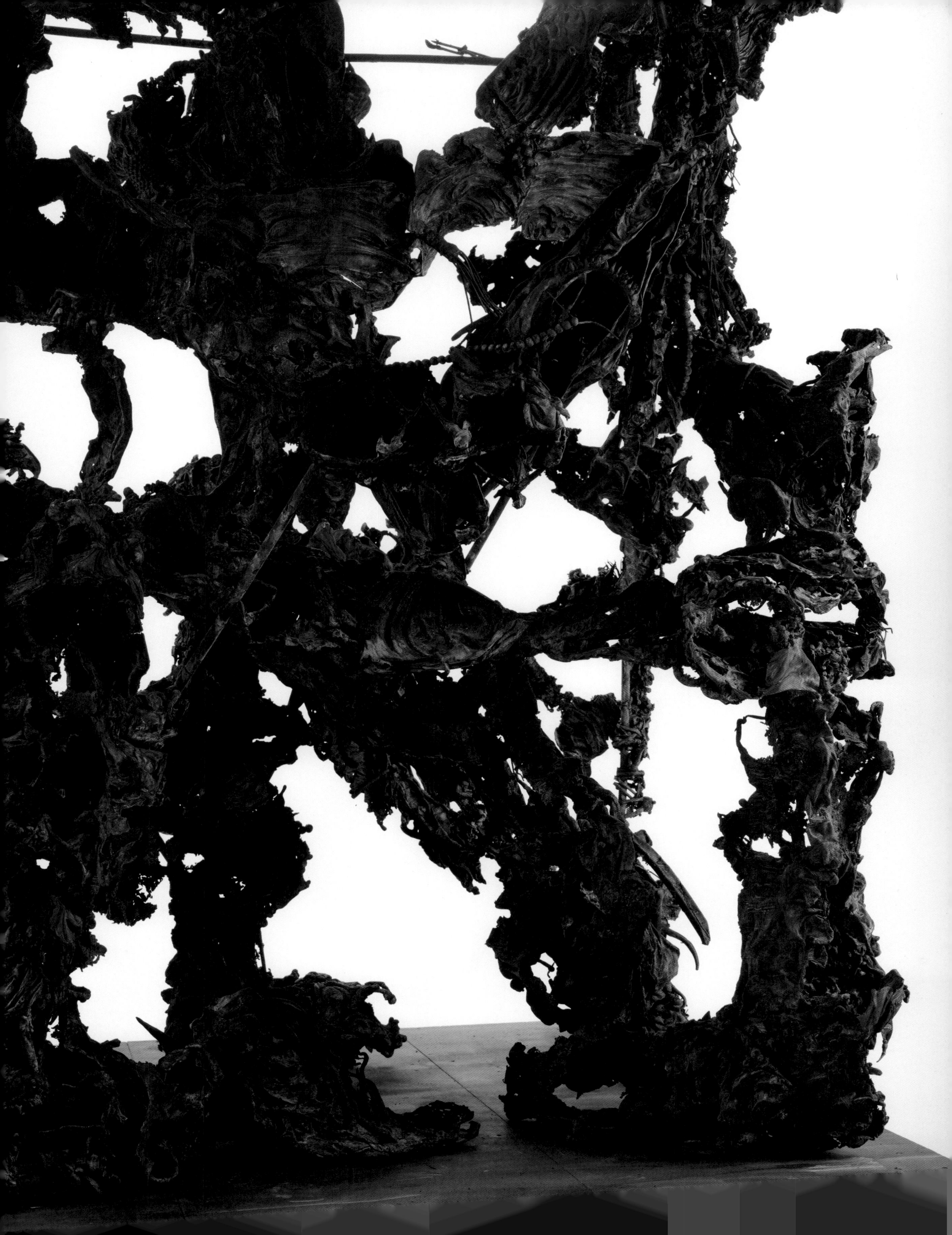

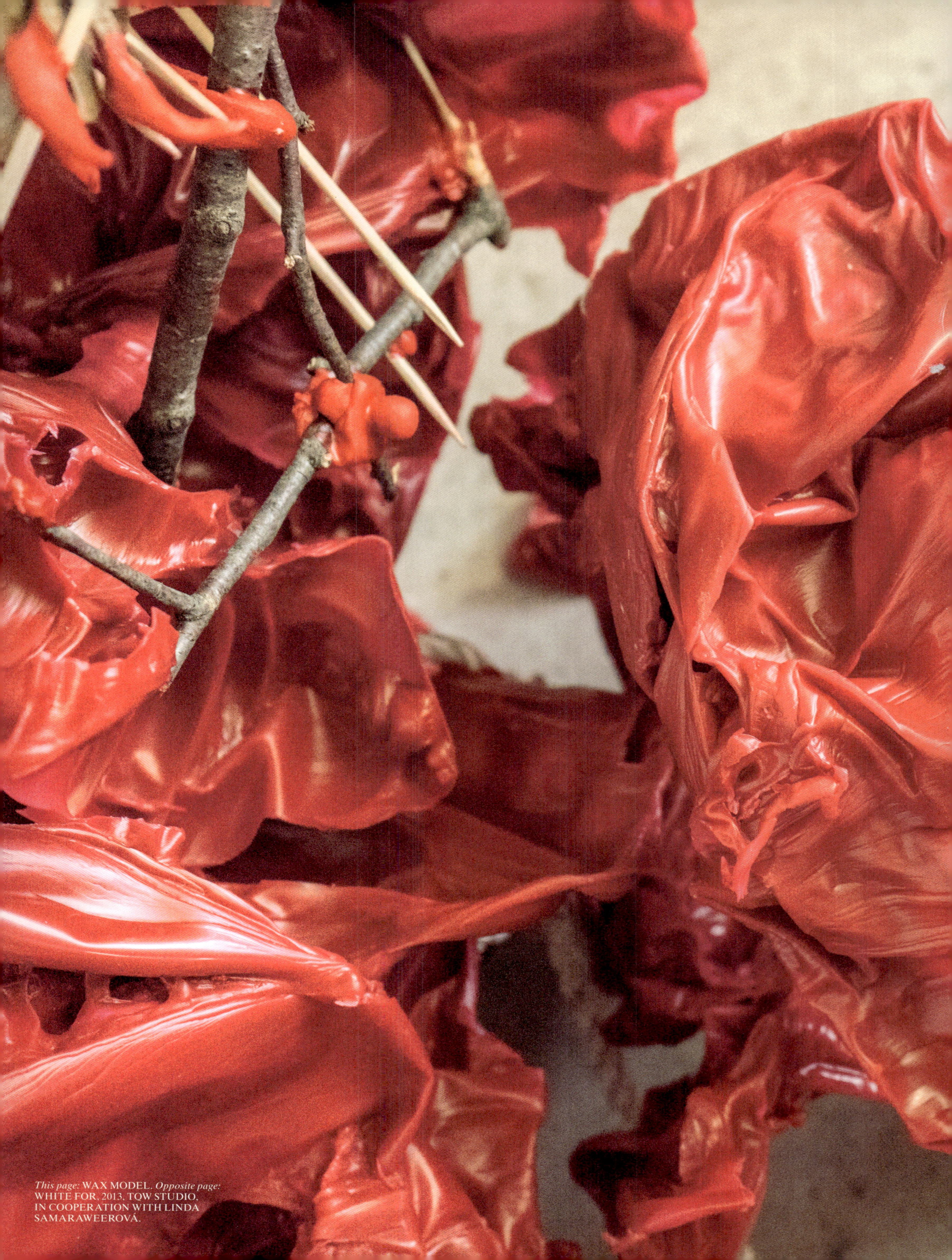

*This page:* WAX MODEL. *Opposite page:* WHITE FOR, 2013, TOW STUDIO, IN COOPERATION WITH LINDA SAMARAWEEROVÁ.

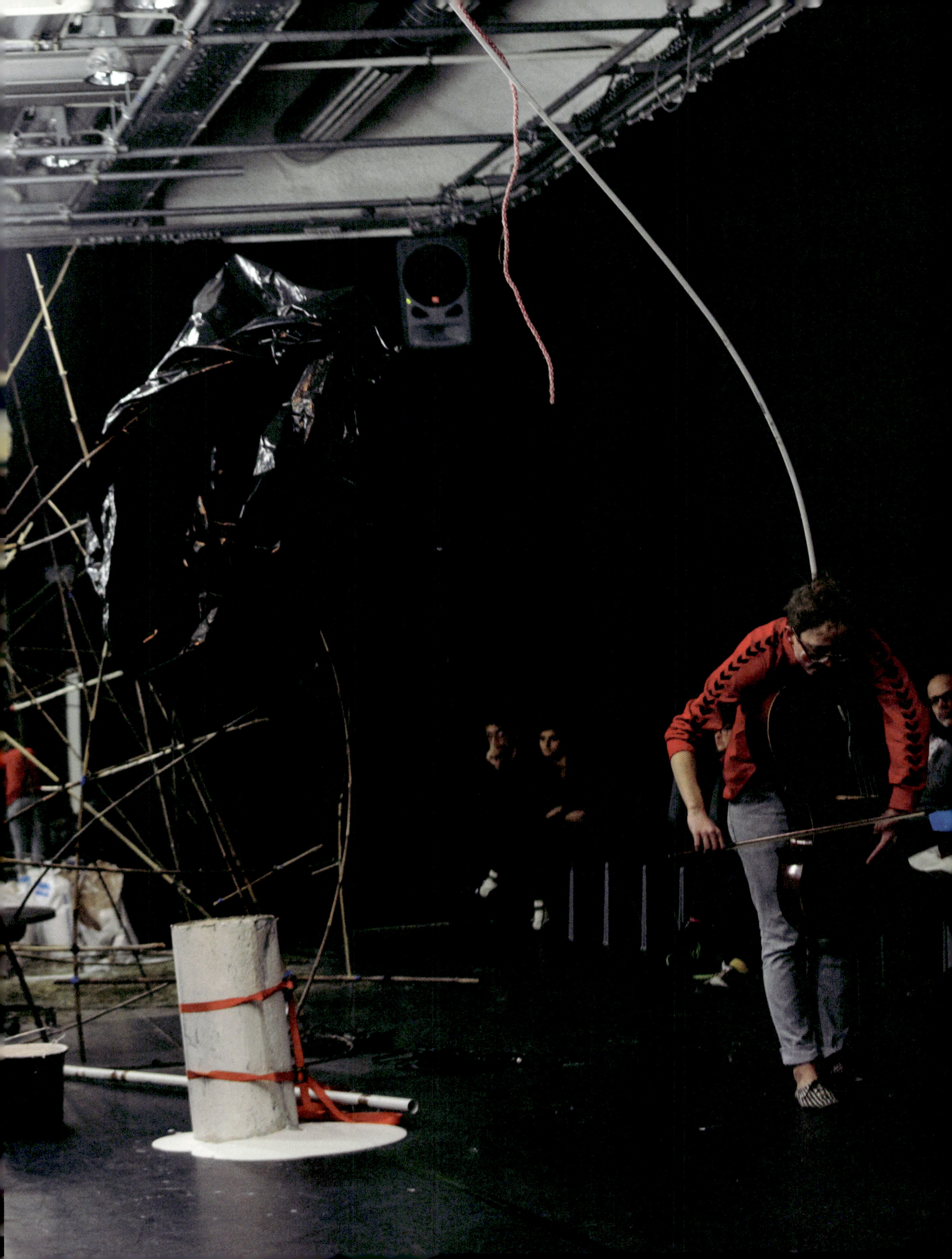

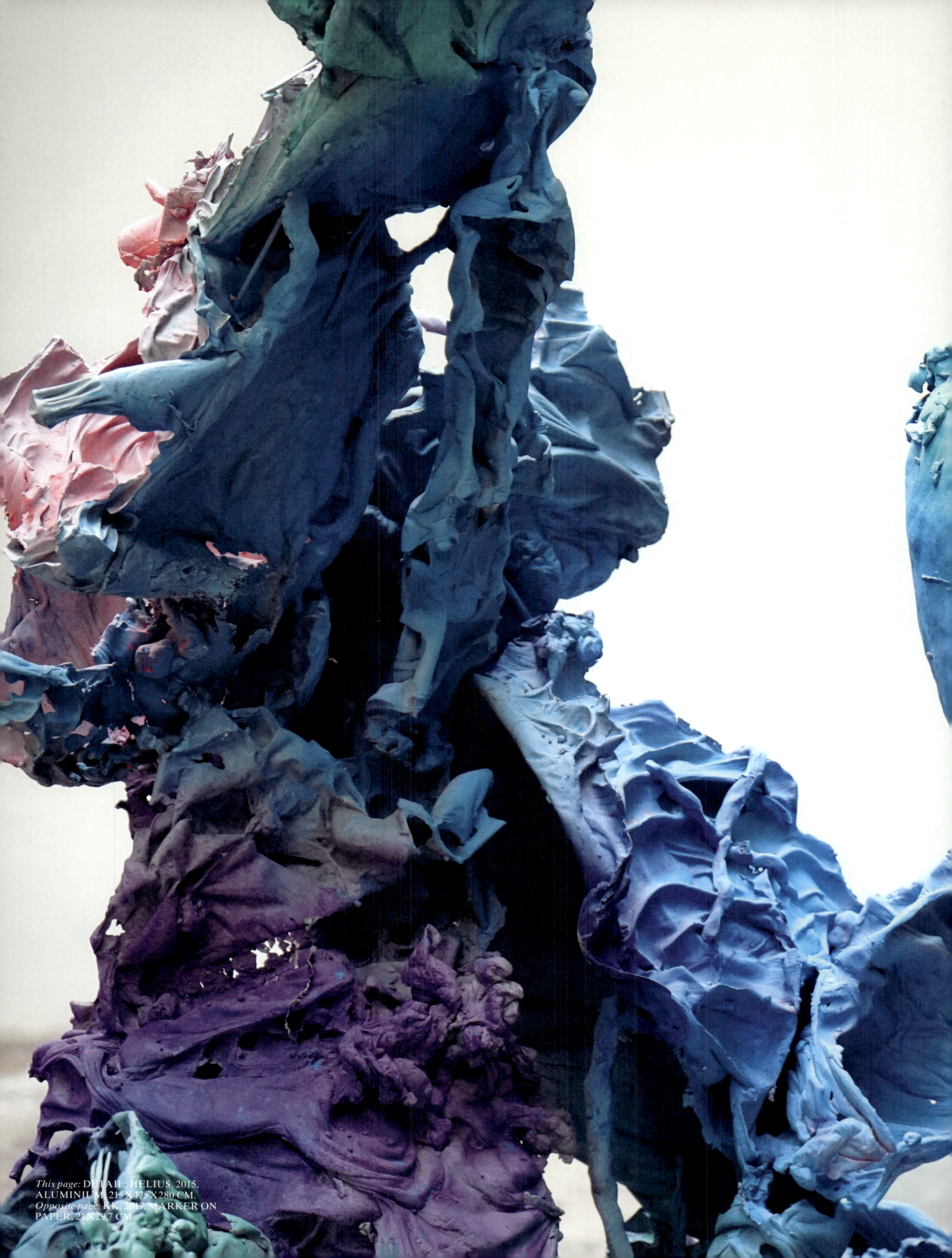

*This page:* DETAIL, HELIUS, 2015, ALUMINIUM, 215 X 175 X 280 CM.
*Opposite page:* KK, 2017, MARKER ON PAPER, 21 X 29,7 CM.

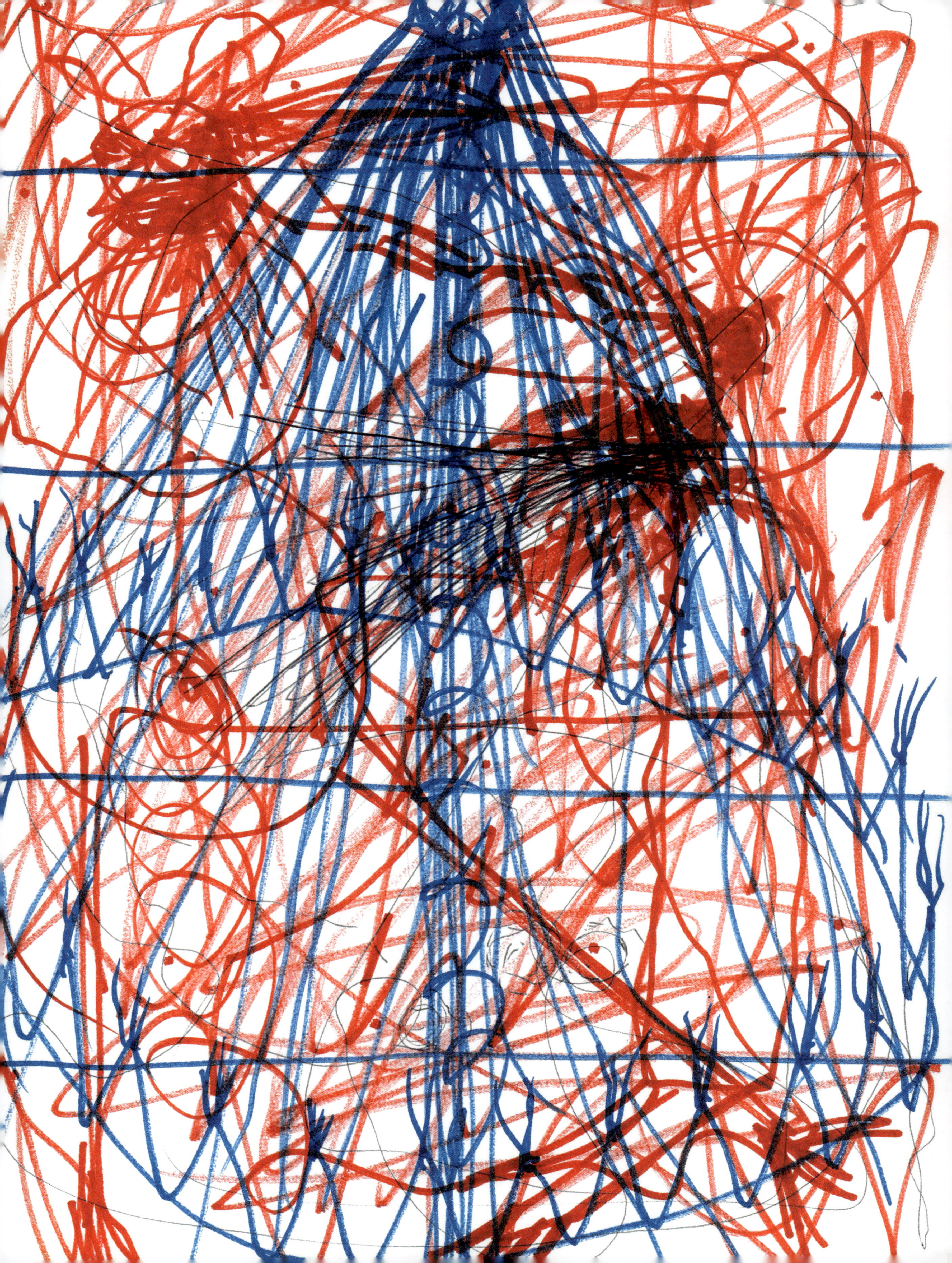

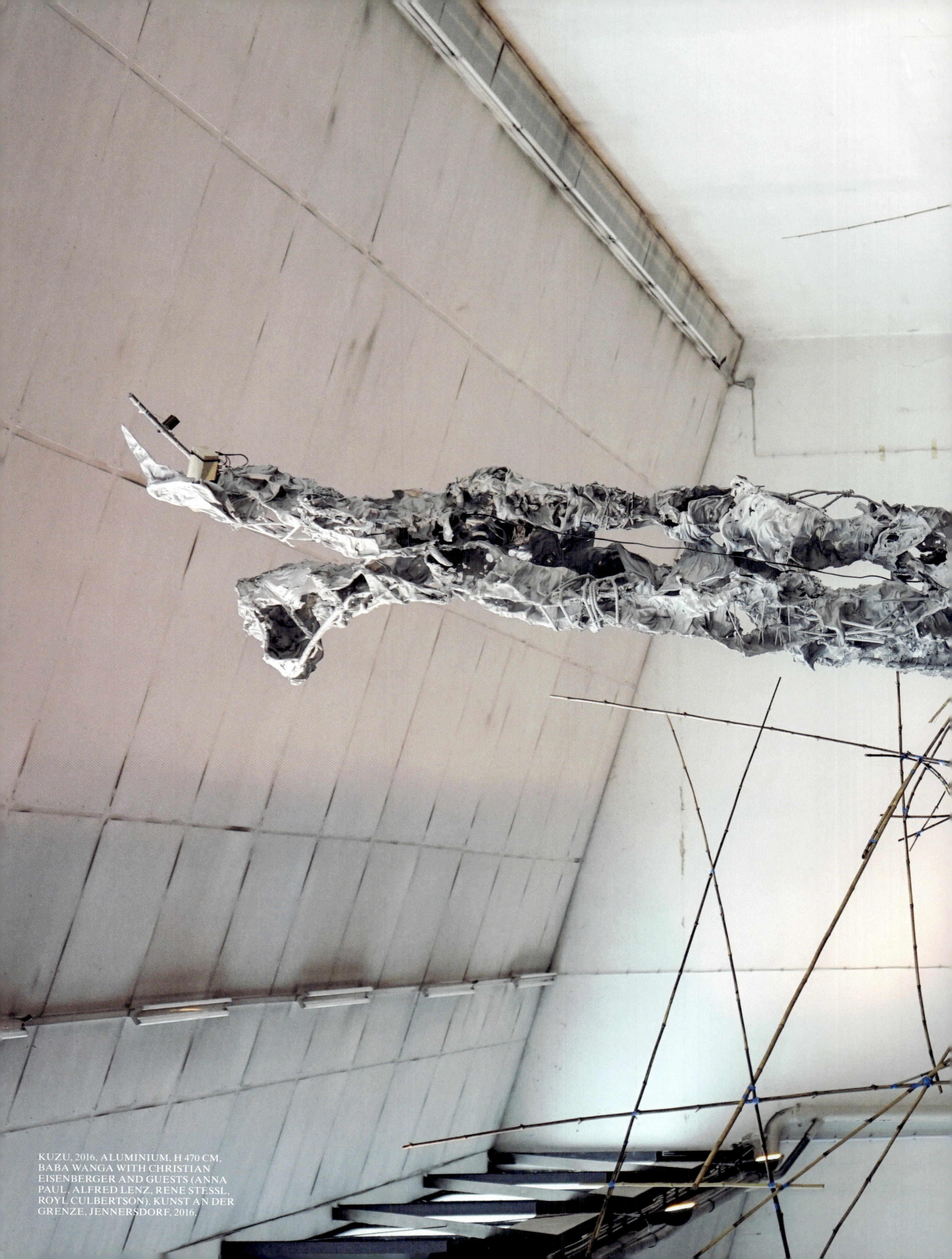

KUZU, 2016, ALUMINIUM, H 470 CM, BABA WANGA WITH CHRISTIAN EISENBERGER AND GUESTS (ANNA PAUL, ALFRED LENZ, RENE STESSL, ROYL CULBERTSON), KUNST AN DER GRENZE, JENNERSDORF, 2016.

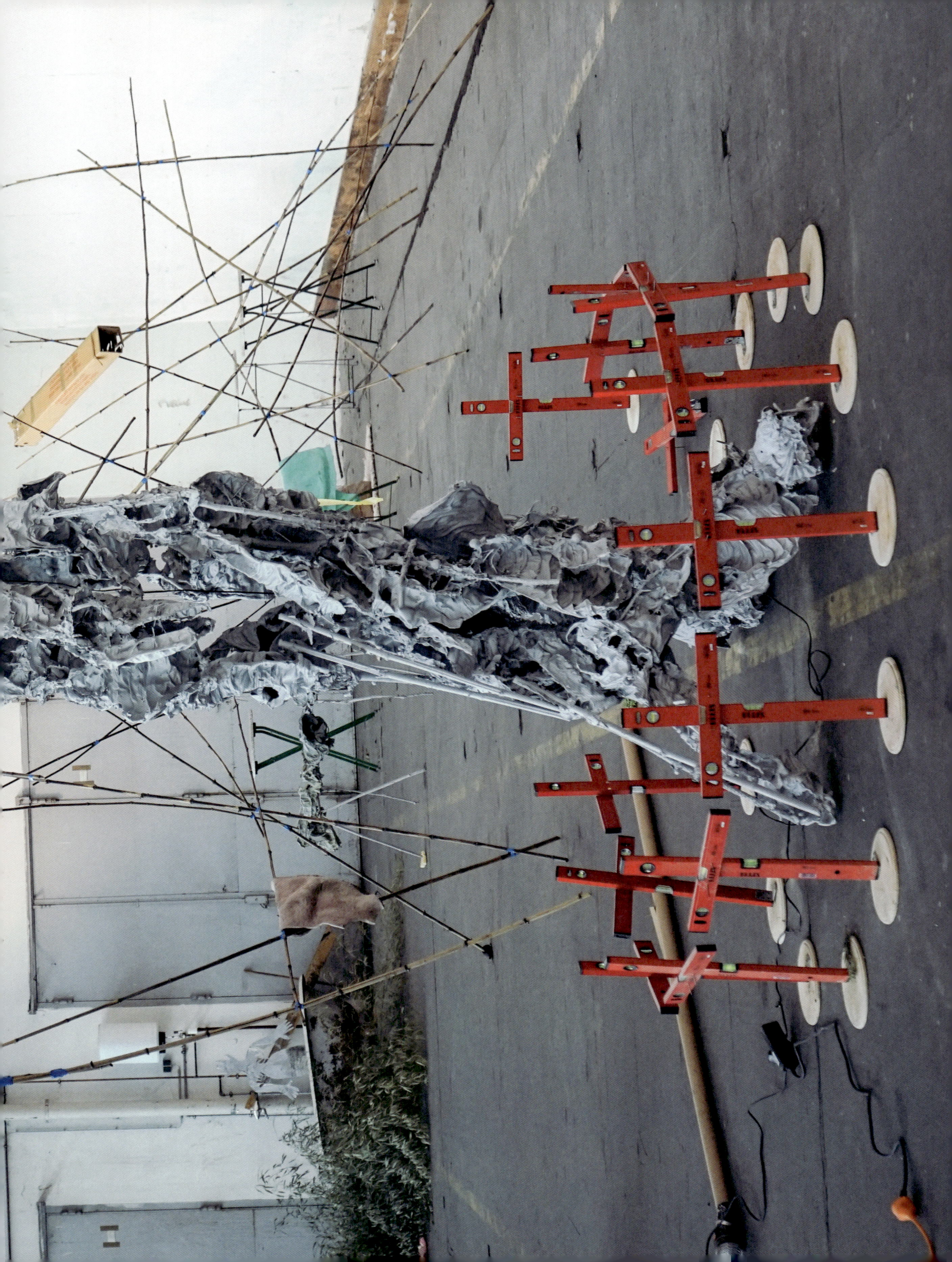

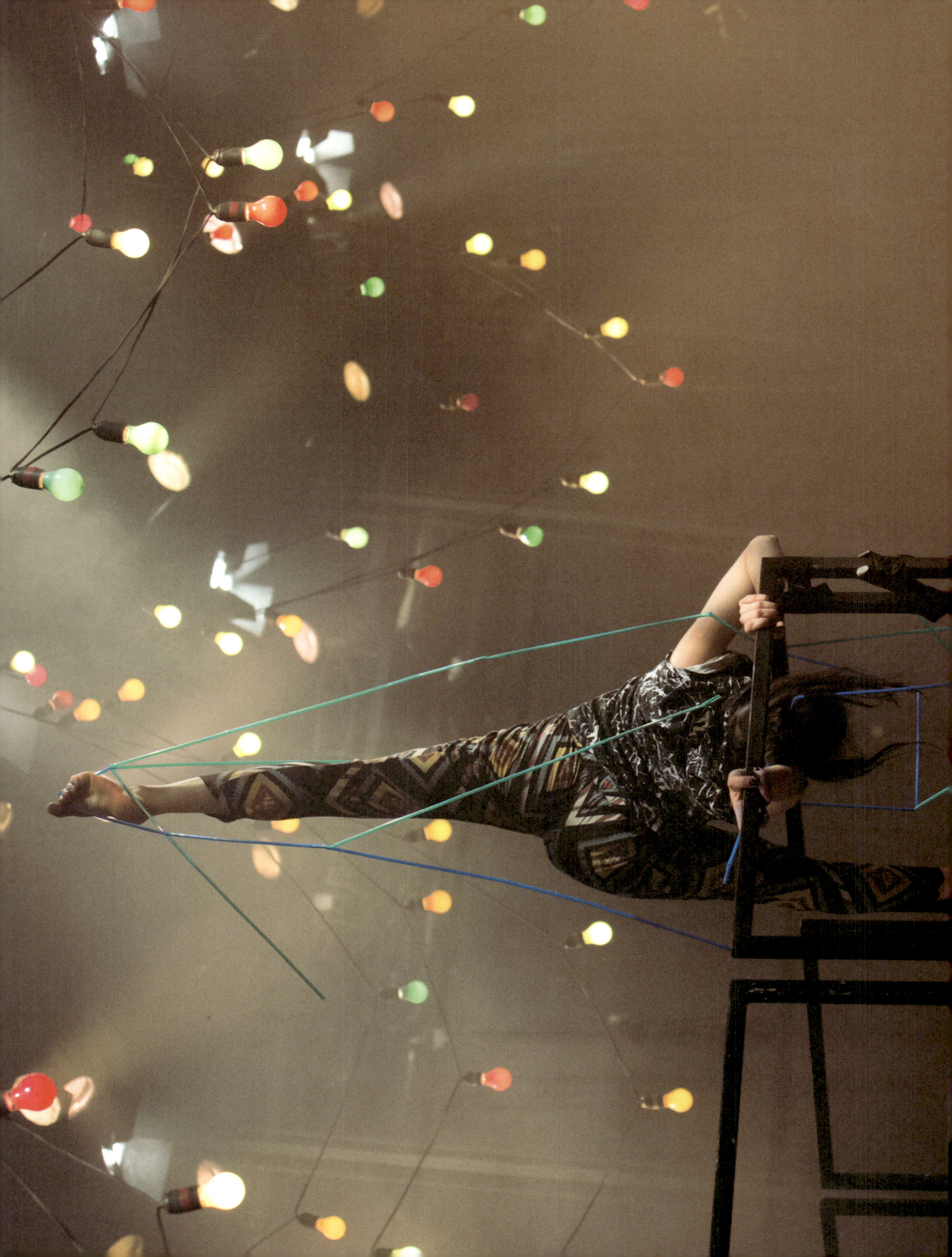

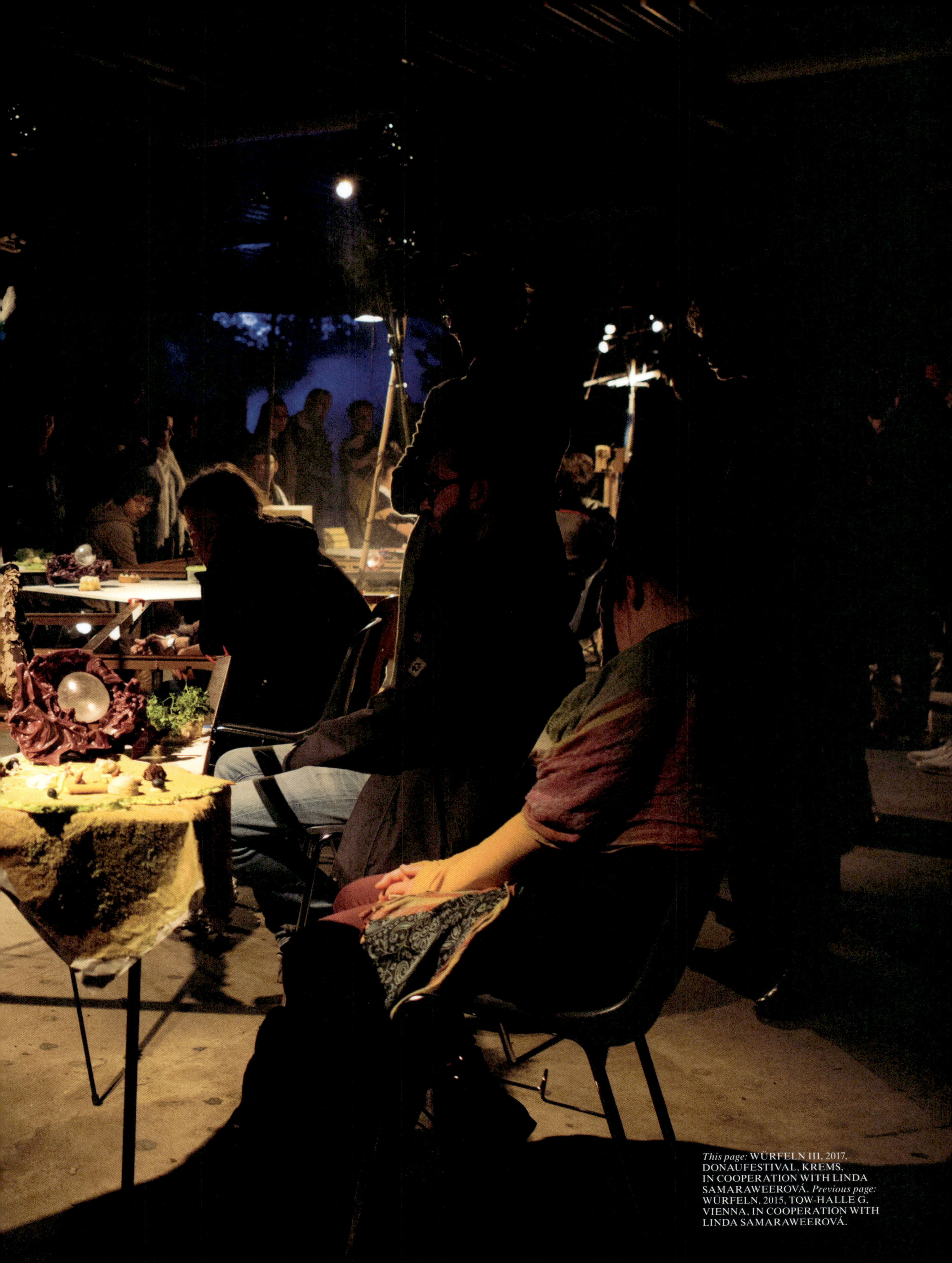

*This page:* WÜRFELN III, 2017, DONAUFESTIVAL, KREMS, IN COOPERATION WITH LINDA SAMARAWEEROVÁ. *Previous page:* WÜRFELN, 2015, TQW-HALLE G, VIENNA, IN COOPERATION WITH LINDA SAMARAWEEROVÁ.

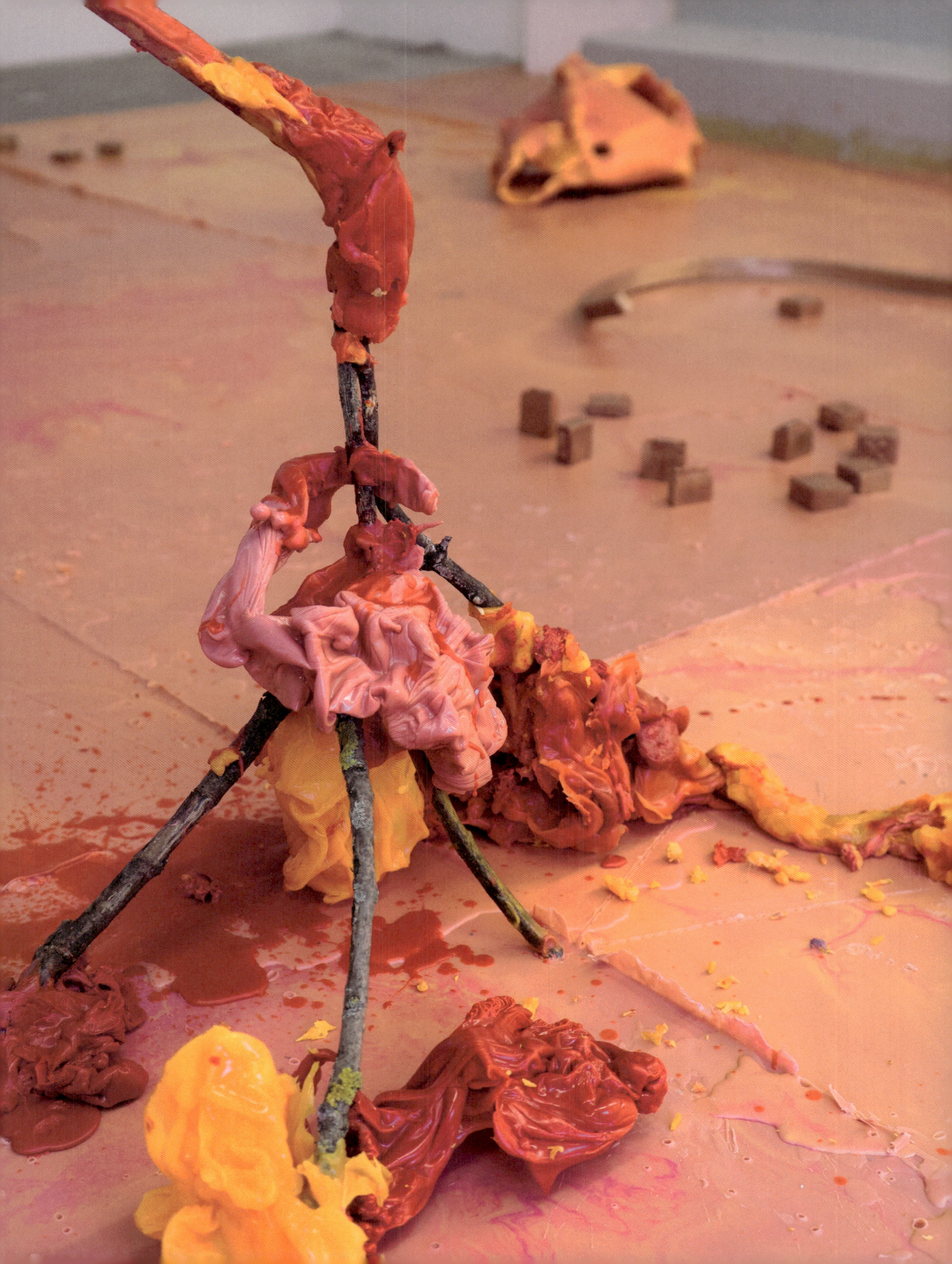

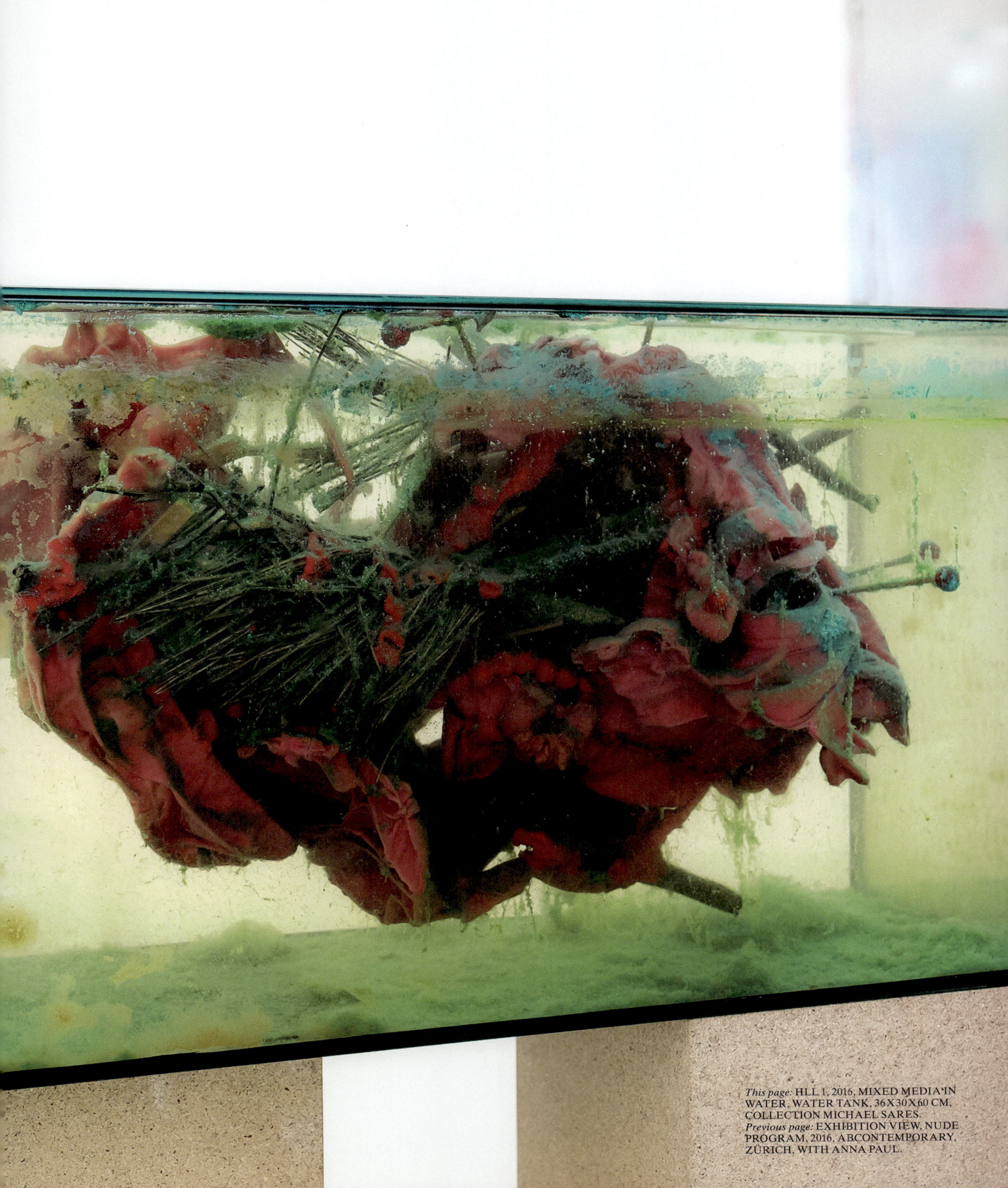

*This page:* HLL 1, 2016, MIXED MEDIA IN WATER, WATER TANK, 36 X 30 X 60 CM, COLLECTION MICHAEL SARES.
*Previous page:* EXHIBITION VIEW, NUDE PROGRAM, 2016, ABCONTEMPORARY, ZÜRICH, WITH ANNA PAUL.

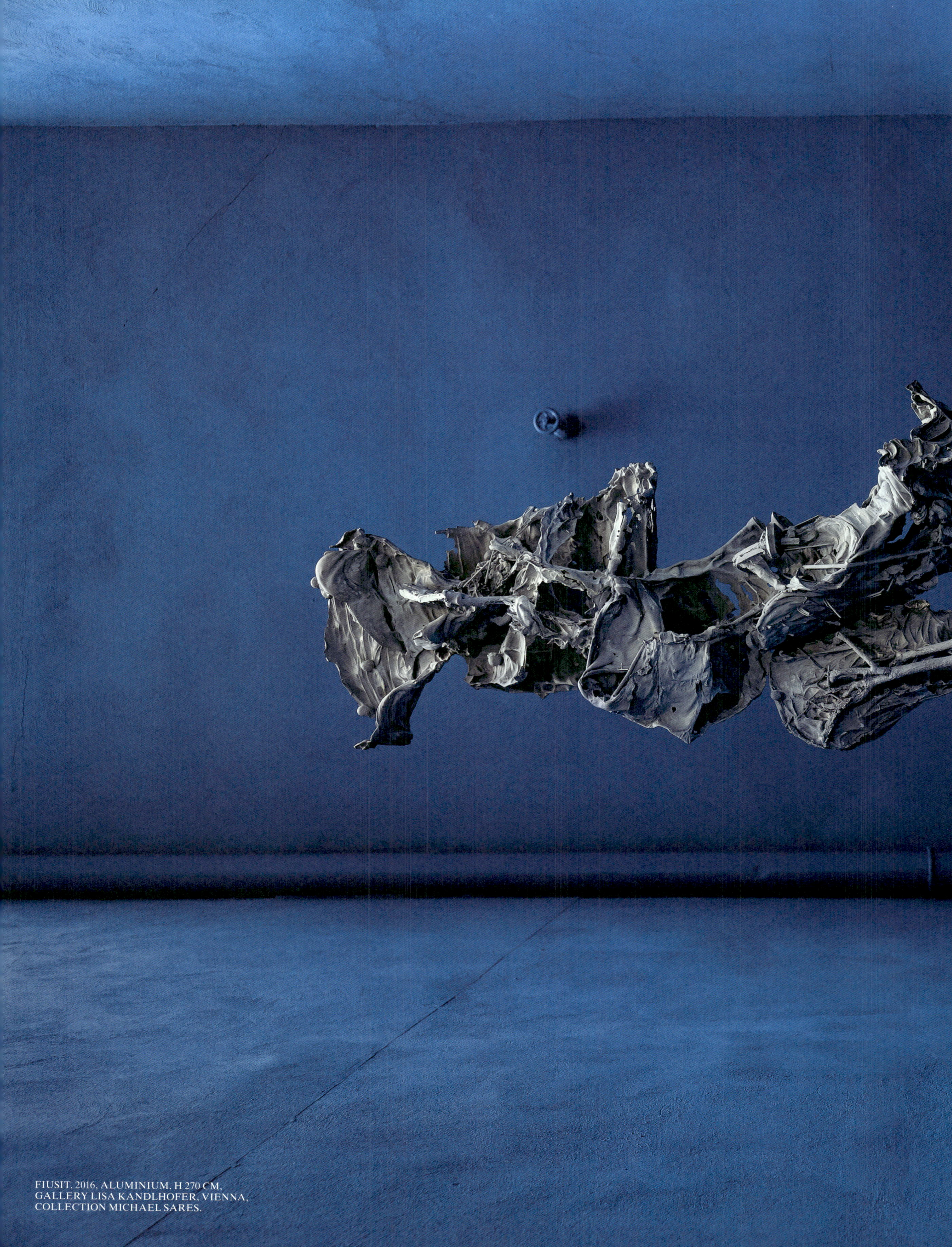

FIUSIT, 2016, ALUMINIUM, H 270 CM,
GALLERY LISA KANDLHOFER, VIENNA,
COLLECTION MICHAEL SARES.

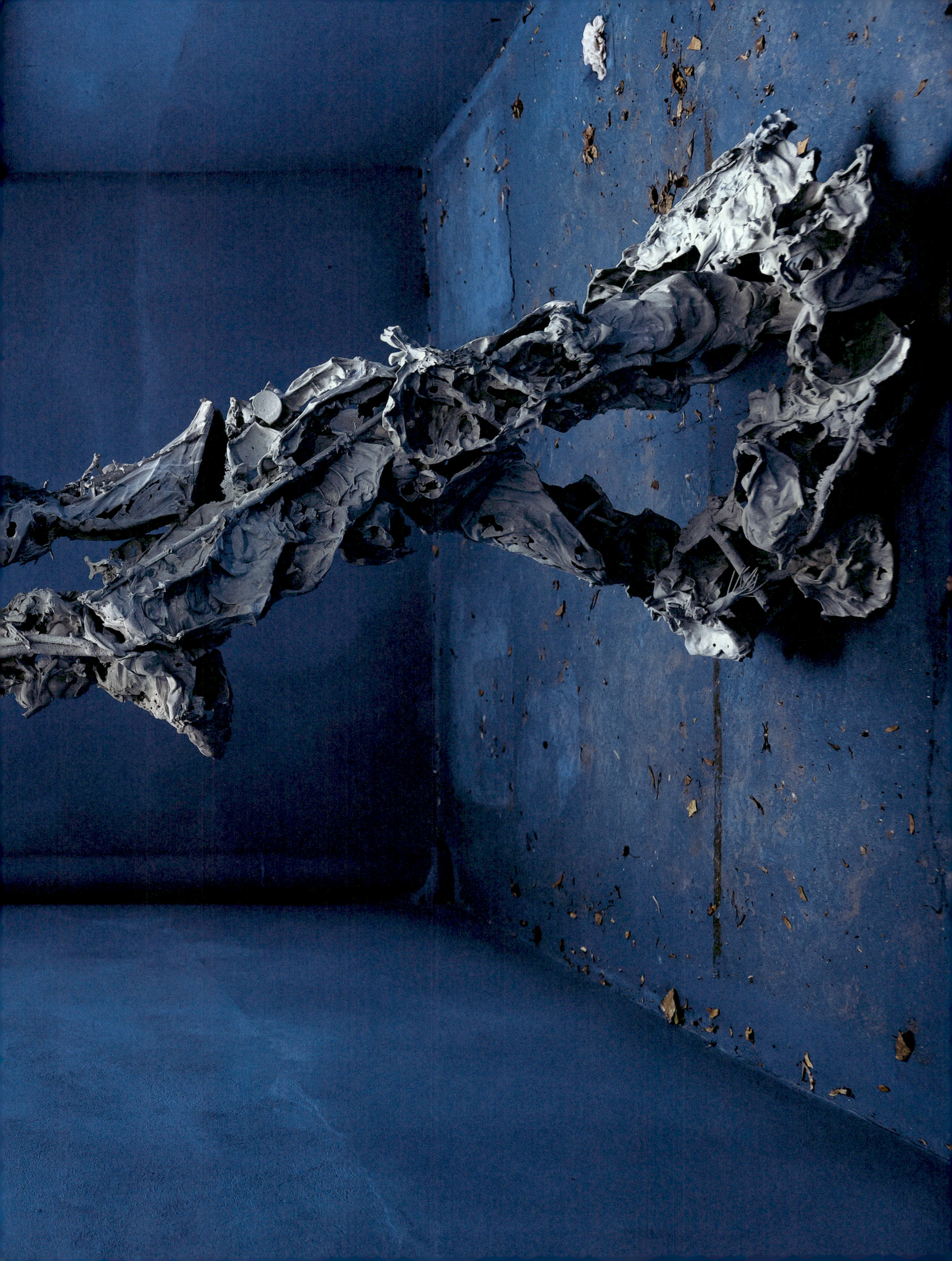

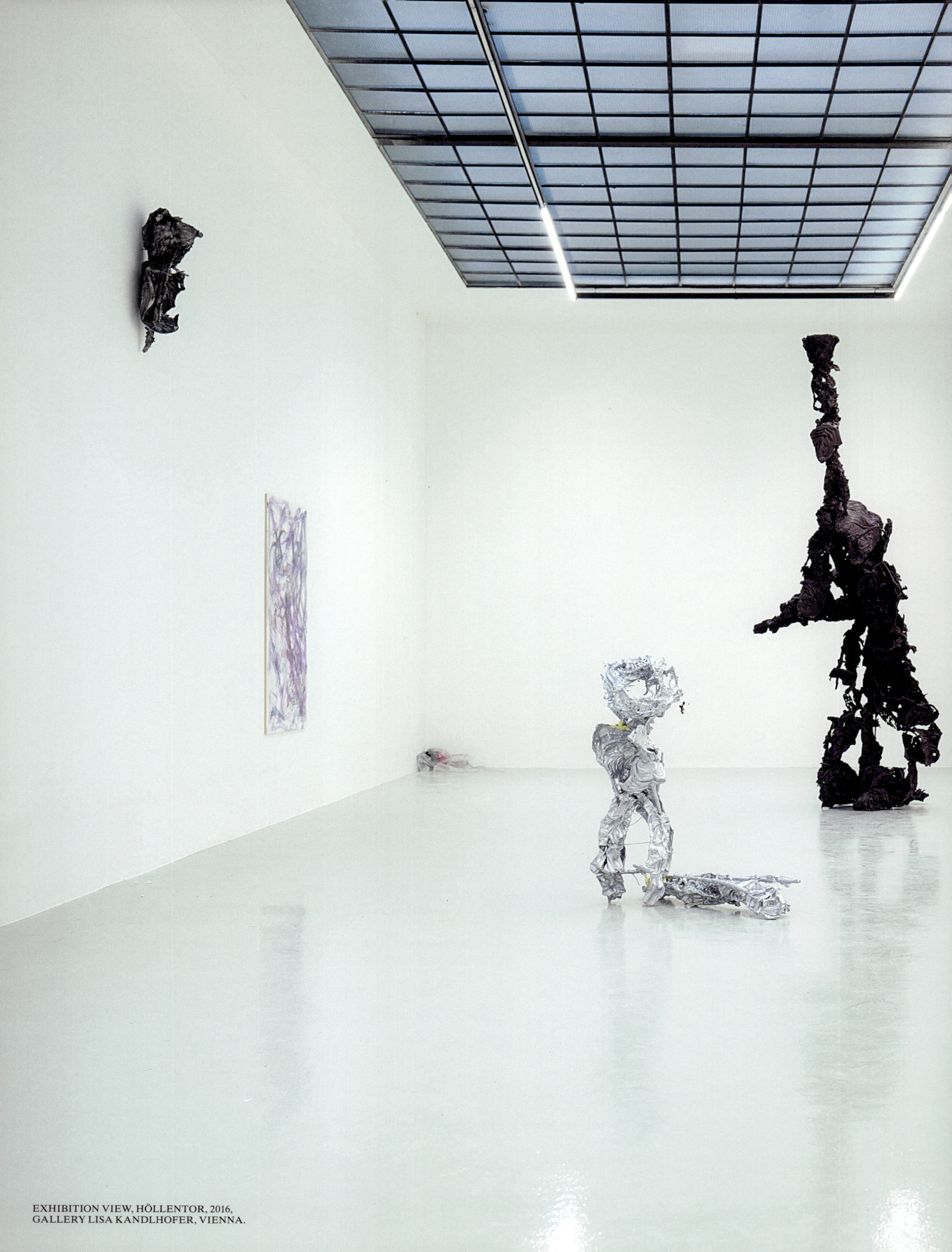

EXHIBITION VIEW, HÖLLENTOR, 2016,
GALLERY LISA KANDLHOFER, VIENNA.

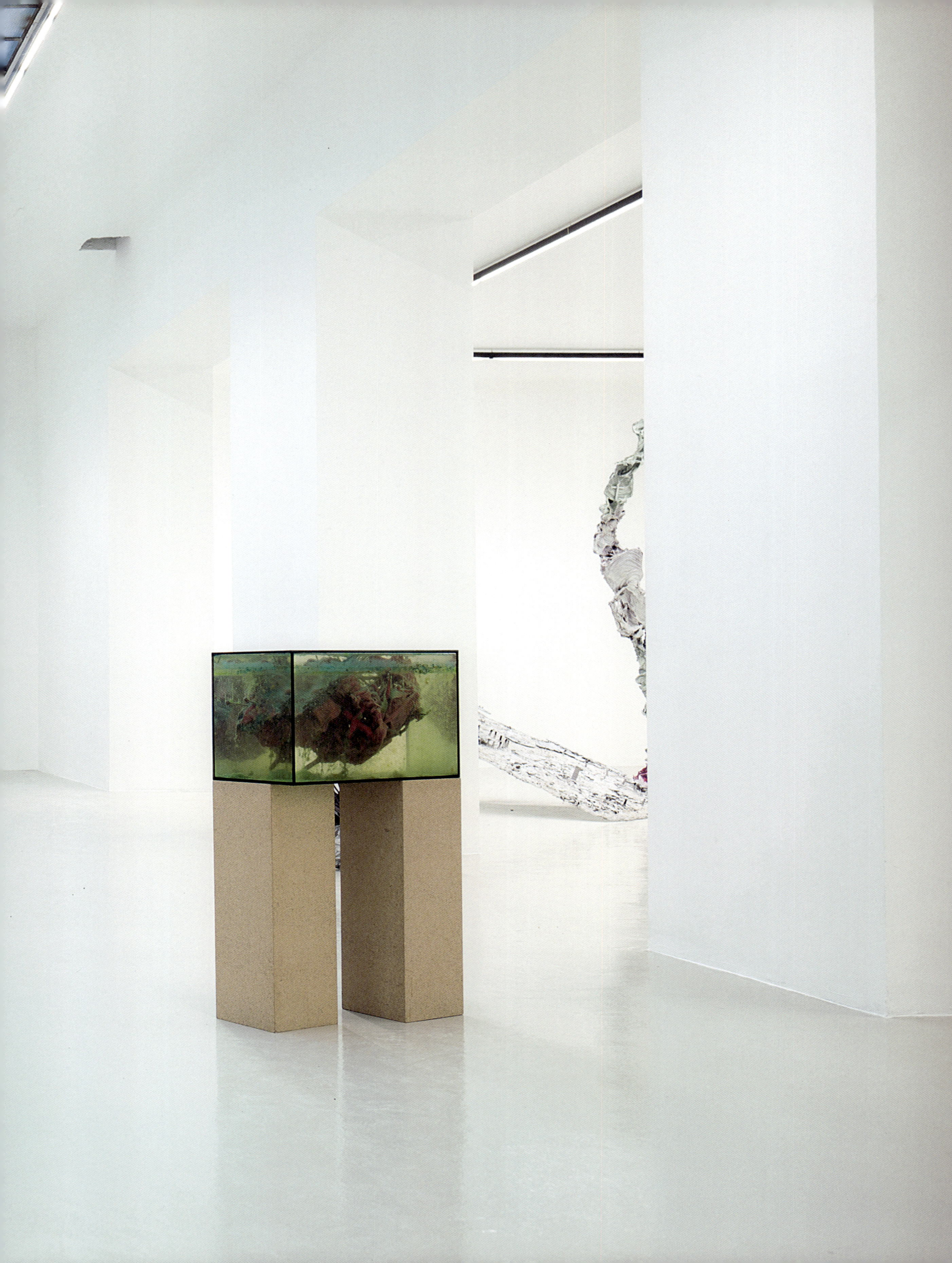

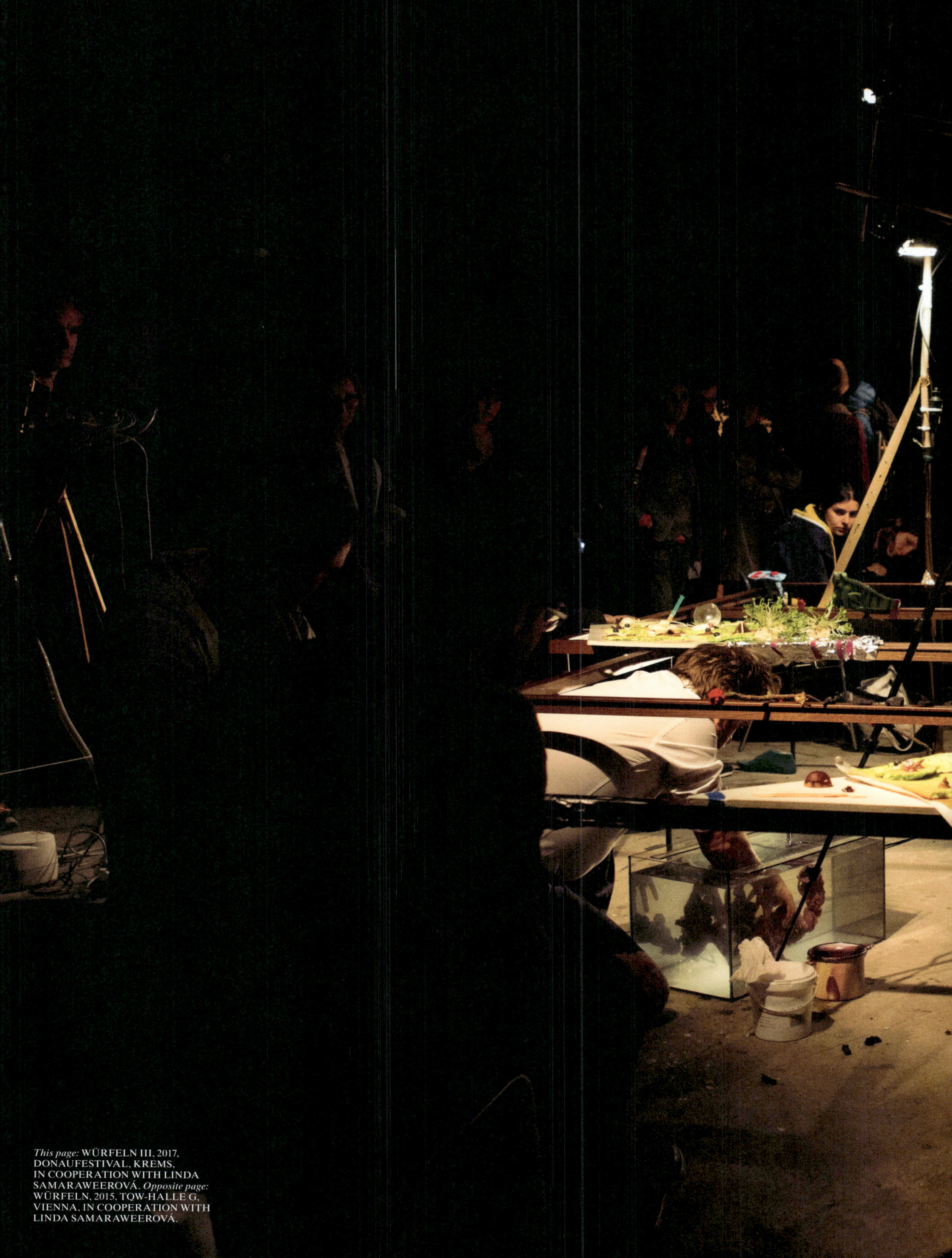

*This page:* WÜRFELN III, 2017, DONAUFESTIVAL, KREMS, IN COOPERATION WITH LINDA SAMARAWEEROVÁ. *Opposite page:* WÜRFELN, 2015, TQW-HALLE G, VIENNA, IN COOPERATION WITH LINDA SAMARAWEEROVÁ.

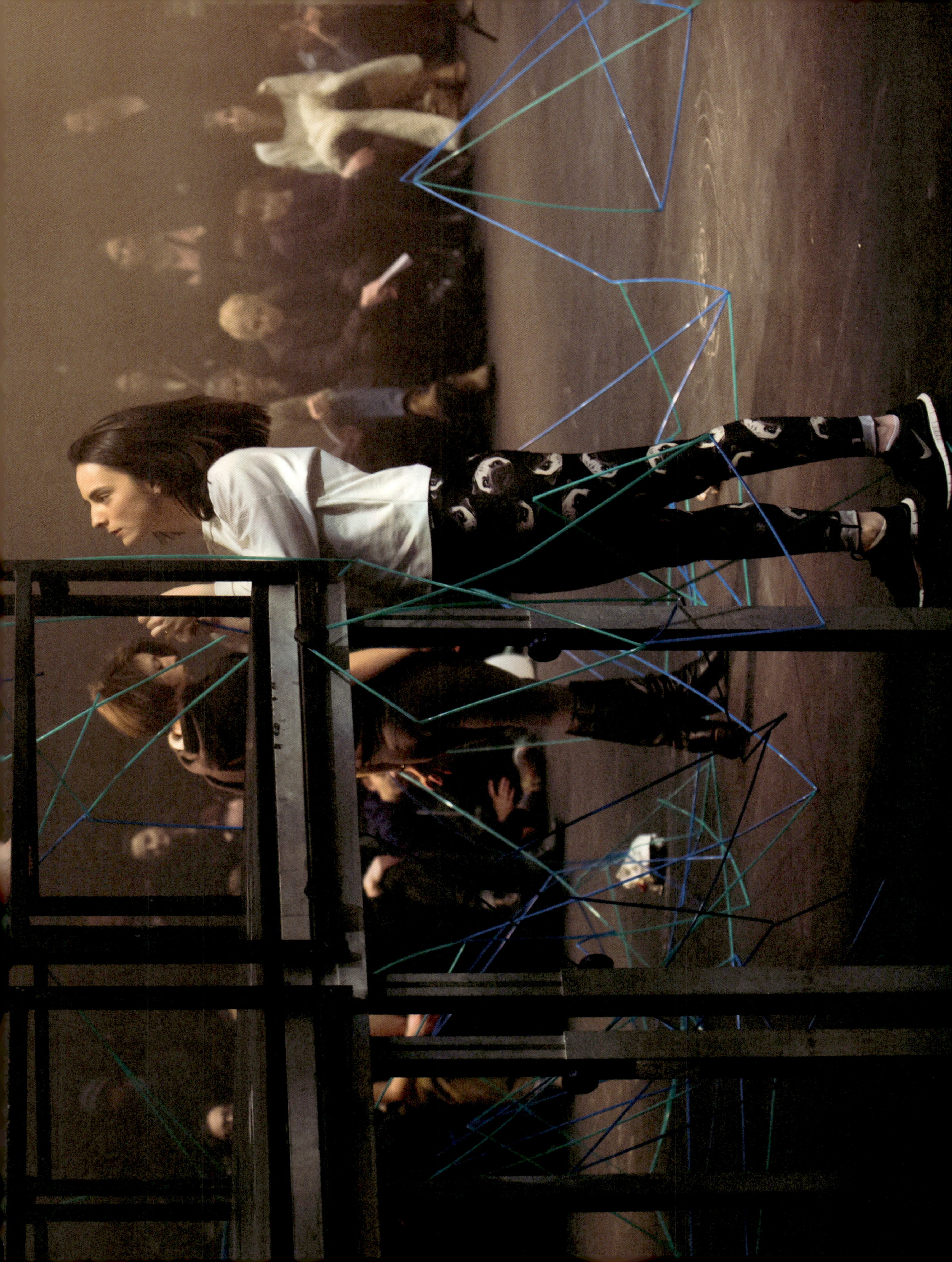

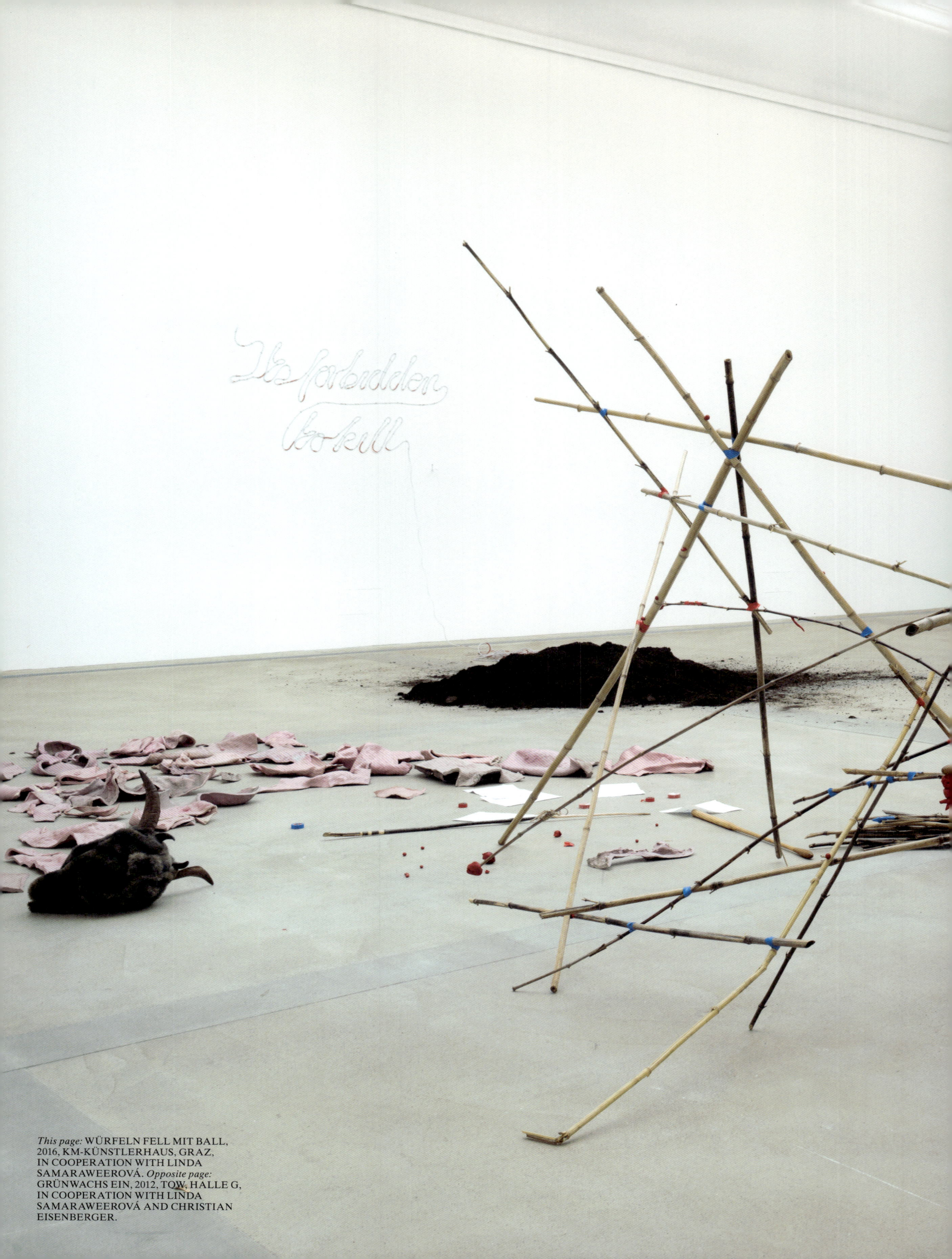


*This page:* WÜRFELN FELL MIT BALL, 2016, KM-KÜNSTLERHAUS, GRAZ, IN COOPERATION WITH LINDA SAMARAWEEROVÁ. *Opposite page:* GRÜNWACHS EIN, 2012, TQW, HALLE G, IN COOPERATION WITH LINDA SAMARAWEEROVÁ AND CHRISTIAN EISENBERGER.

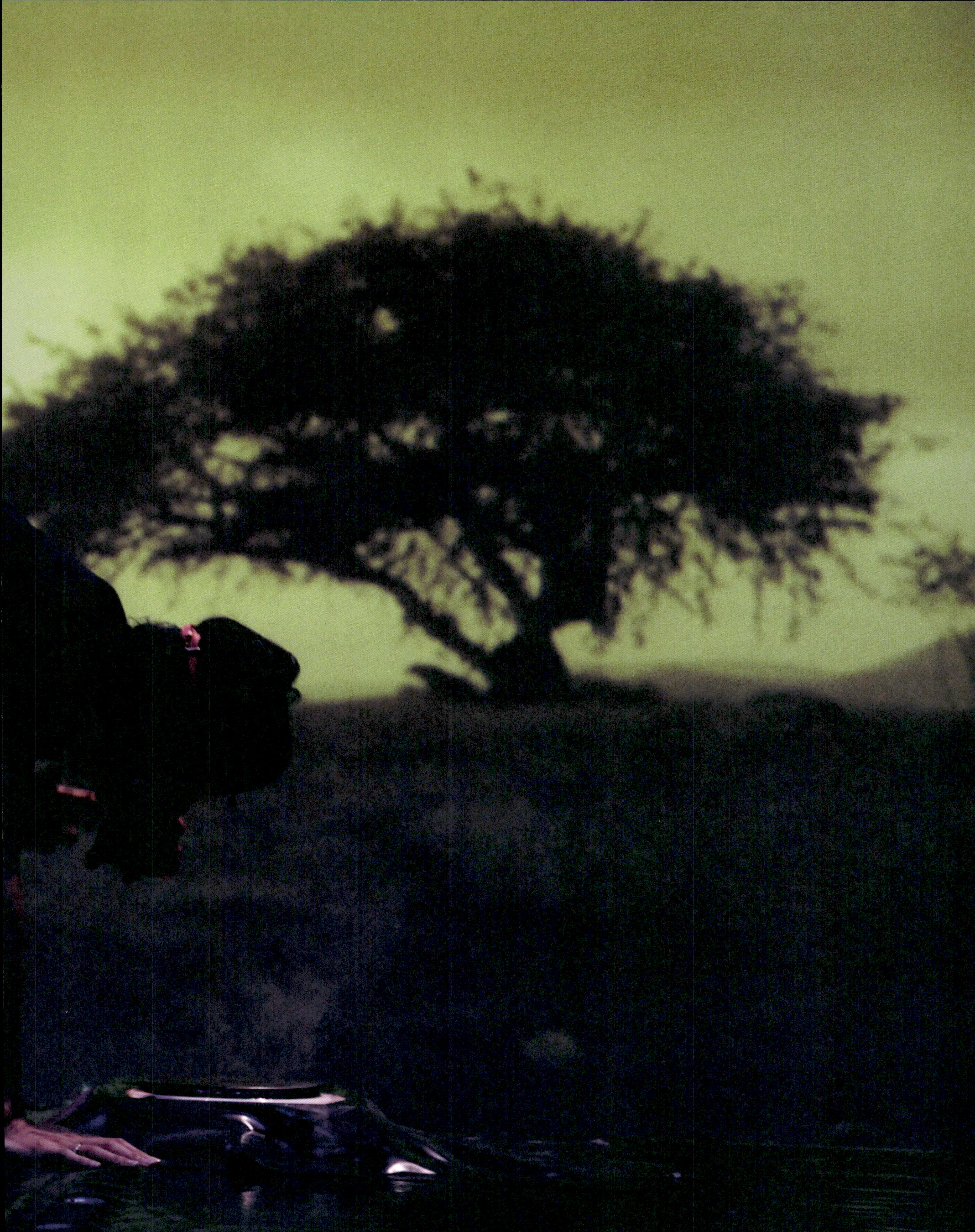

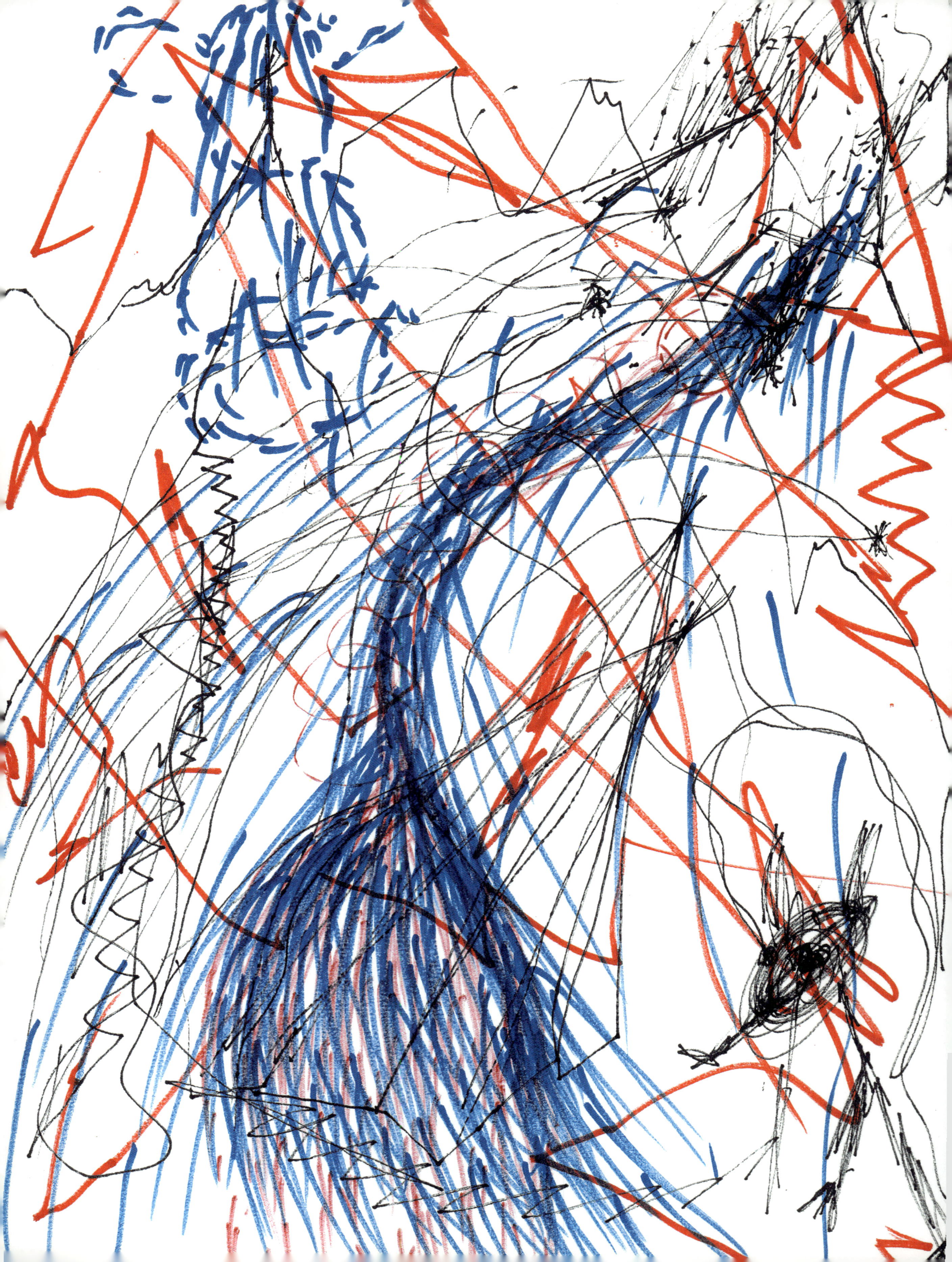

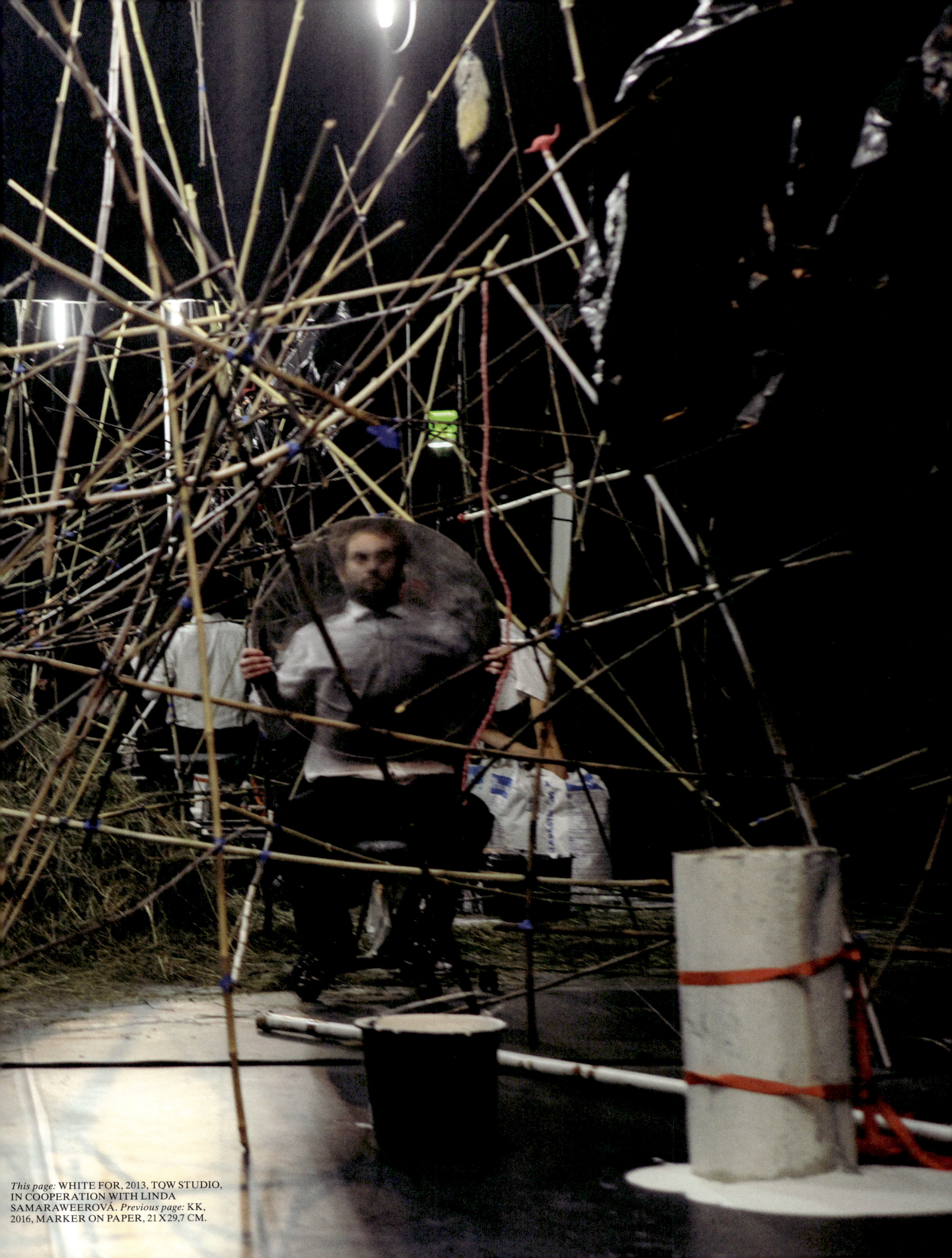

*This page:* WHITE FOR, 2013, TQW STUDIO, IN COOPERATION WITH LINDA SAMARAWEEROVÁ. *Previous page:* KK, 2016, MARKER ON PAPER, 21 X 29,7 CM.

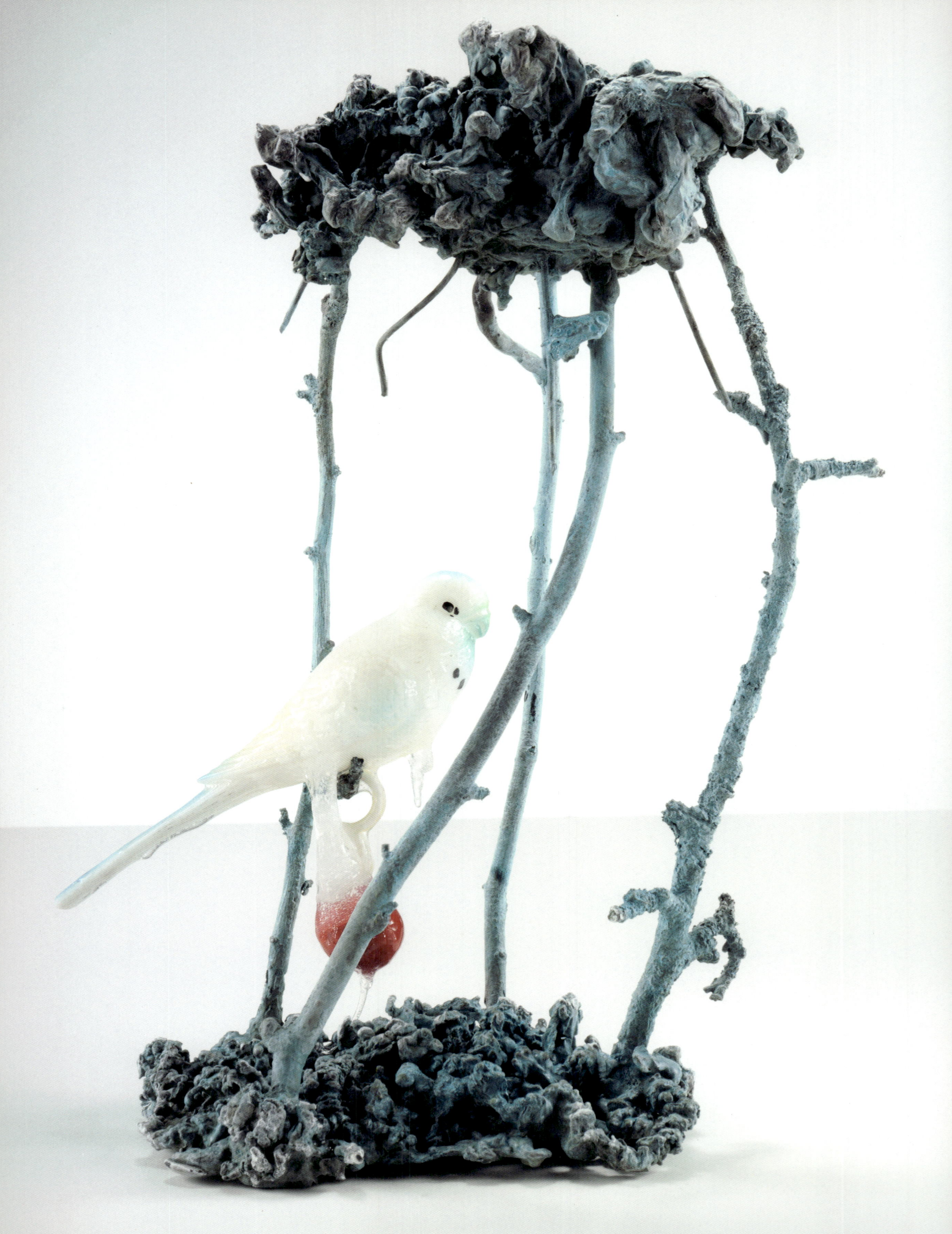

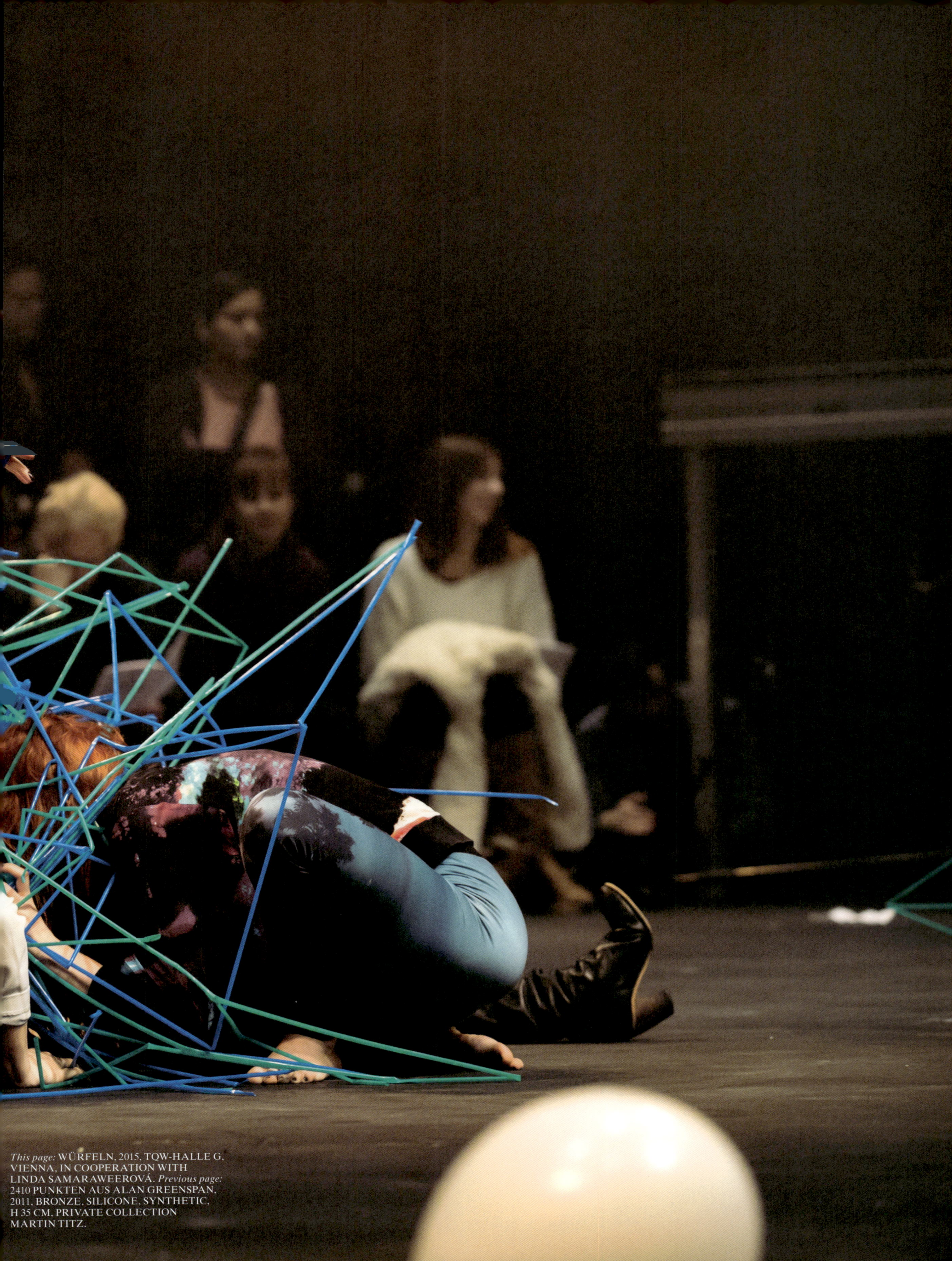

*This page:* WÜRFELN, 2015, TQW-HALLE G, VIENNA, IN COOPERATION WITH LINDA SAMARAWEEROVÁ. *Previous page:* 2410 PUNKTEN AUS ALAN GREENSPAN, 2011, BRONZE, SILICONE, SYNTHETIC, H 35 CM, PRIVATE COLLECTION MARTIN TITZ.

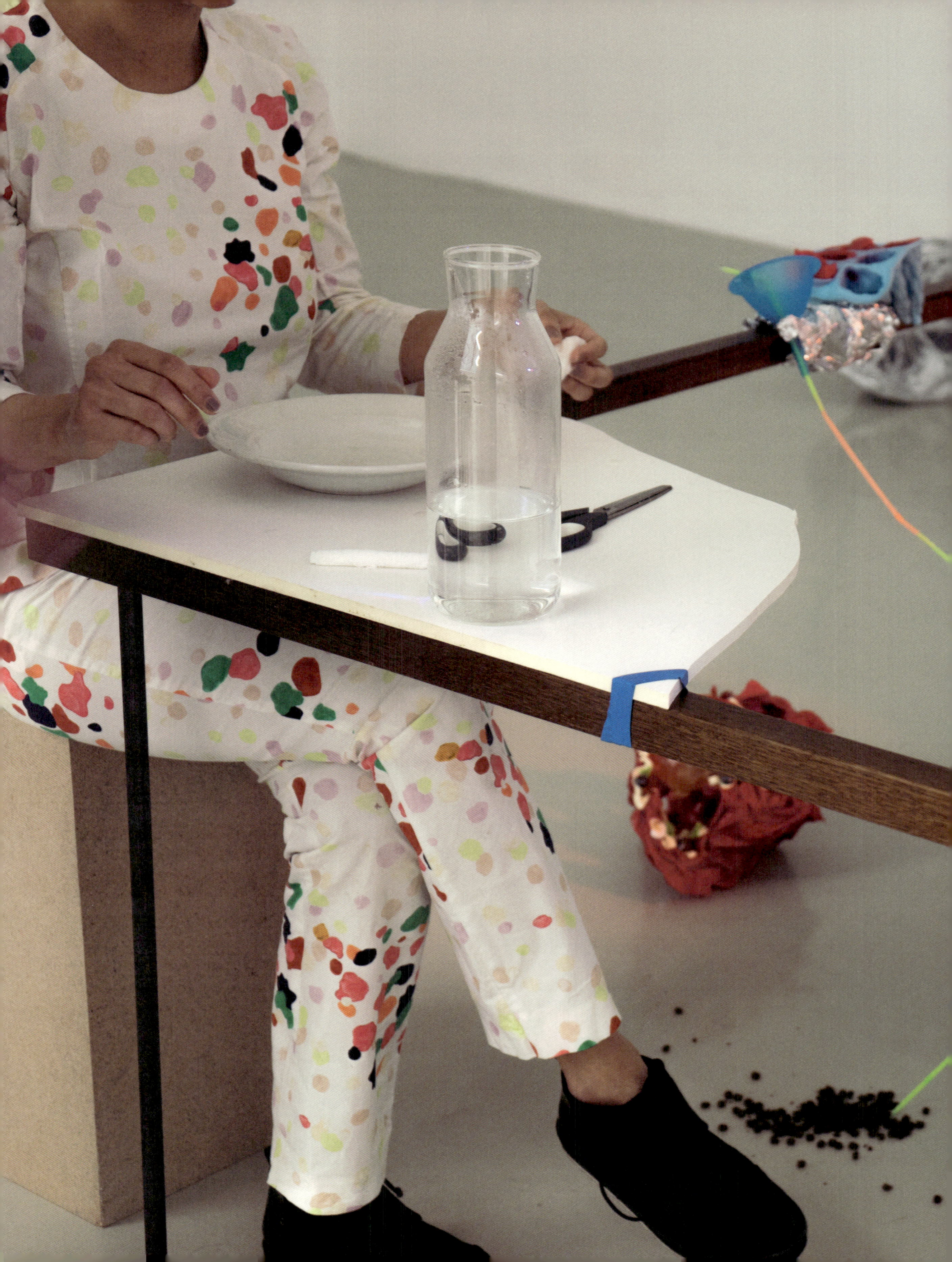

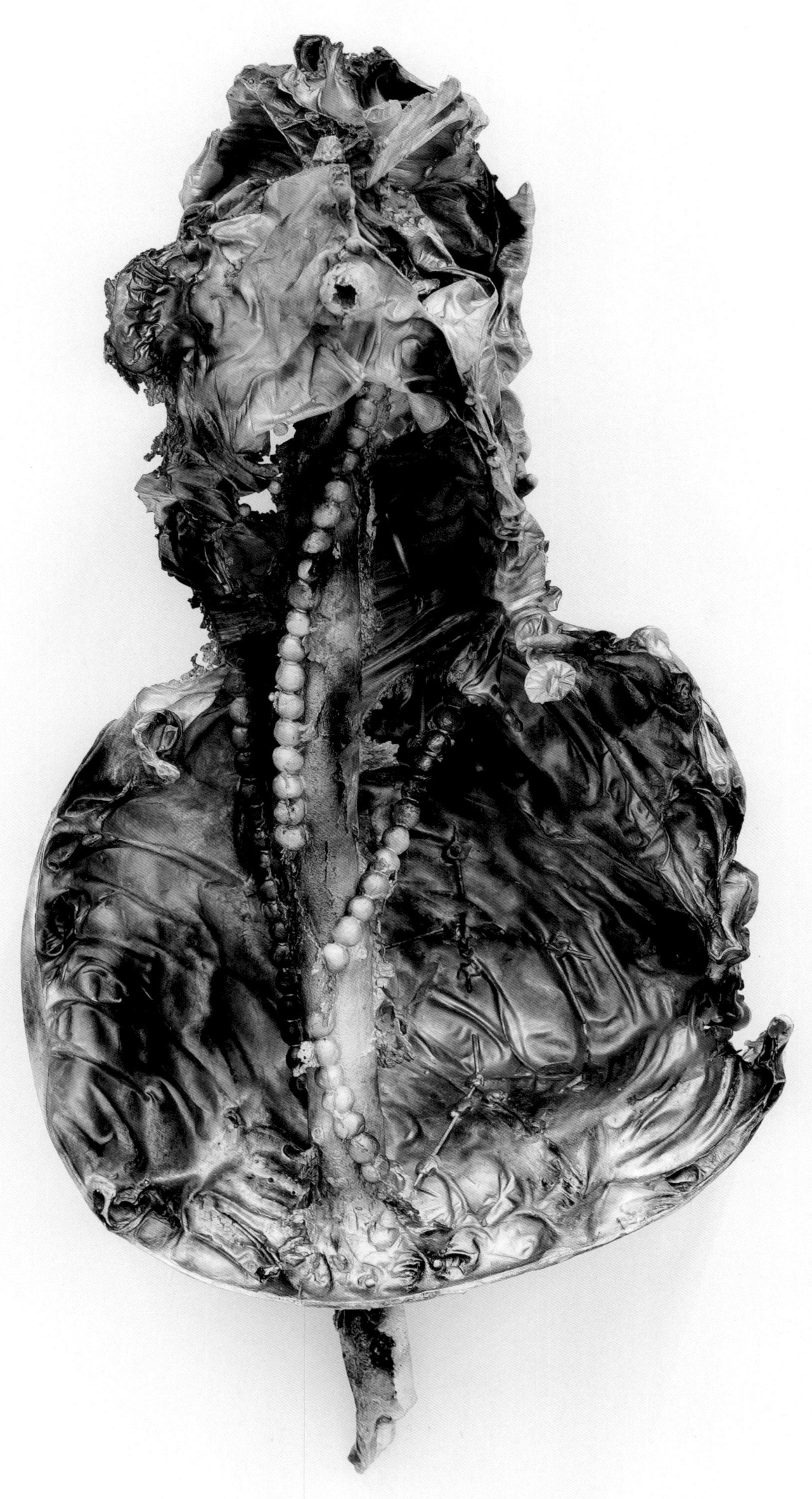

*This page:* PERLRUSS, 2016, ALUMINIUM, 33 X 67 X 29 CM, COLLECTION HEINZ NEUMANN. *Previous page:* WÜRFELN III, 2017, GALLERY LISA KANDLHOFER, VIENNA, IN COOPERATION WITH LINDA SAMARAWEEROVÁ.

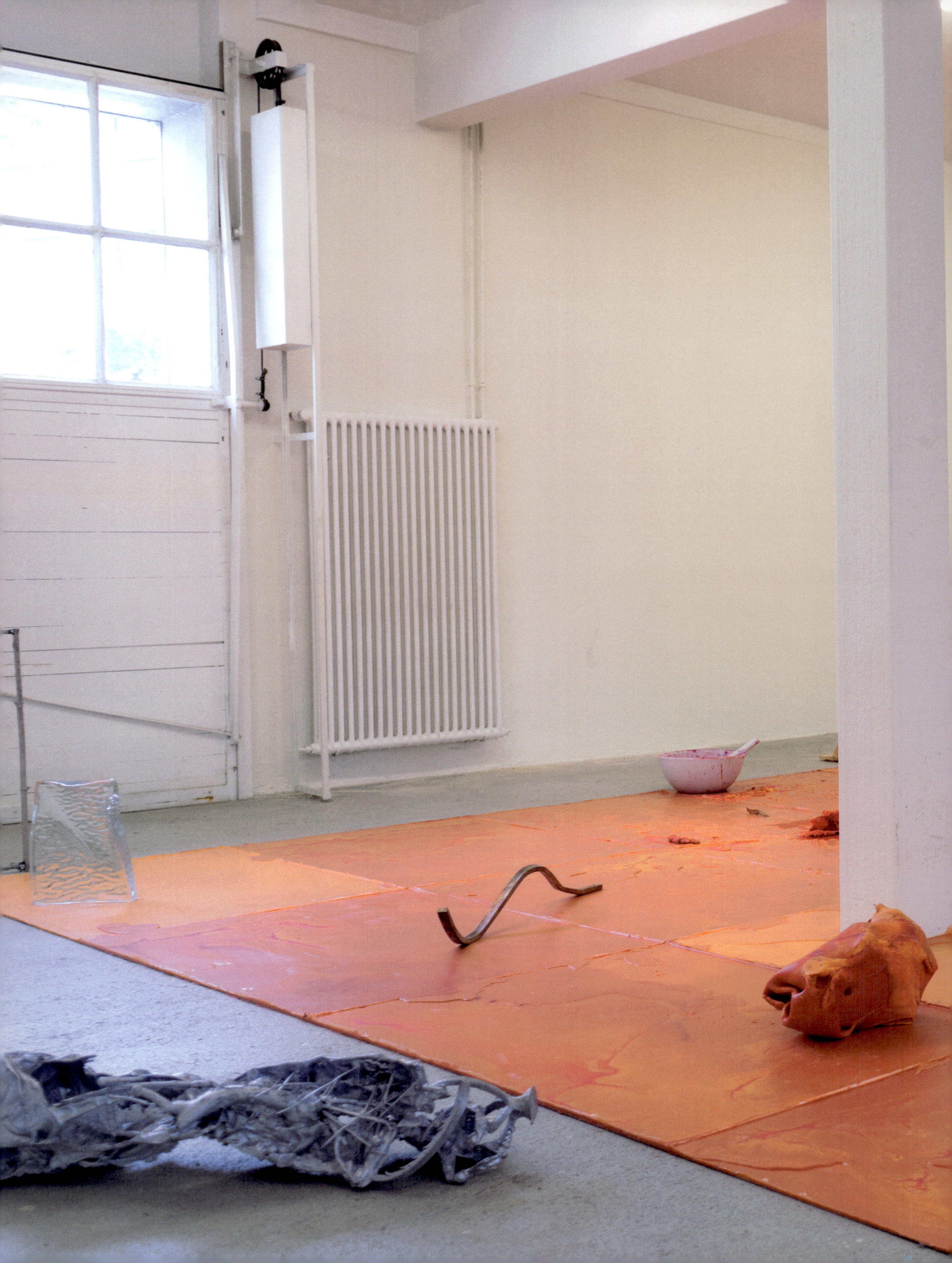

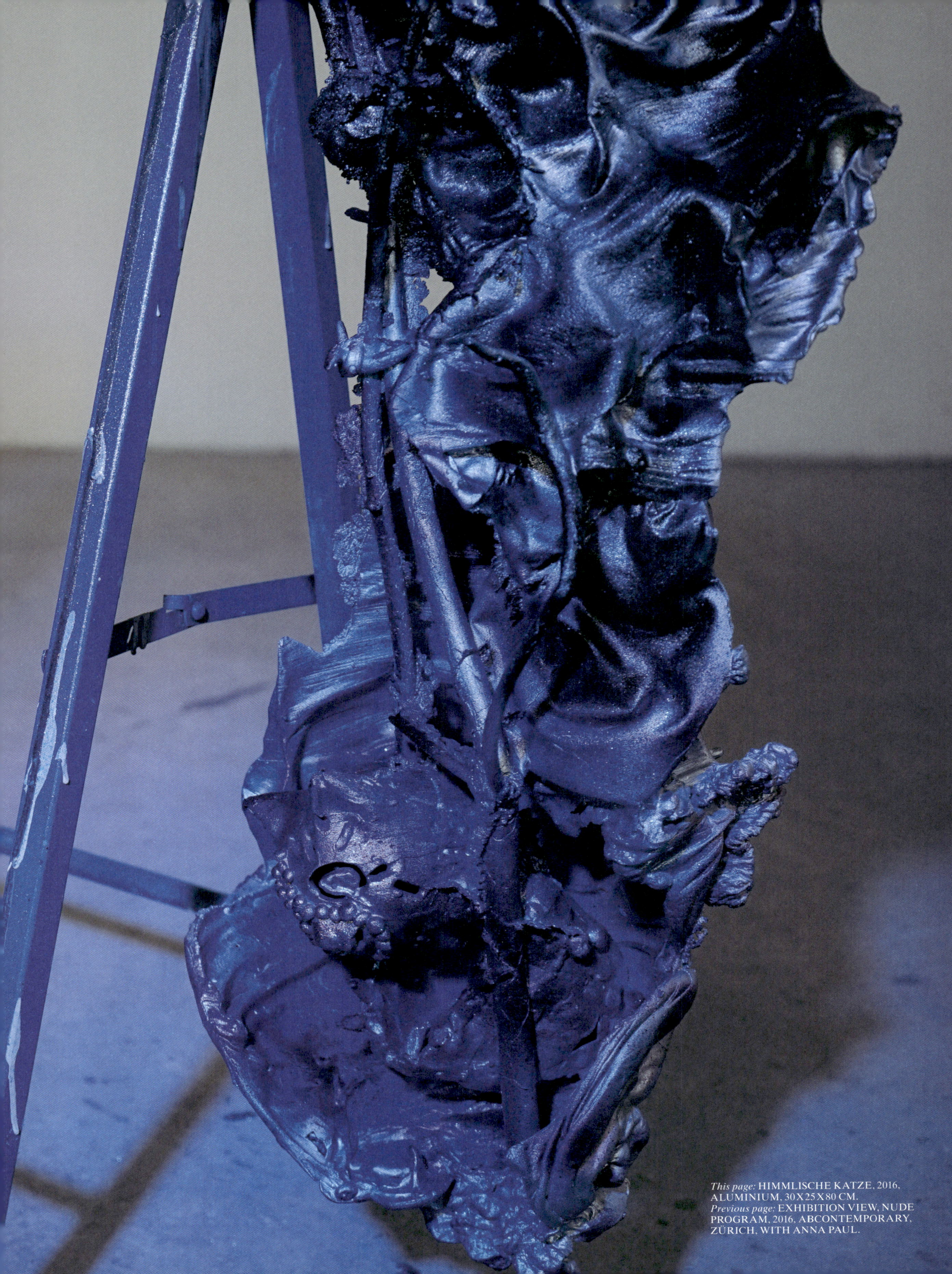

*This page:* HIMMLISCHE KATZE, 2016, ALUMINIUM, 30X25X80 CM.
*Previous page:* EXHIBITION VIEW, NUDE PROGRAM, 2016, ABCONTEMPORARY, ZÜRICH, WITH ANNA PAUL.

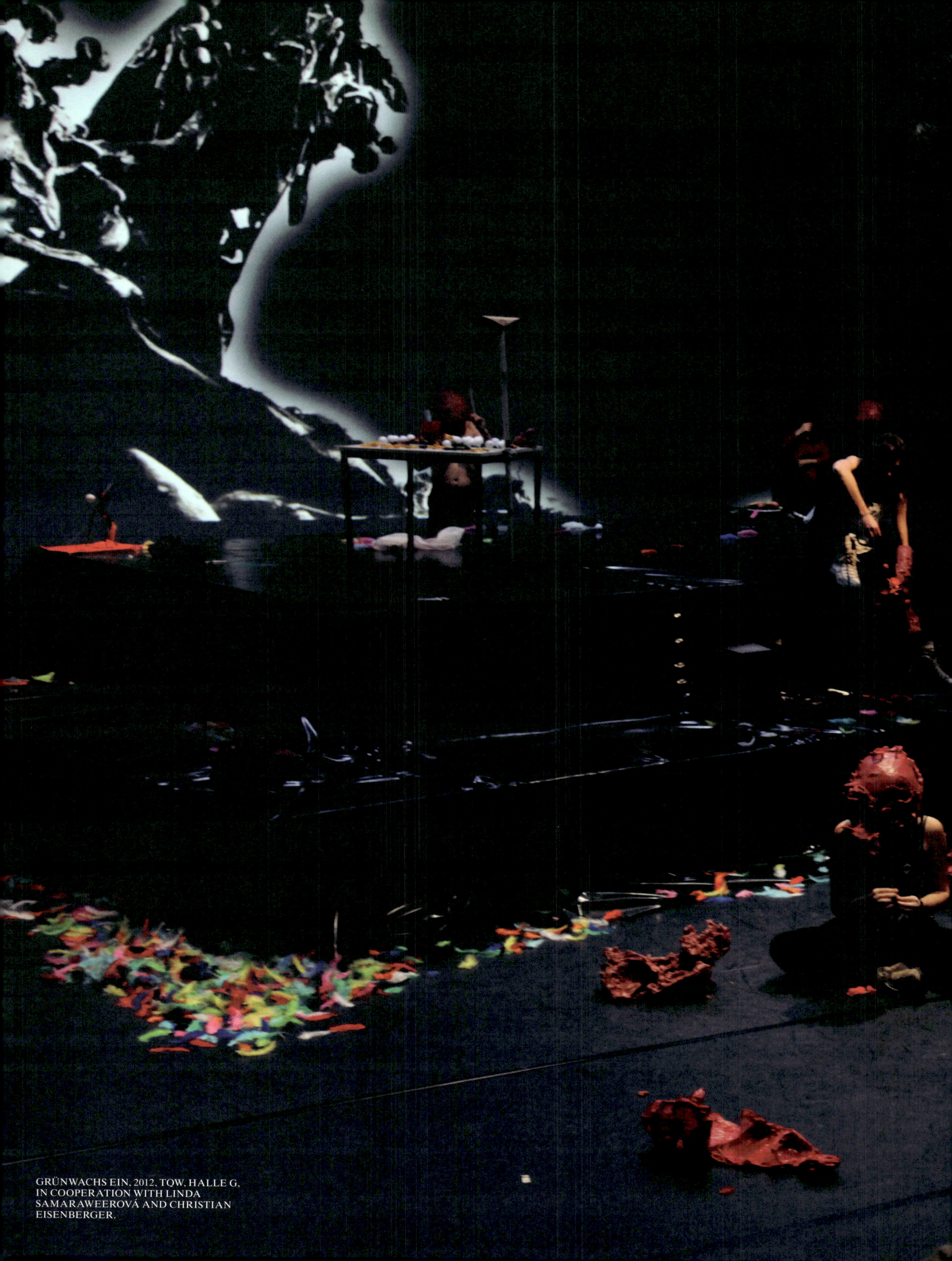

GRÜNWACHS EIN, 2012, TQW, HALLE G, IN COOPERATION WITH LINDA SAMARAWEEROVÁ AND CHRISTIAN EISENBERGER.

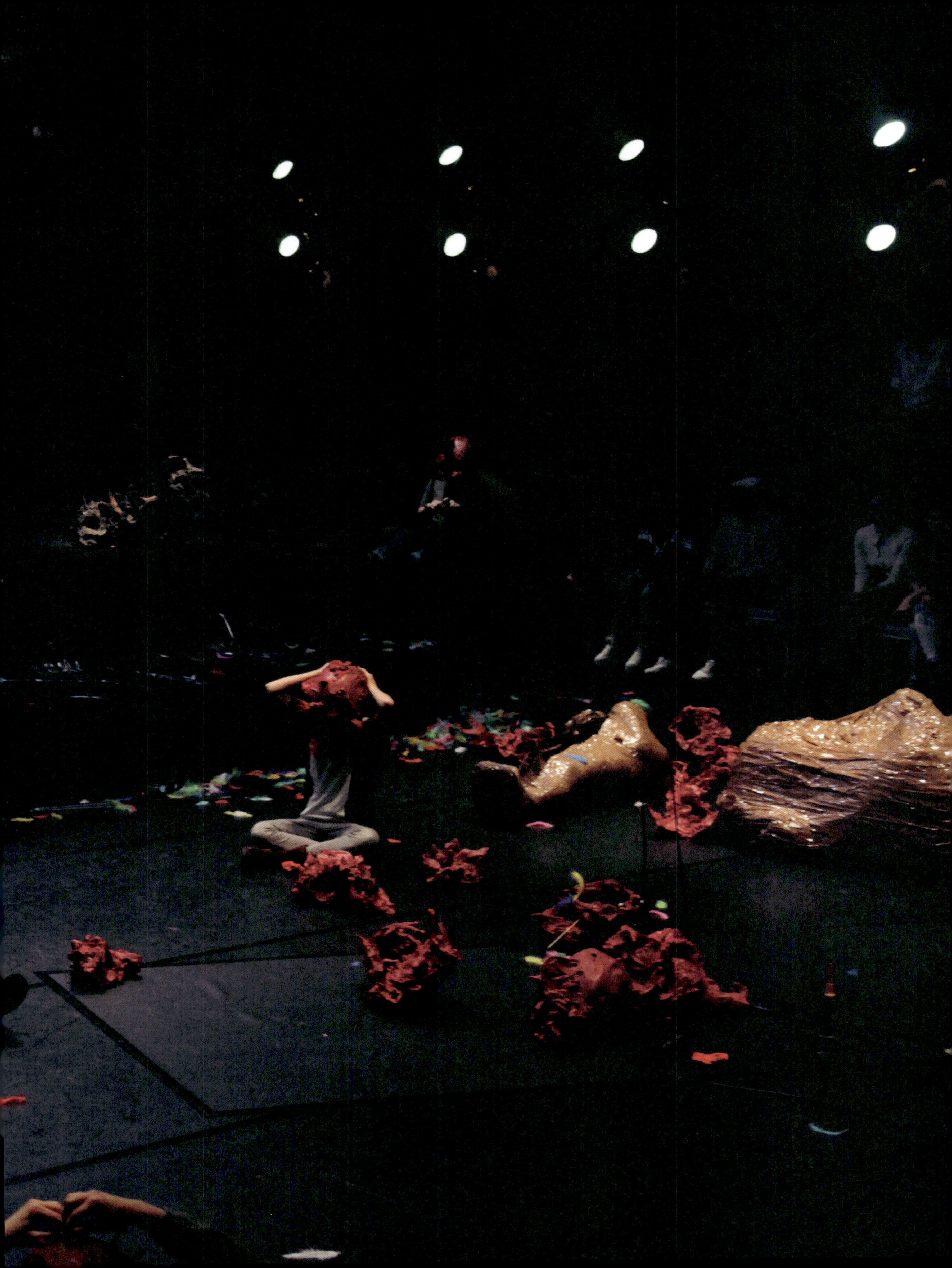

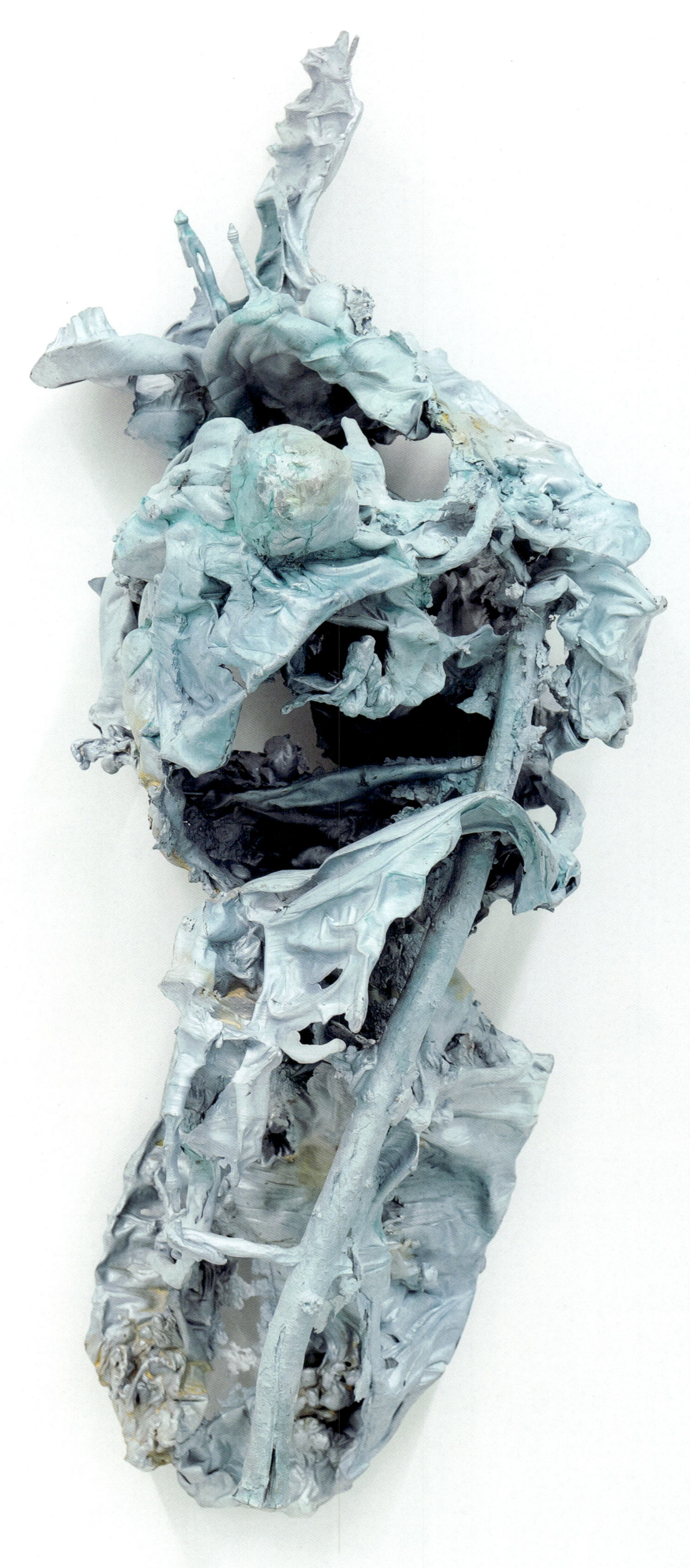

*This page:* SILVER K, 2016, SPRAY PAINT ON ALUMINIUM, 36 X 82 X 28 CM.
*Opposite page:* EXHIBITION VIEW, NUDE PROGRAM, 2016, ABCONTEMPORARY, ZÜRICH, WITH ANNA PAUL.

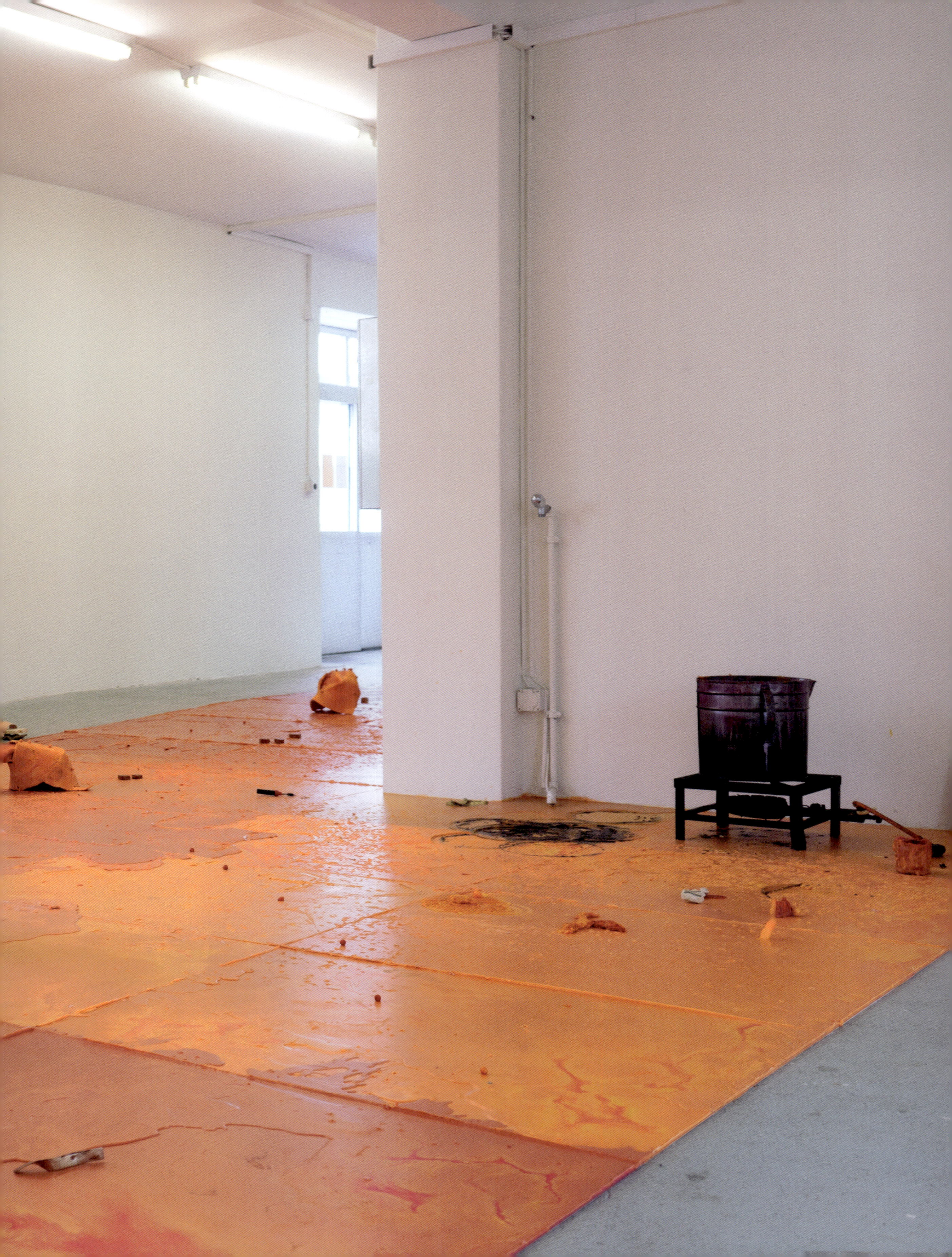

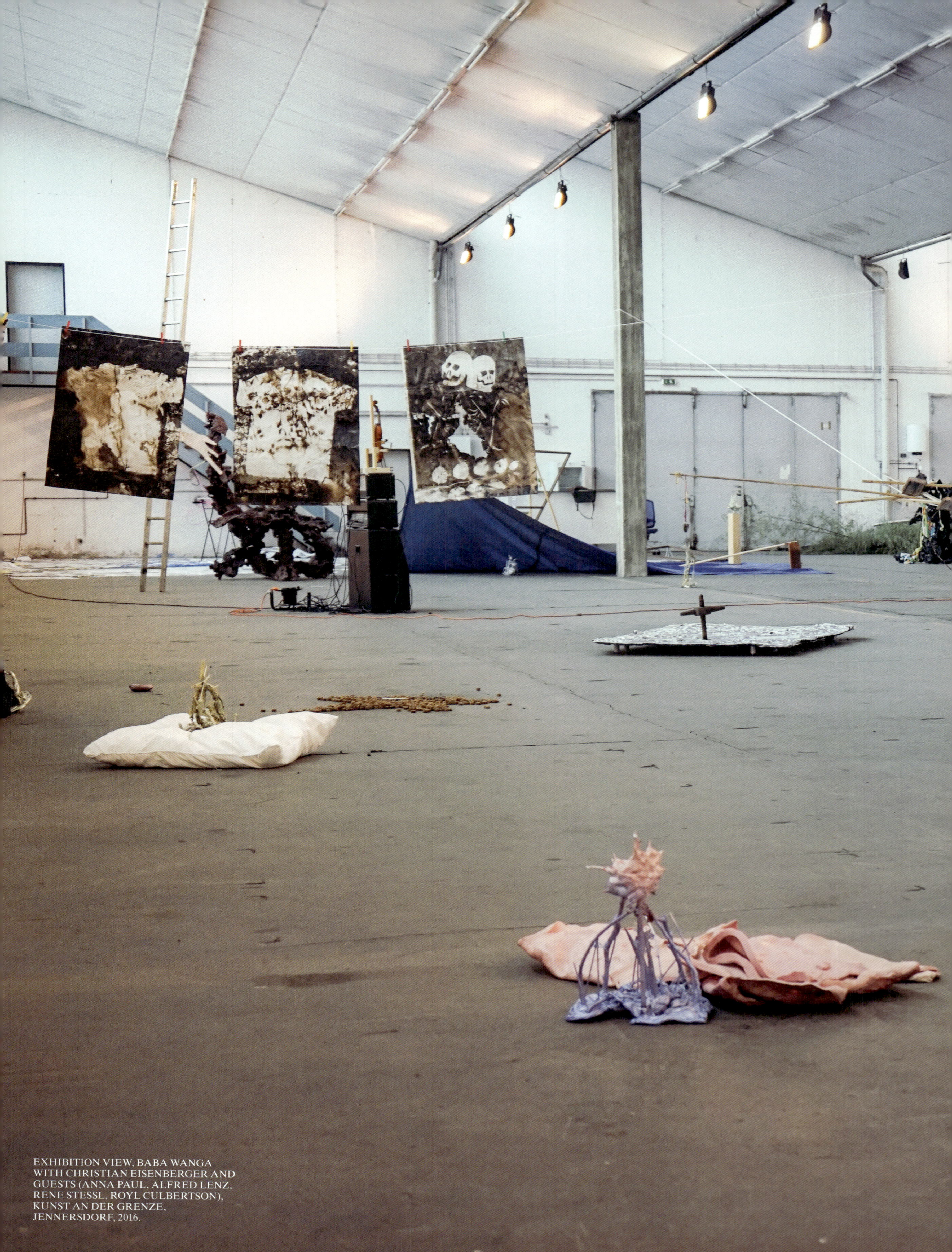

EXHIBITION VIEW, BABA WANGA WITH CHRISTIAN EISENBERGER AND GUESTS (ANNA PAUL, ALFRED LENZ, RENE STESSL, ROYL CULBERTSON), KUNST AN DER GRENZE, JENNERSDORF, 2016.

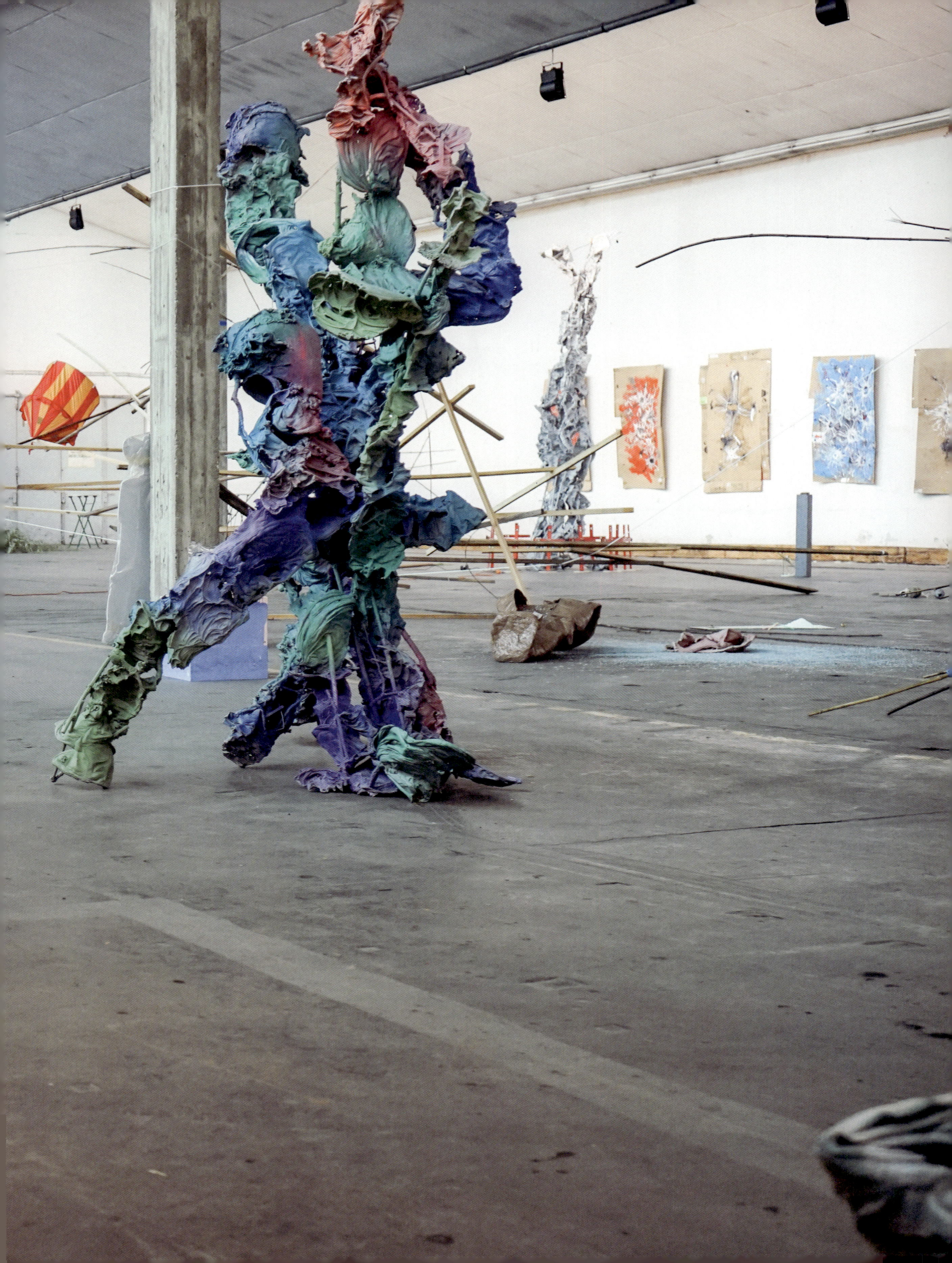

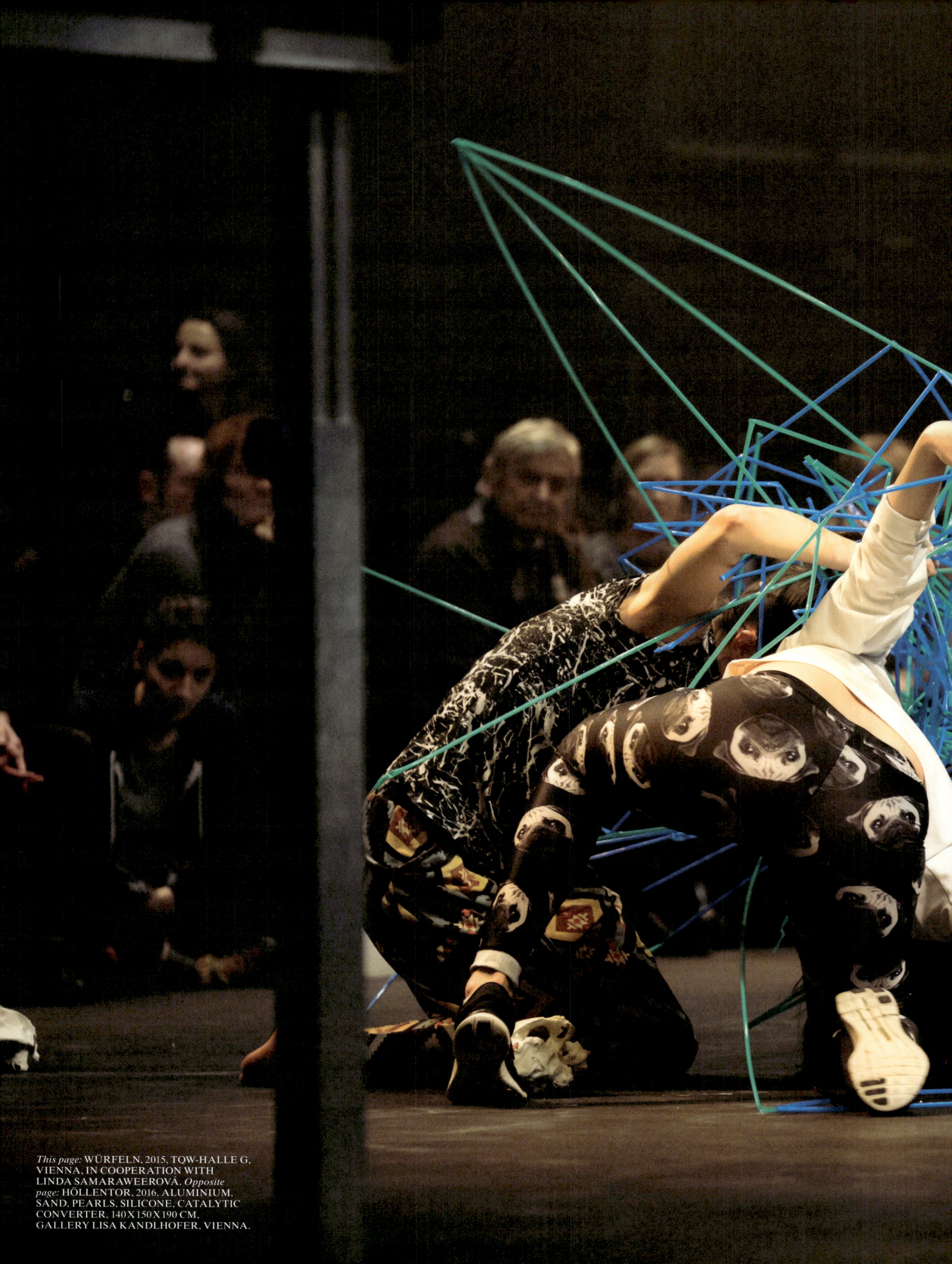

*This page:* WÜRFELN, 2015, TQW-HALLE G, VIENNA, IN COOPERATION WITH LINDA SAMARAWEEROVÁ. *Opposite page:* HÖLLENTOR, 2016, ALUMINIUM, SAND, PEARLS, SILICONE, CATALYTIC CONVERTER, 140 X 150 X 190 CM, GALLERY LISA KANDLHOFER, VIENNA.

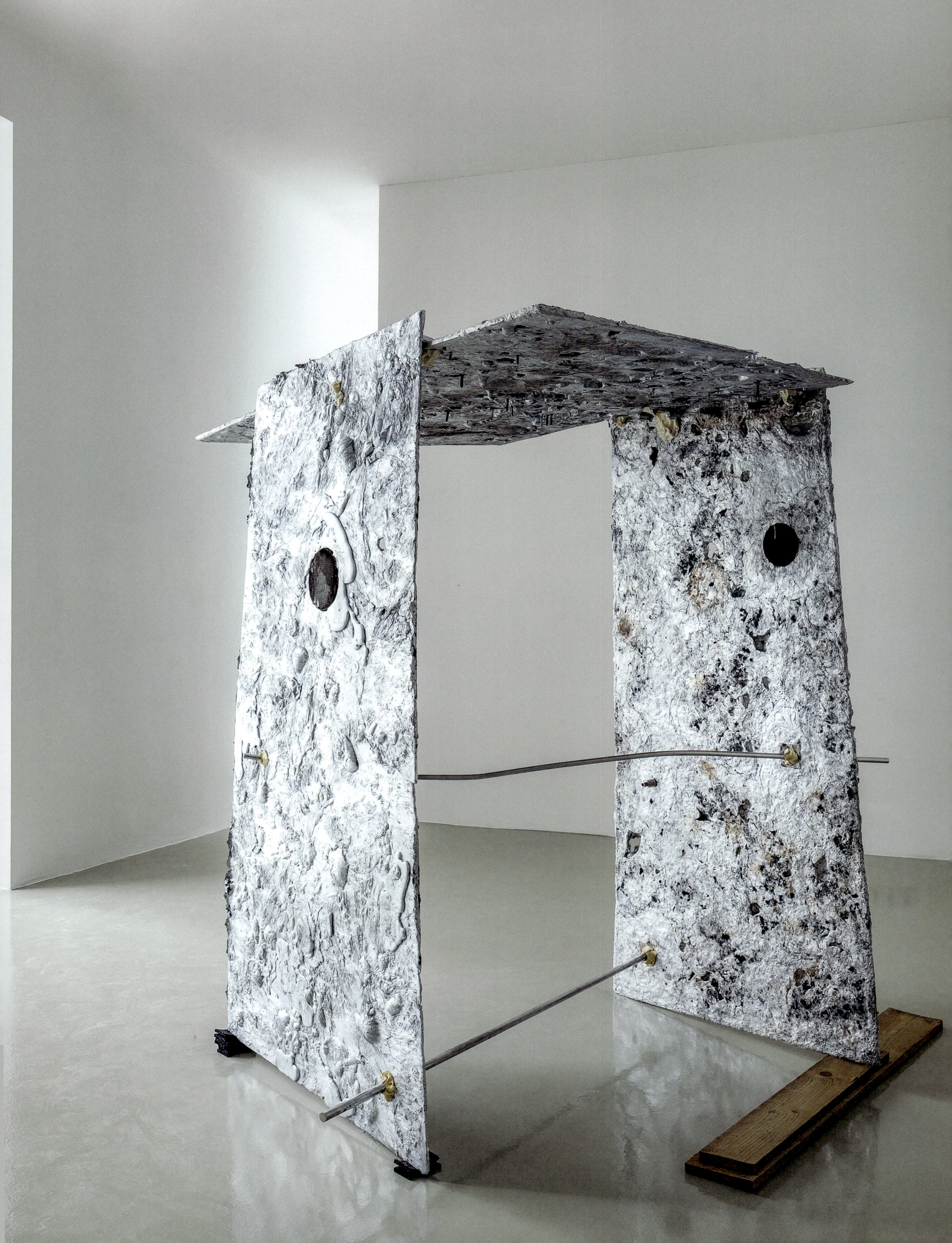

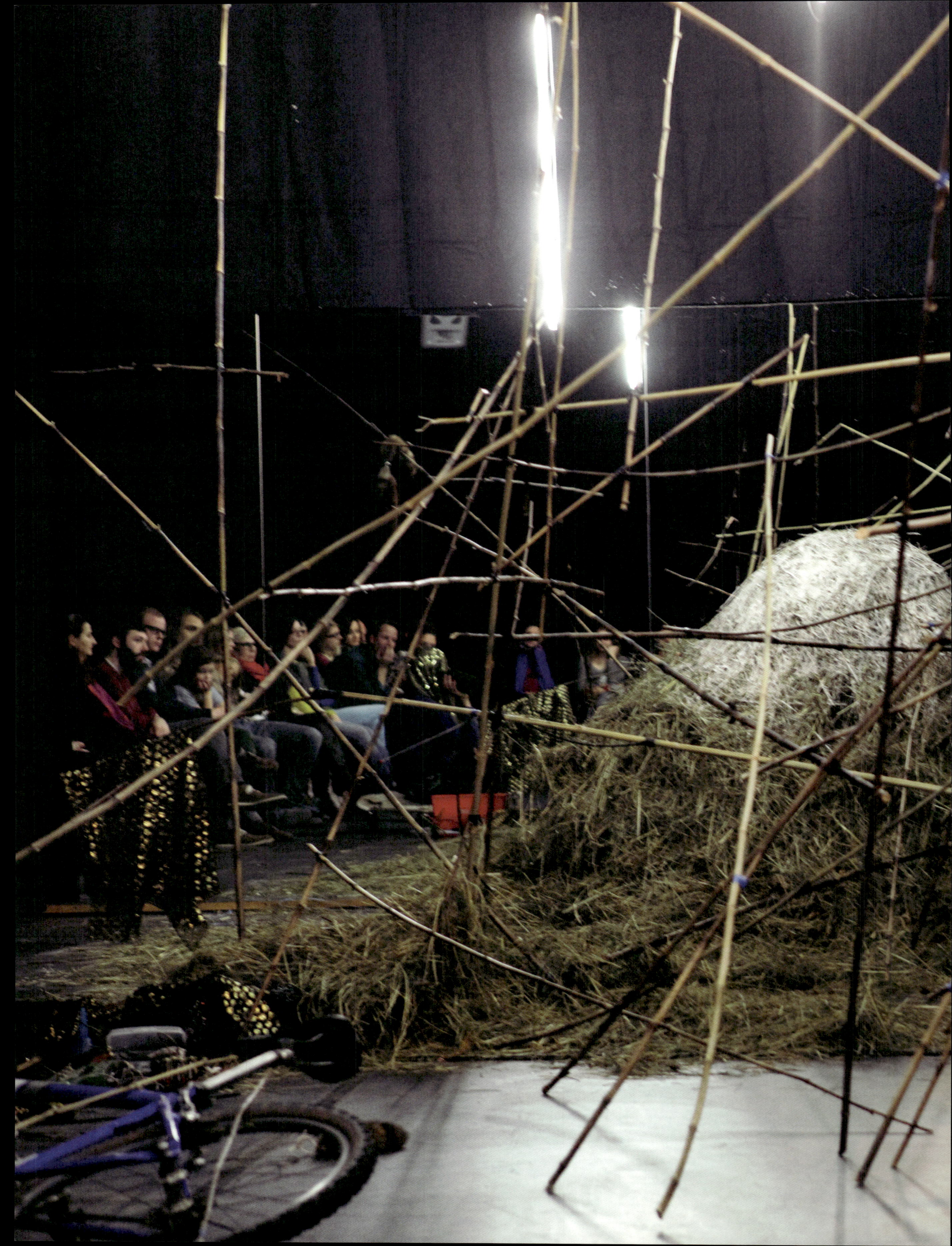

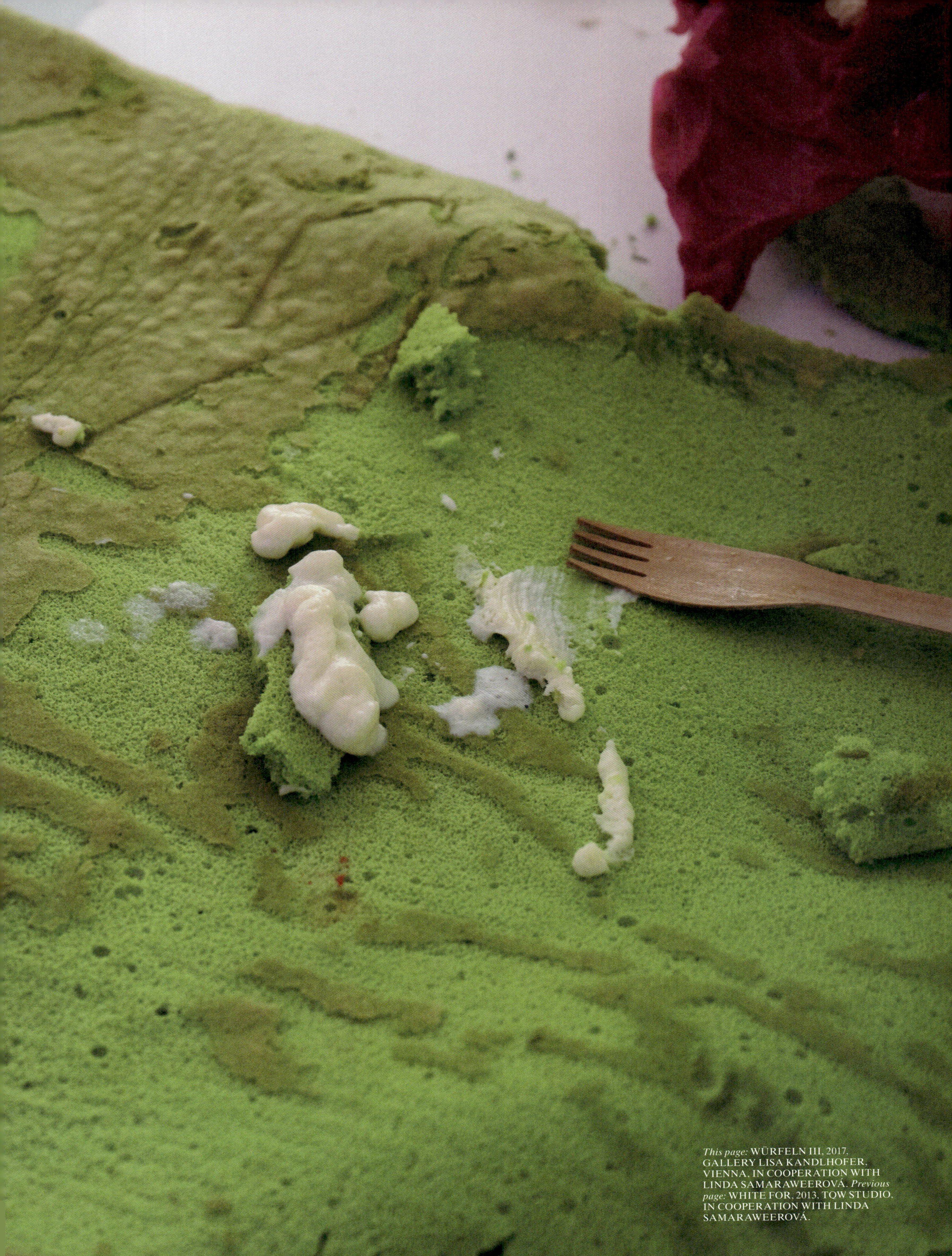

*This page:* WÜRFELN III, 2017, GALLERY LISA KANDLHOFER, VIENNA, IN COOPERATION WITH LINDA SAMARAWEEROVÁ. *Previous page:* WHITE FOR, 2013, TQW STUDIO, IN COOPERATION WITH LINDA SAMARAWEEROVÁ.

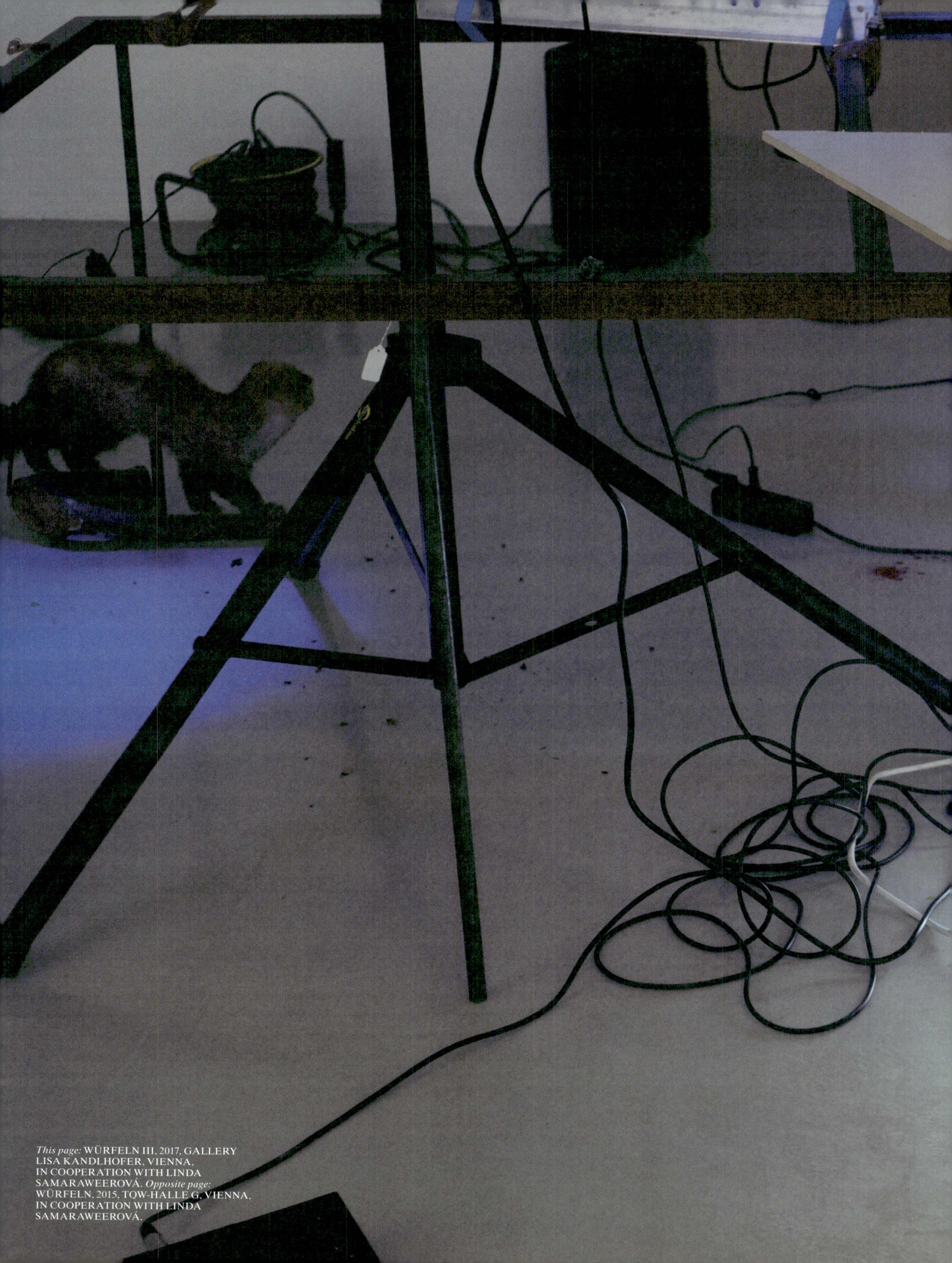

*This page:* WÜRFELN III, 2017, GALLERY LISA KANDLHOFER, VIENNA, IN COOPERATION WITH LINDA SAMARAWEEROVÁ. *Opposite page:* WÜRFELN, 2015, TQW-HALLE G, VIENNA, IN COOPERATION WITH LINDA SAMARAWEEROVÁ.

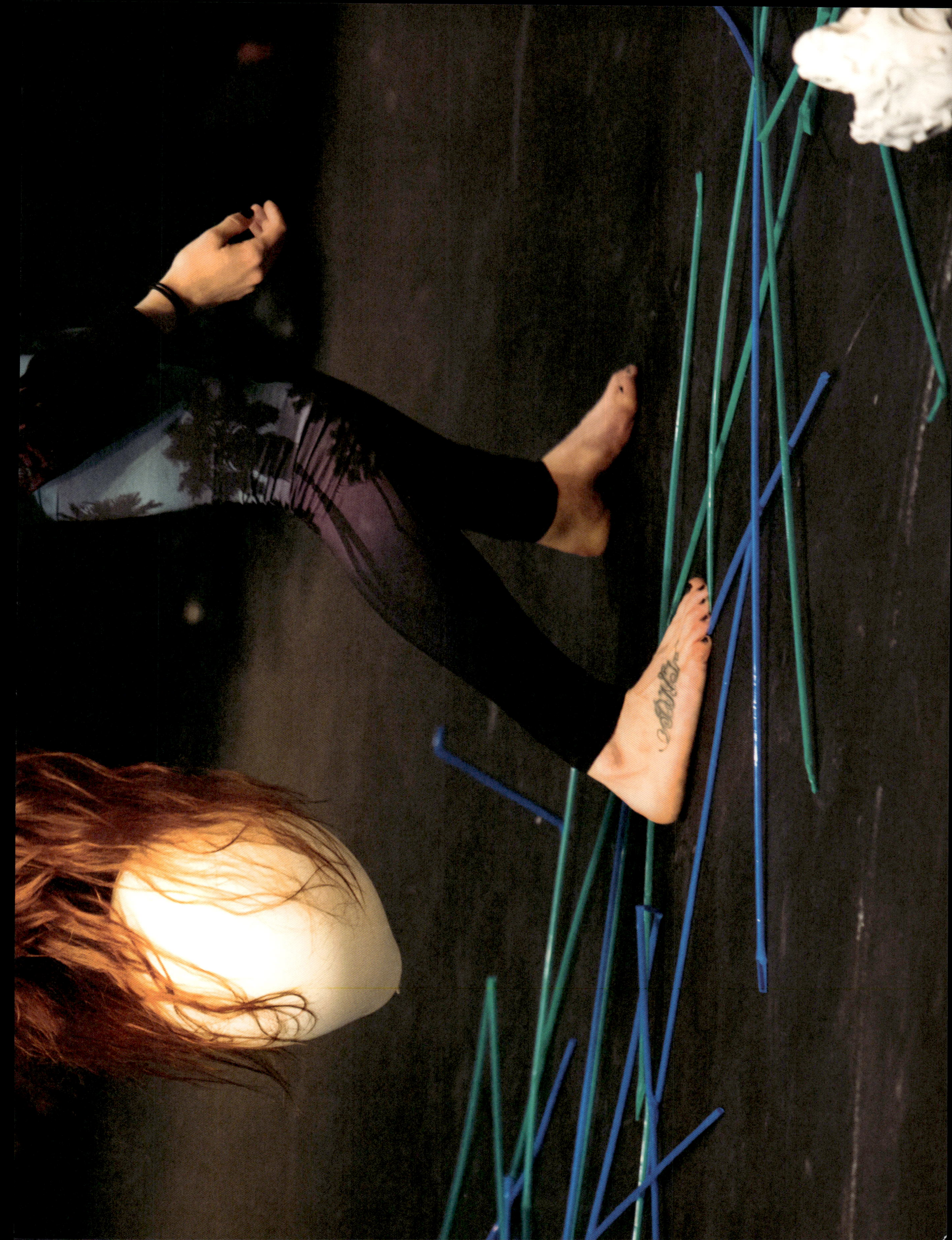

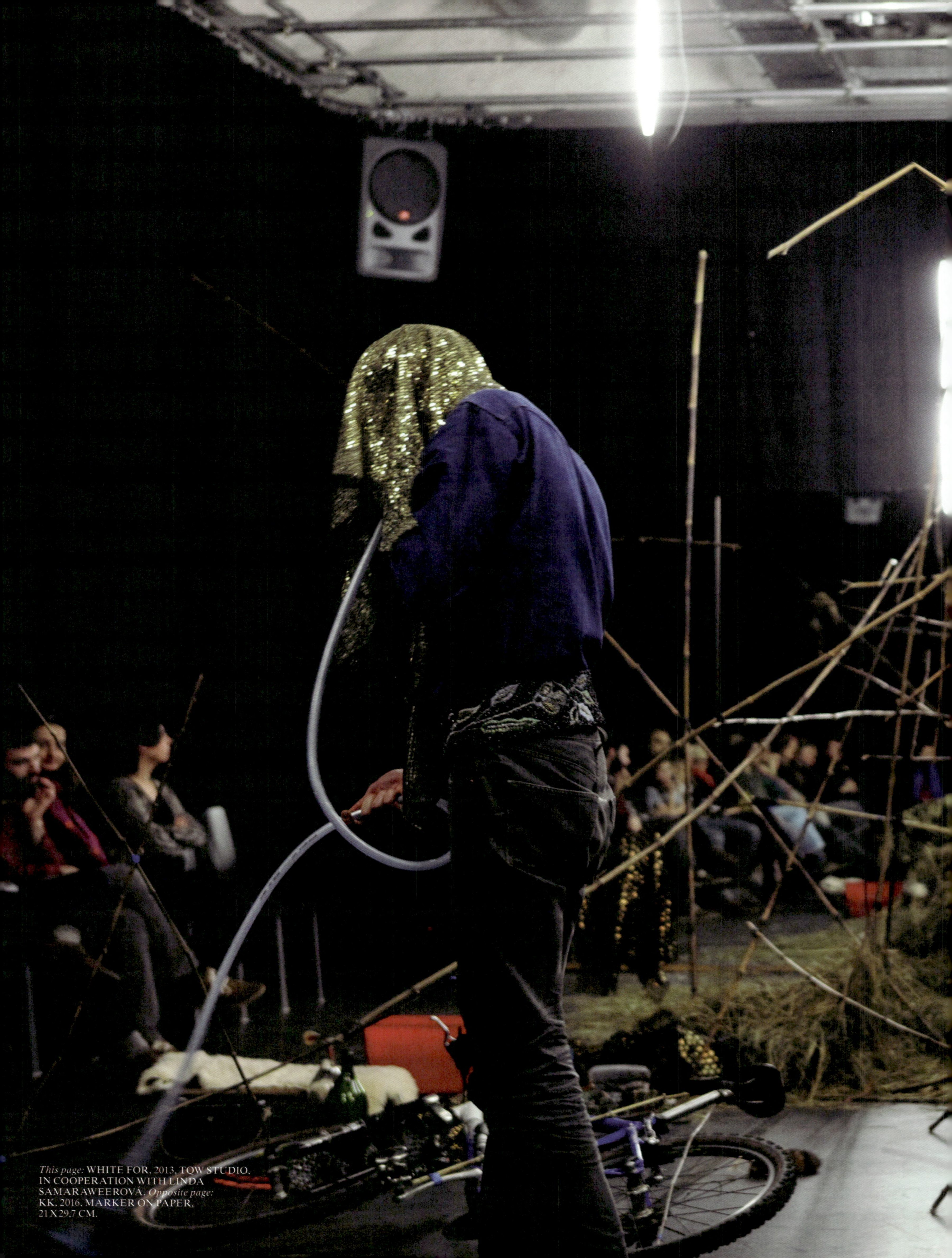

*This page:* WHITE FOR, 2013, TOW STUDIO, IN COOPERATION WITH LINDA SAMARAWEEROVÁ. *Opposite page:* KK, 2016, MARKER ON PAPER, 21X29.7 CM.

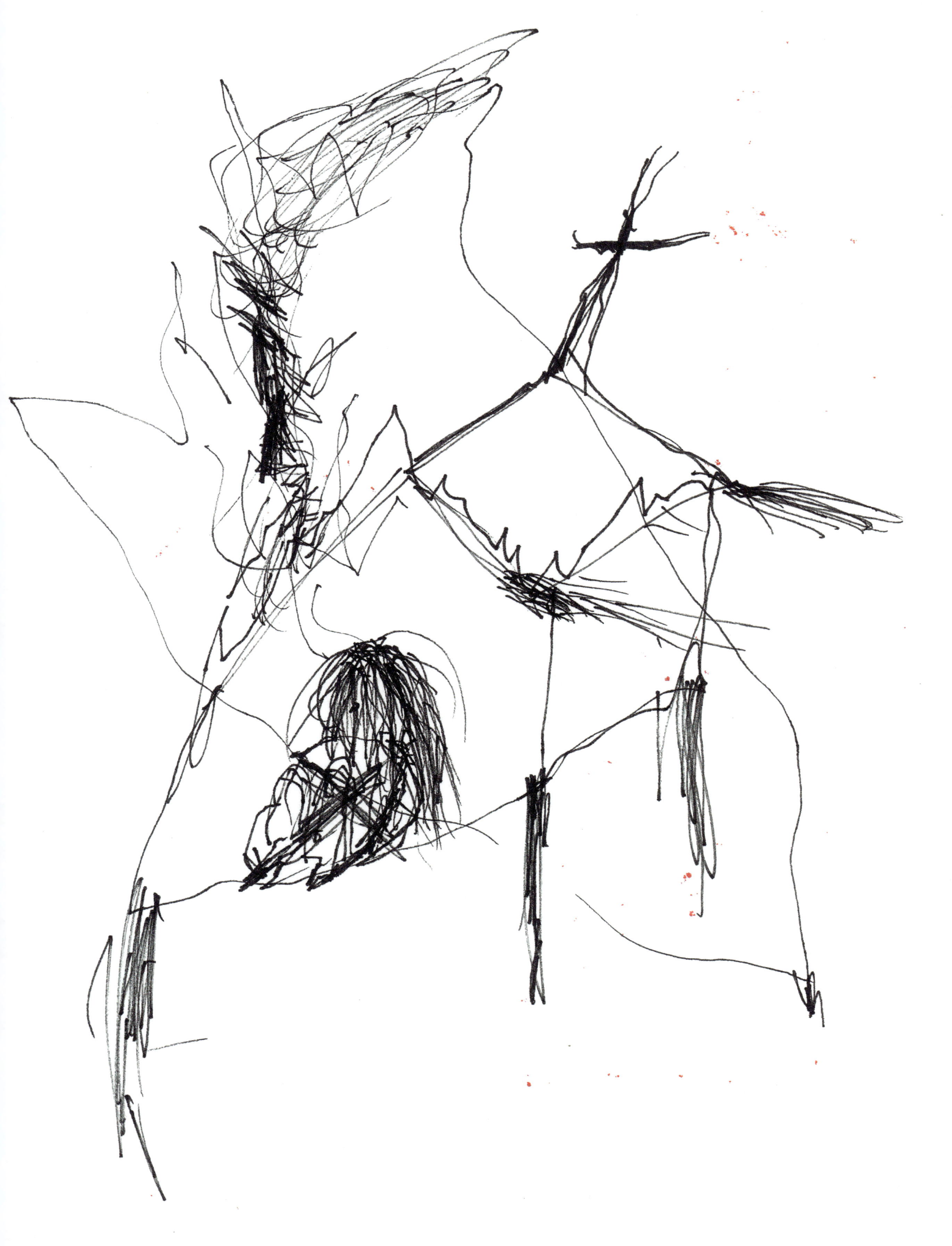

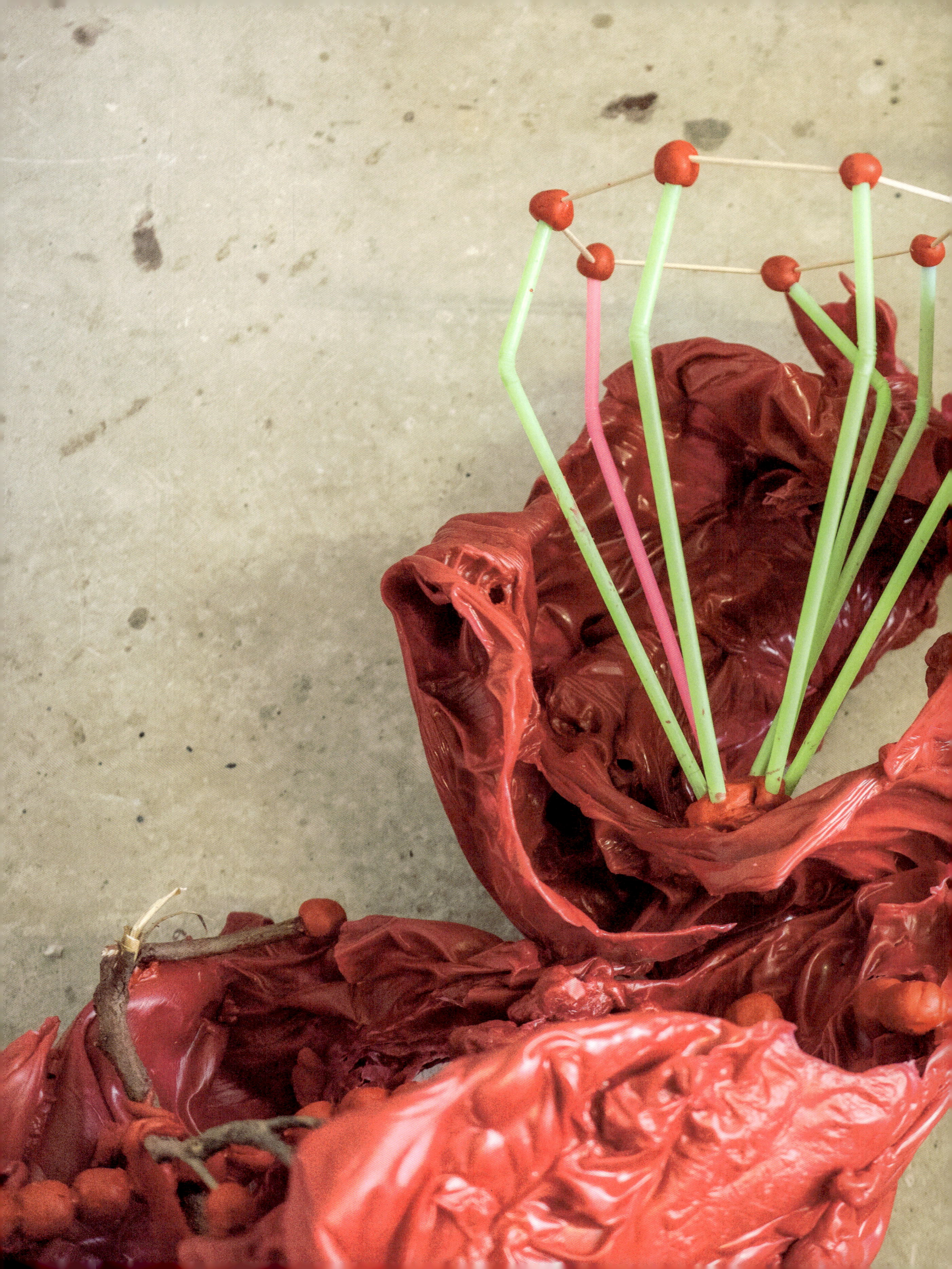

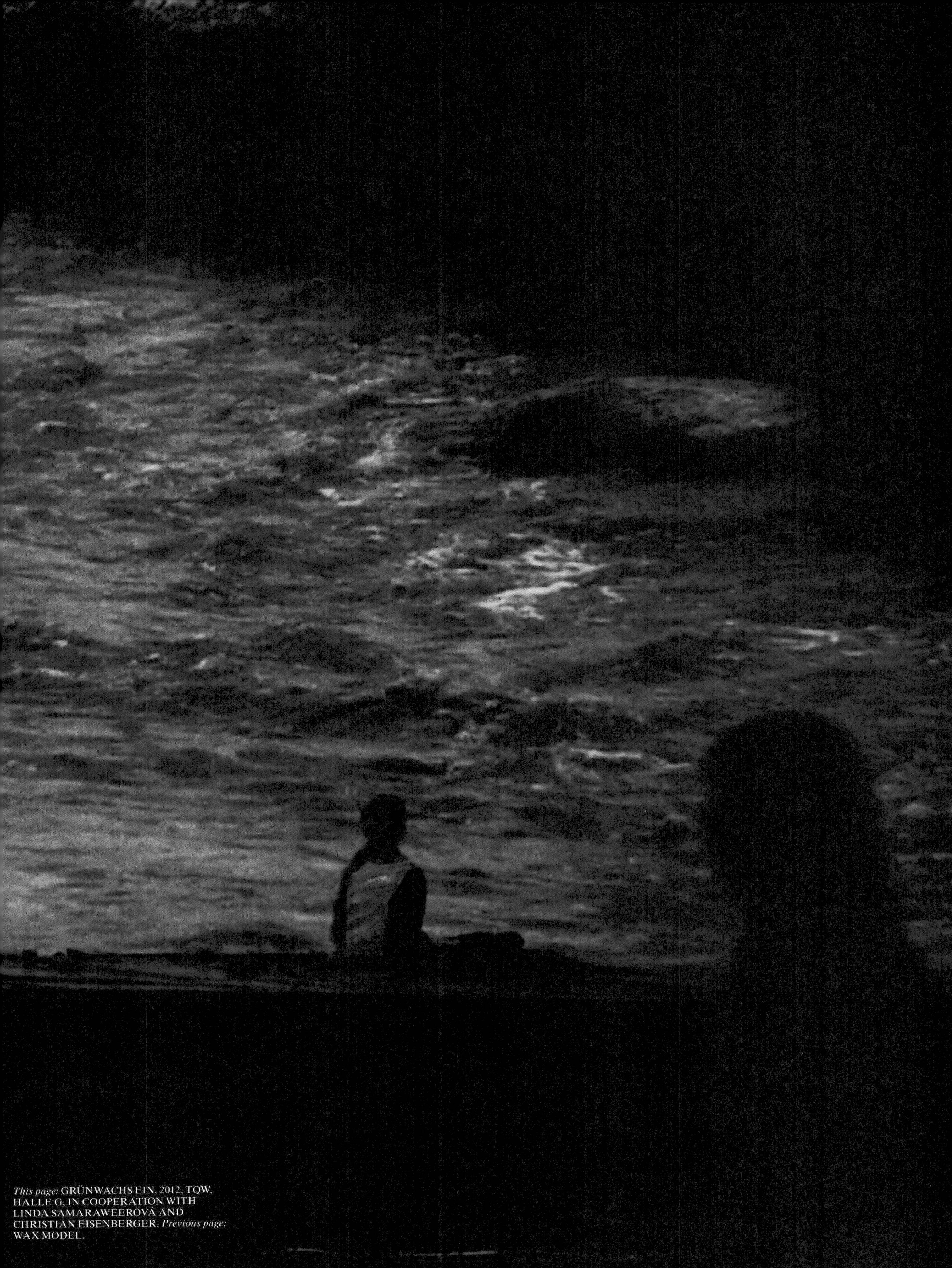

*This page:* GRÜNWACHS EIN, 2012, TQW, HALLE G, IN COOPERATION WITH LINDA SAMARAWEEROVÁ AND CHRISTIAN EISENBERGER. *Previous page:* WAX MODEL.

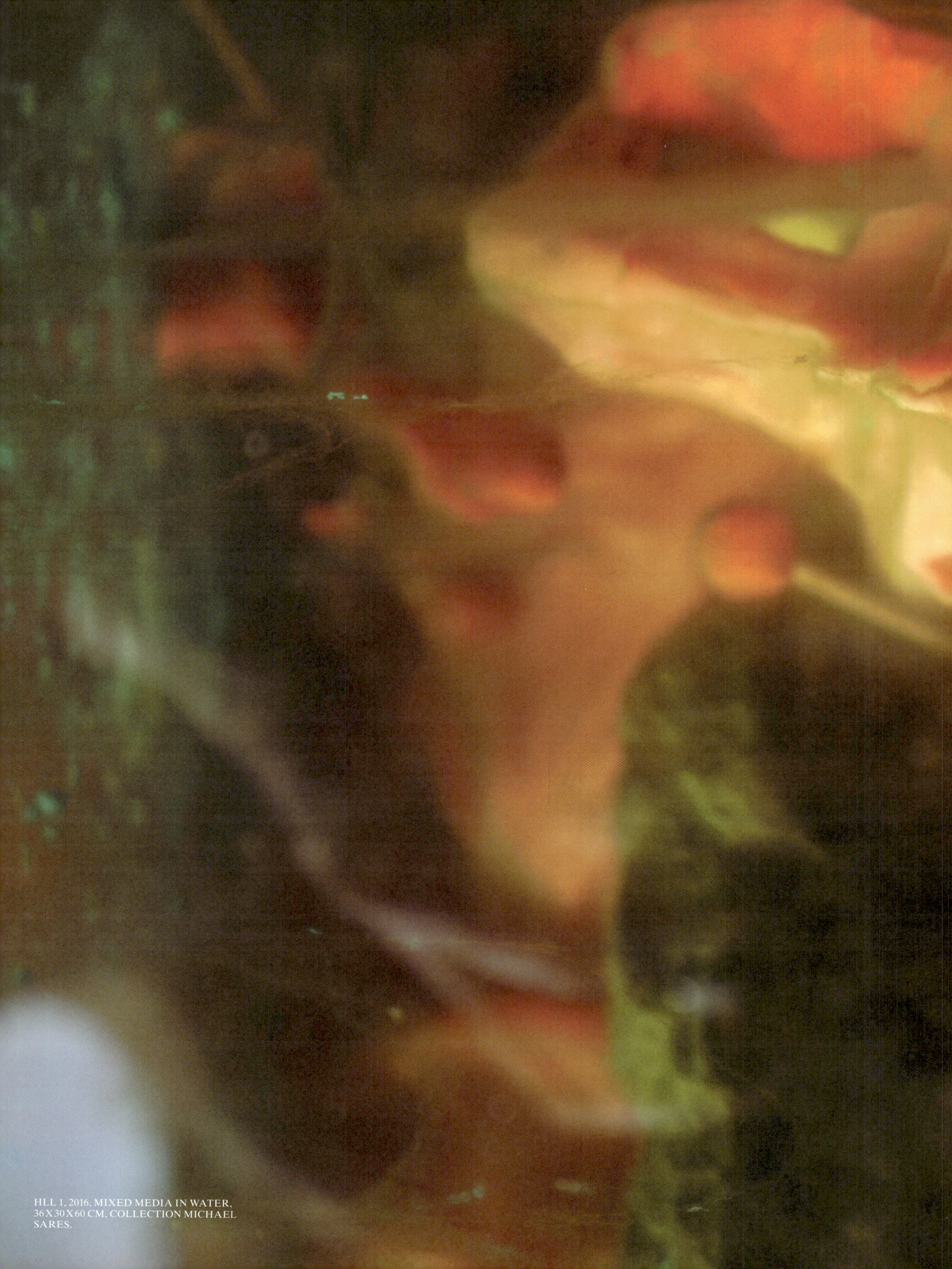

HLL 1, 2016, MIXED MEDIA IN WATER, 36 X 30 X 60 CM, COLLECTION MICHAEL SARES.

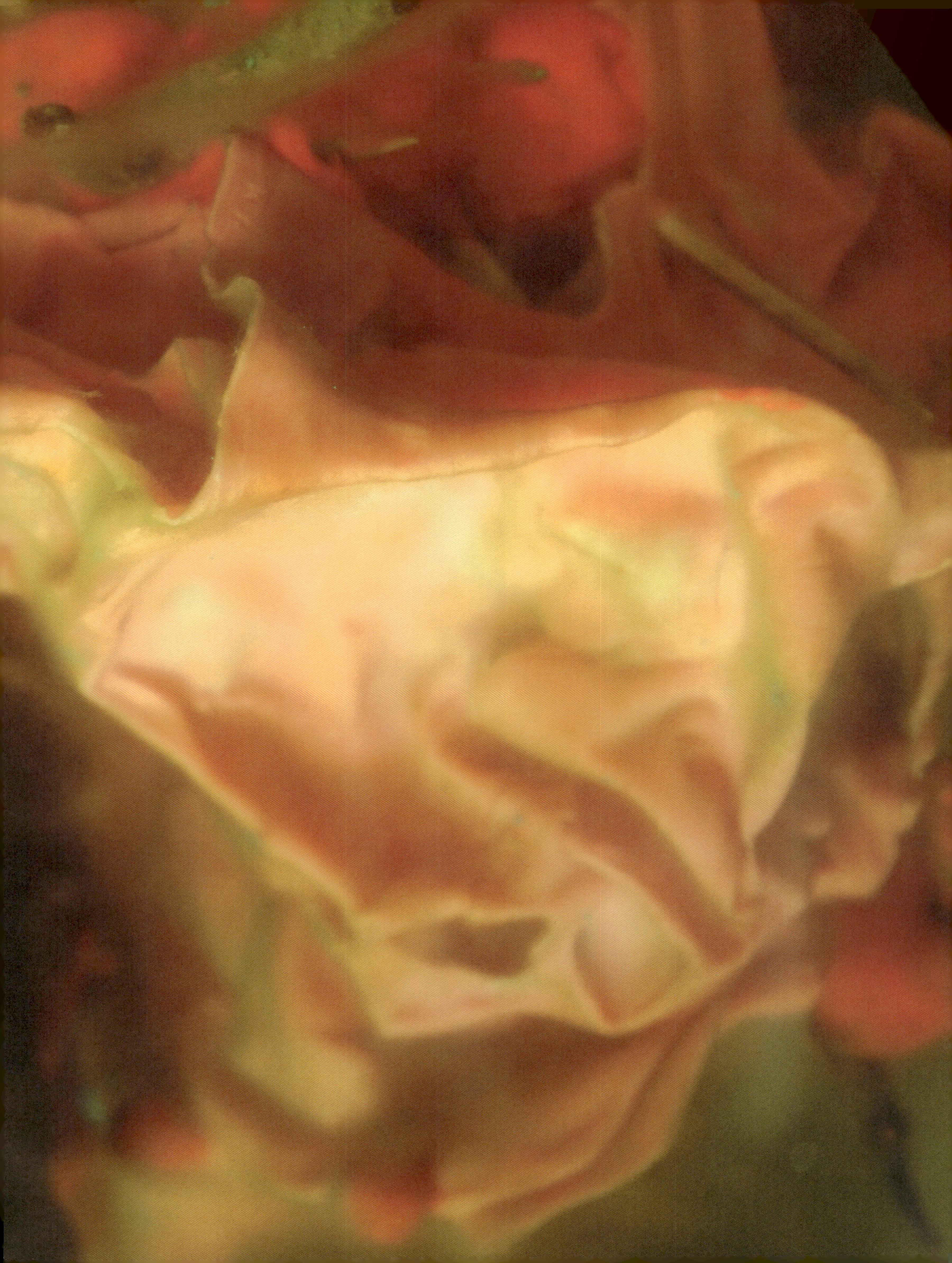

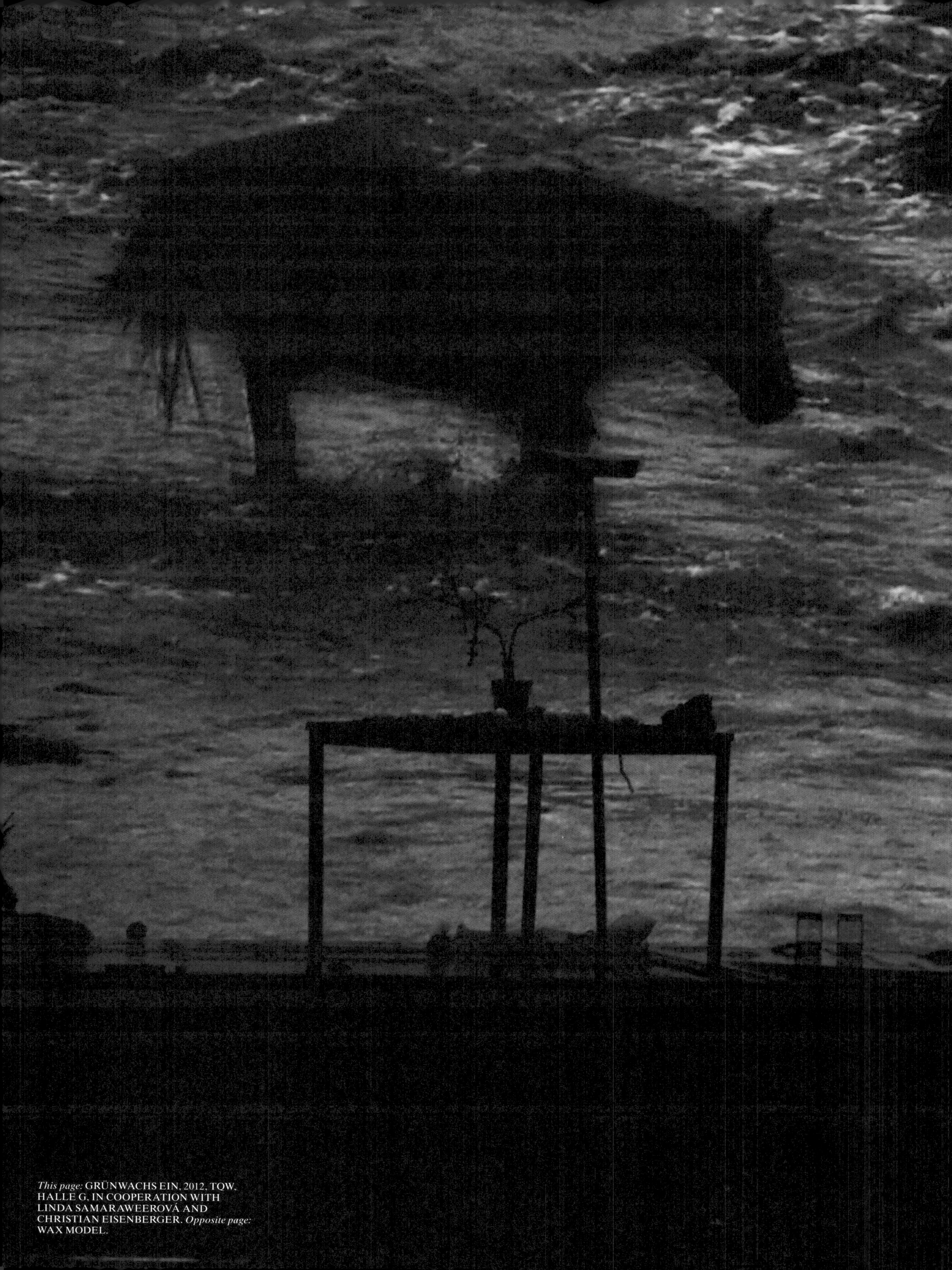

*This page:* GRÜNWACHS EIN, 2012, TQW, HALLE G, IN COOPERATION WITH LINDA SAMARAWEEROVÁ AND CHRISTIAN EISENBERGER. *Opposite page:* WAX MODEL.

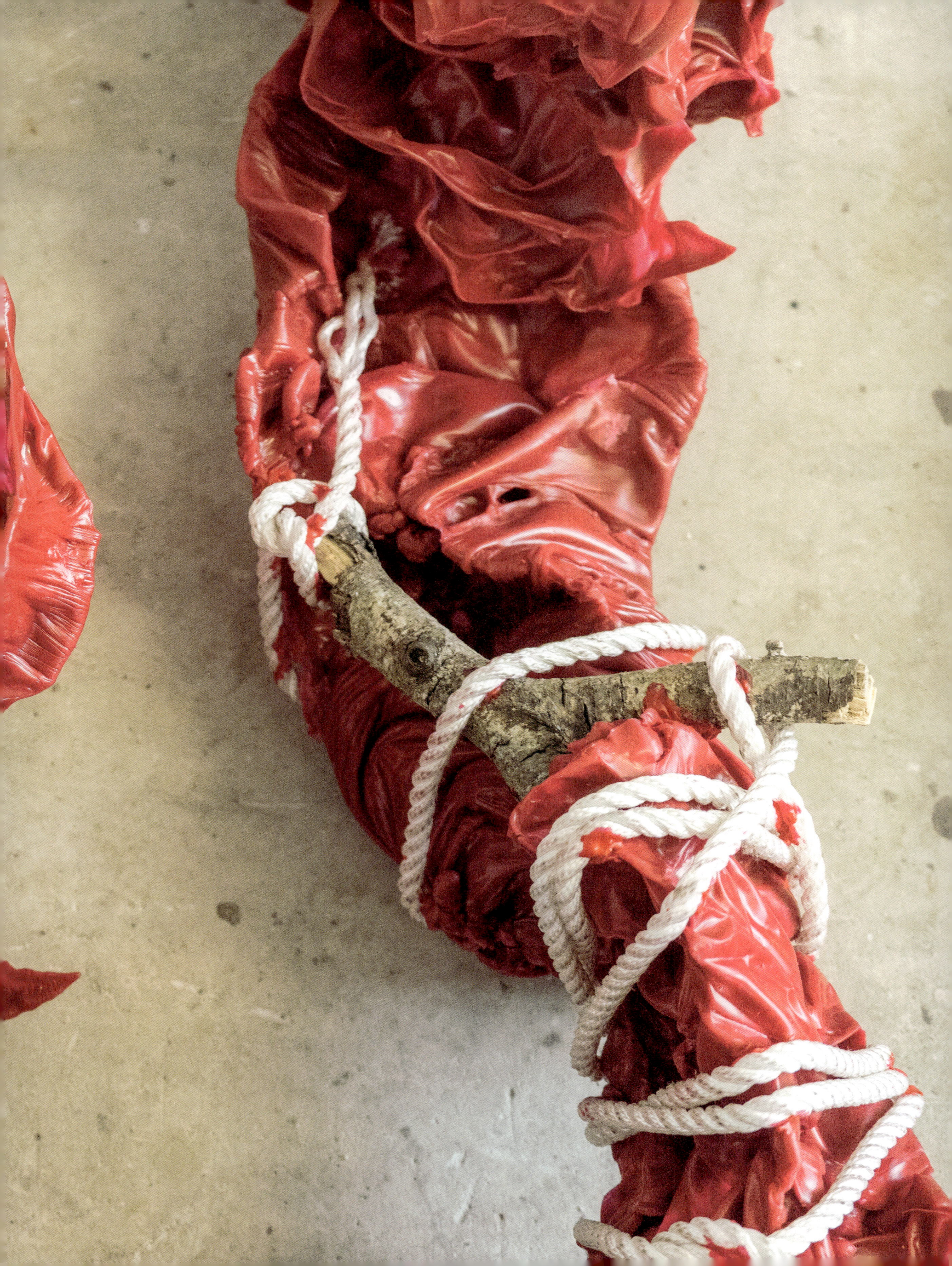

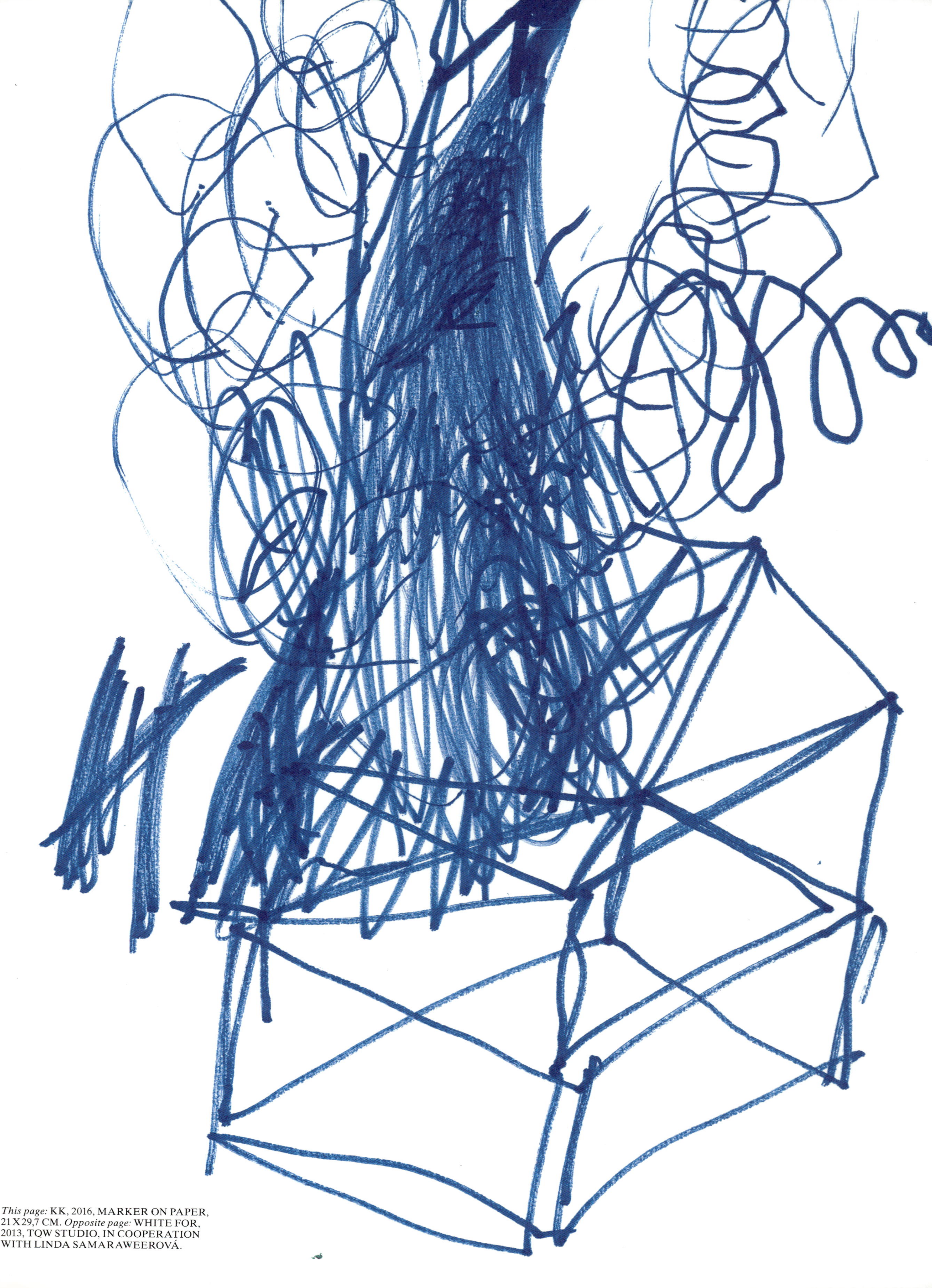

*This page:* KK, 2016, MARKER ON PAPER, 21 X 29,7 CM. *Opposite page:* WHITE FOR, 2013, TQW STUDIO, IN COOPERATION WITH LINDA SAMARAWEEROVÁ.

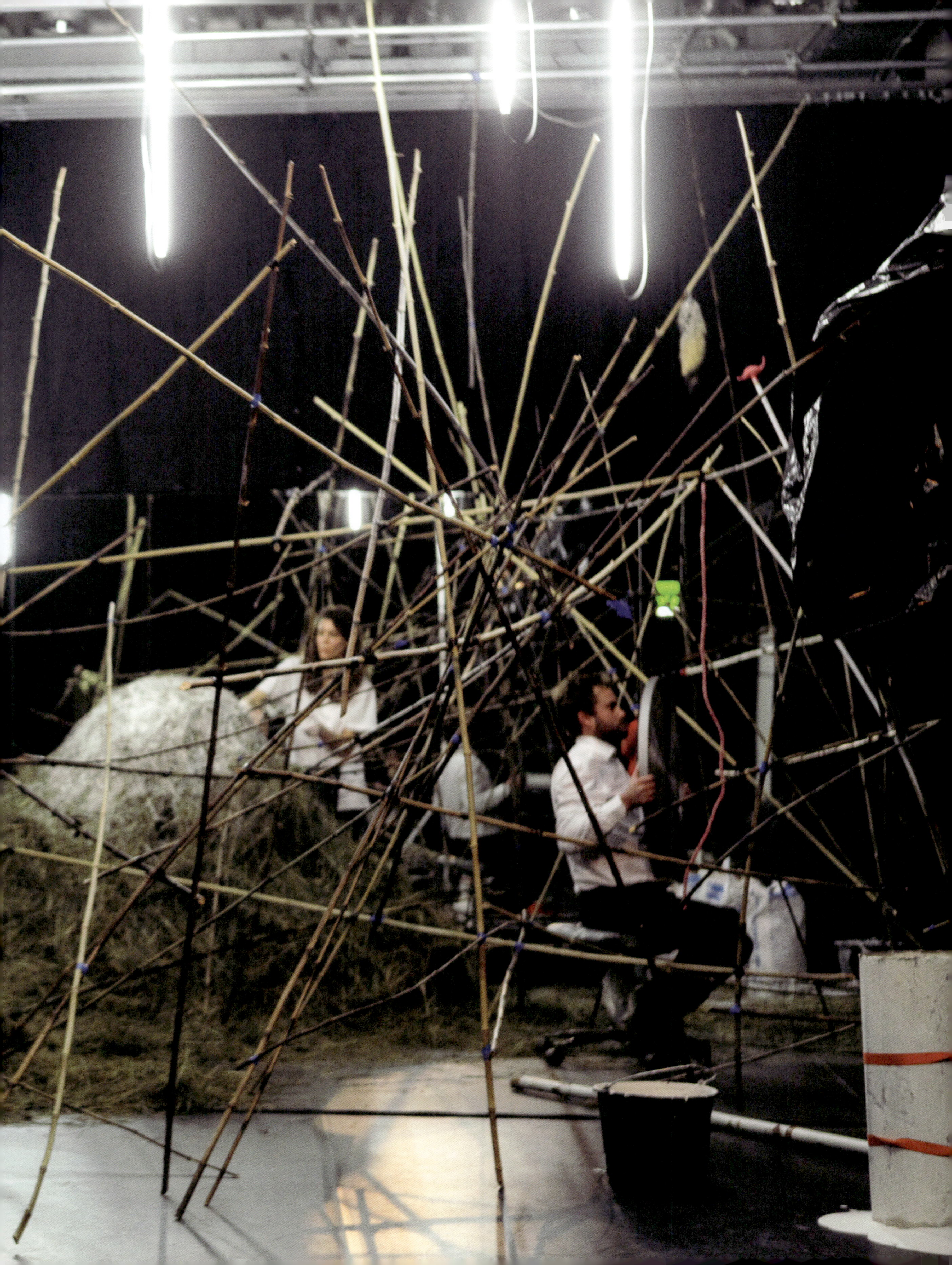

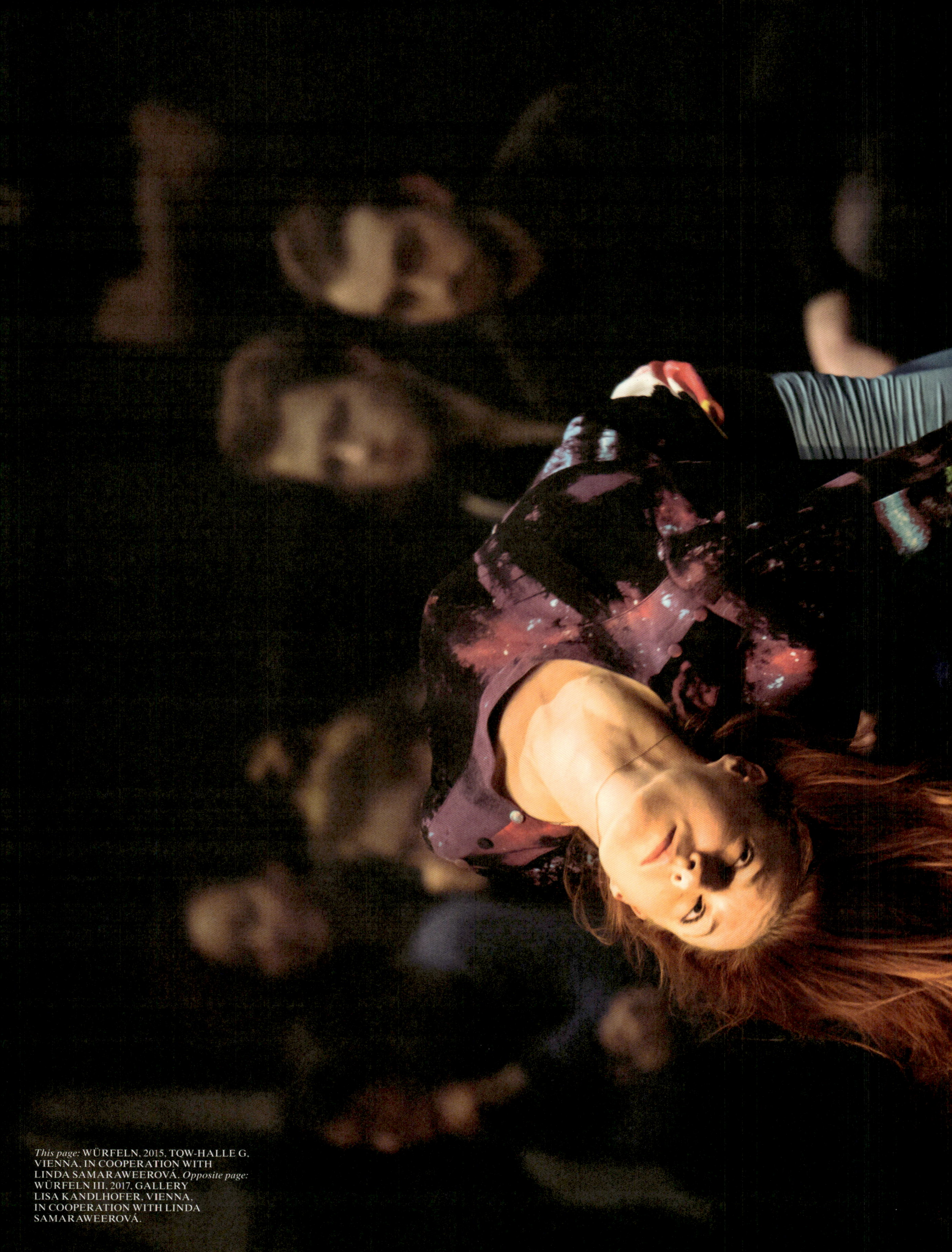

*This page:* WÜRFELN, 2015, TQW-HALLE G, VIENNA, IN COOPERATION WITH LINDA SAMARAWEEROVÁ. *Opposite page:* WÜRFELN III, 2017, GALLERY LISA KANDLHOFER, VIENNA, IN COOPERATION WITH LINDA SAMARAWEEROVÁ.

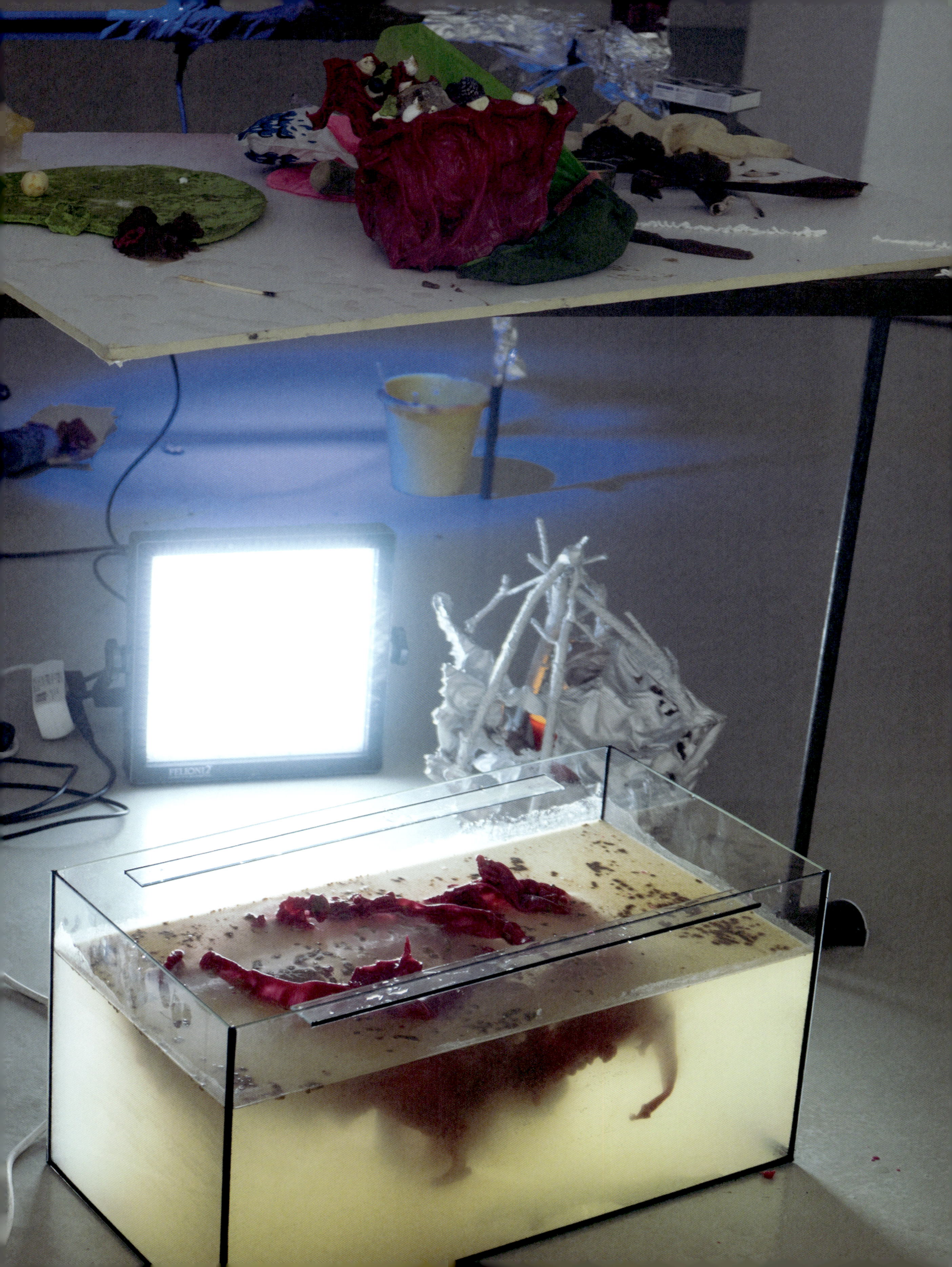

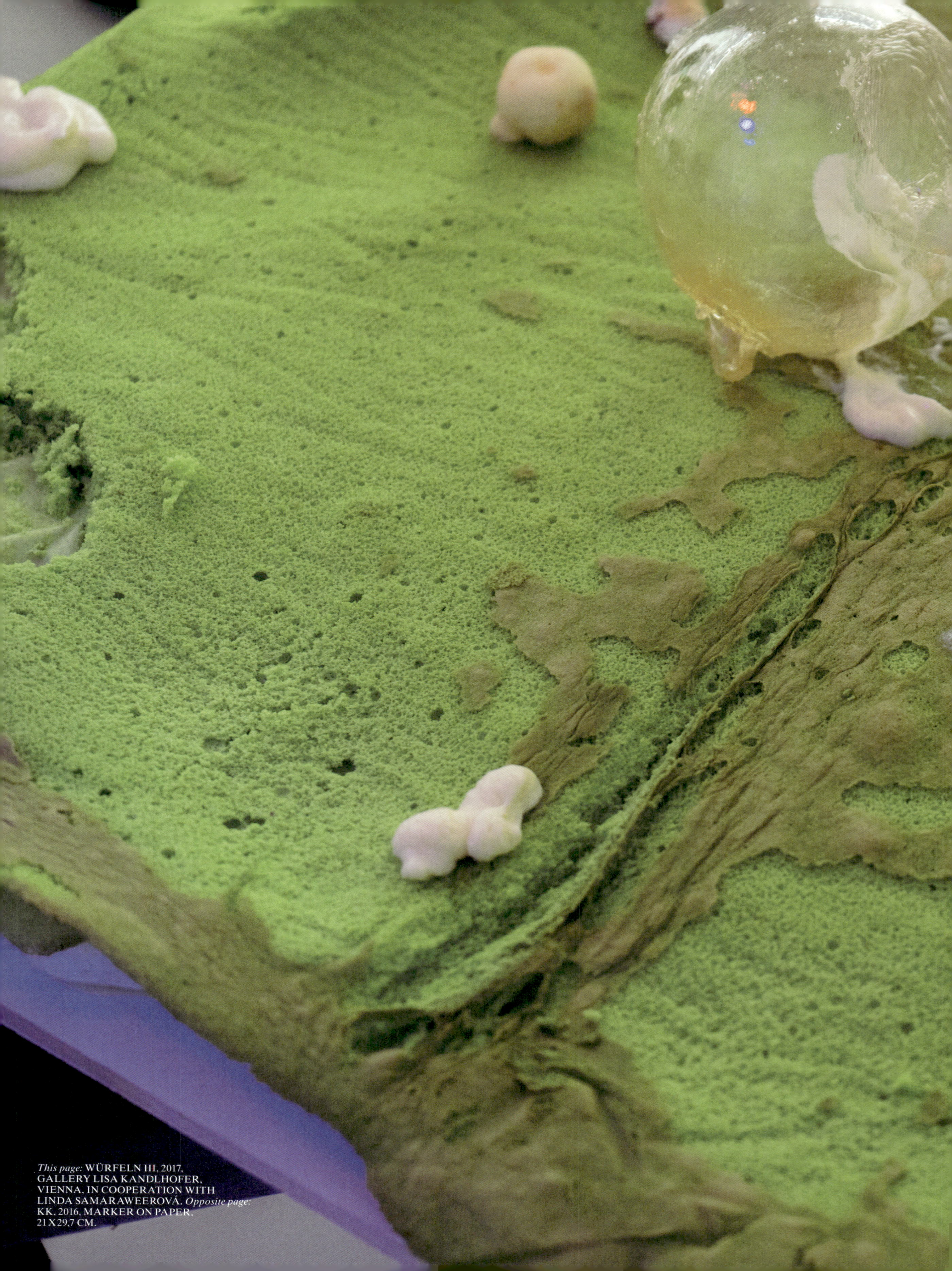

*This page:* WÜRFELN III, 2017, GALLERY LISA KANDLHOFER, VIENNA, IN COOPERATION WITH LINDA SAMARAWEEROVÁ. *Opposite page:* KK, 2016, MARKER ON PAPER, 21 X 29,7 CM.

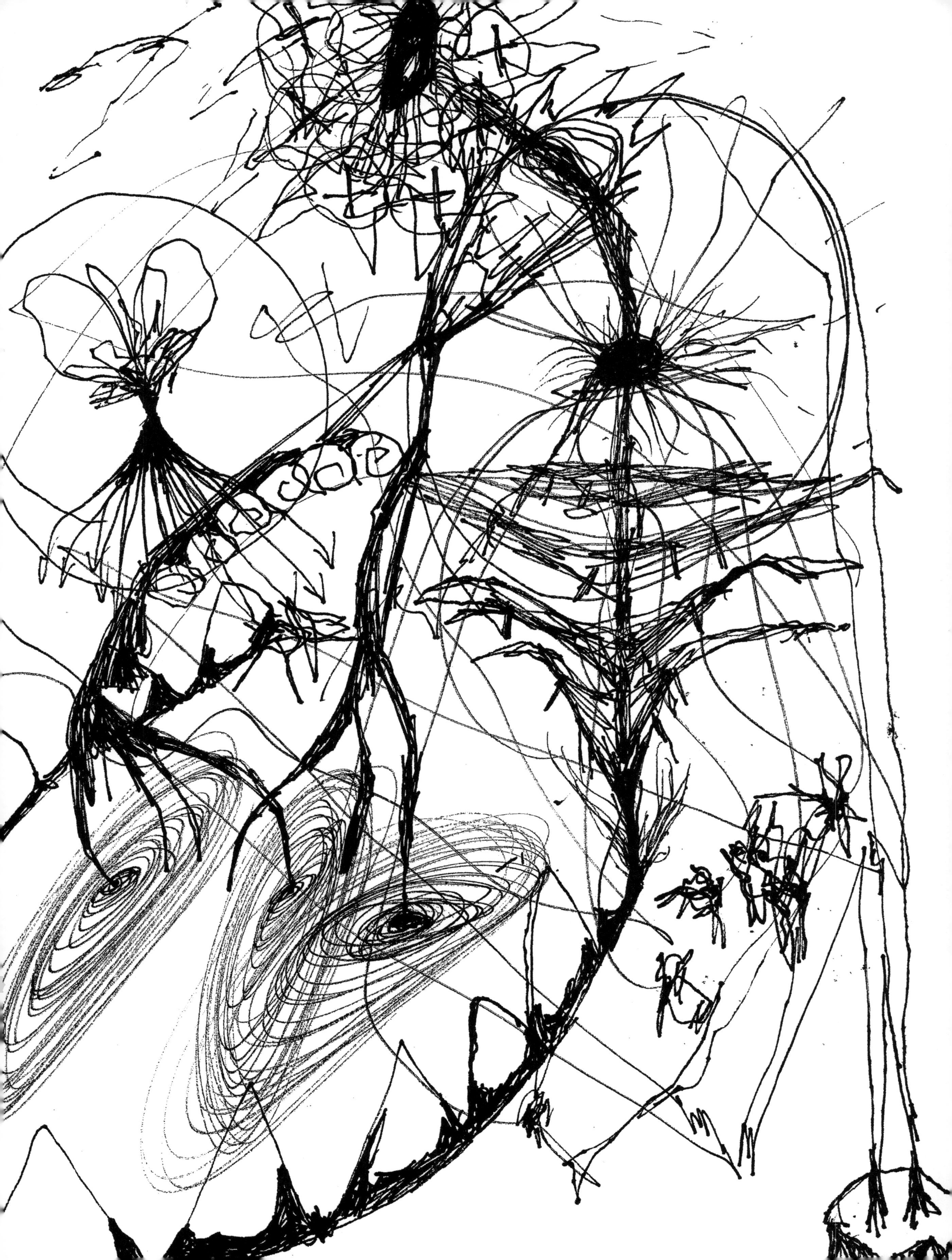

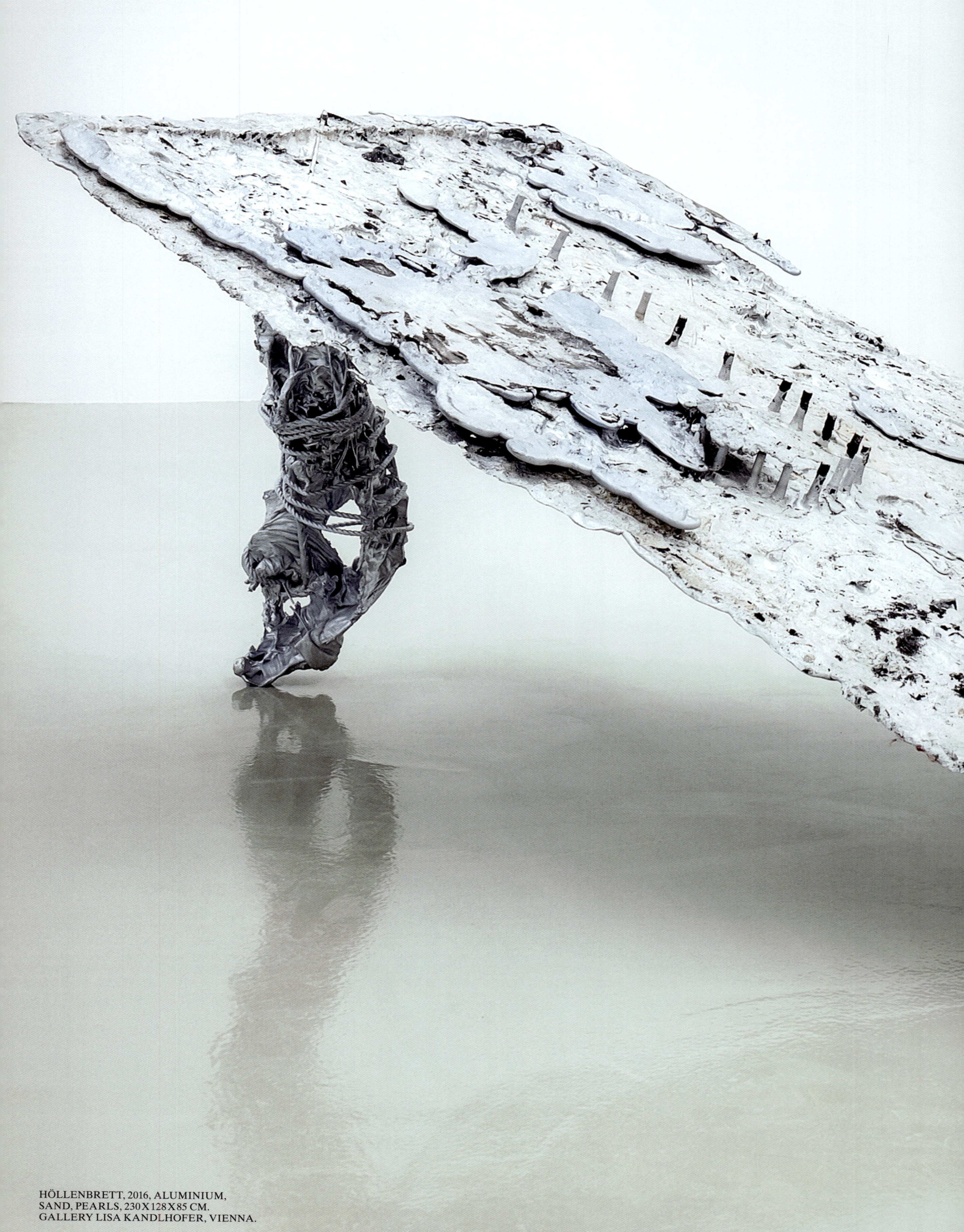

HÖLLENBRETT, 2016, ALUMINIUM,
SAND, PEARLS, 230 X 128 X 85 CM.
GALLERY LISA KANDLHOFER, VIENNA.

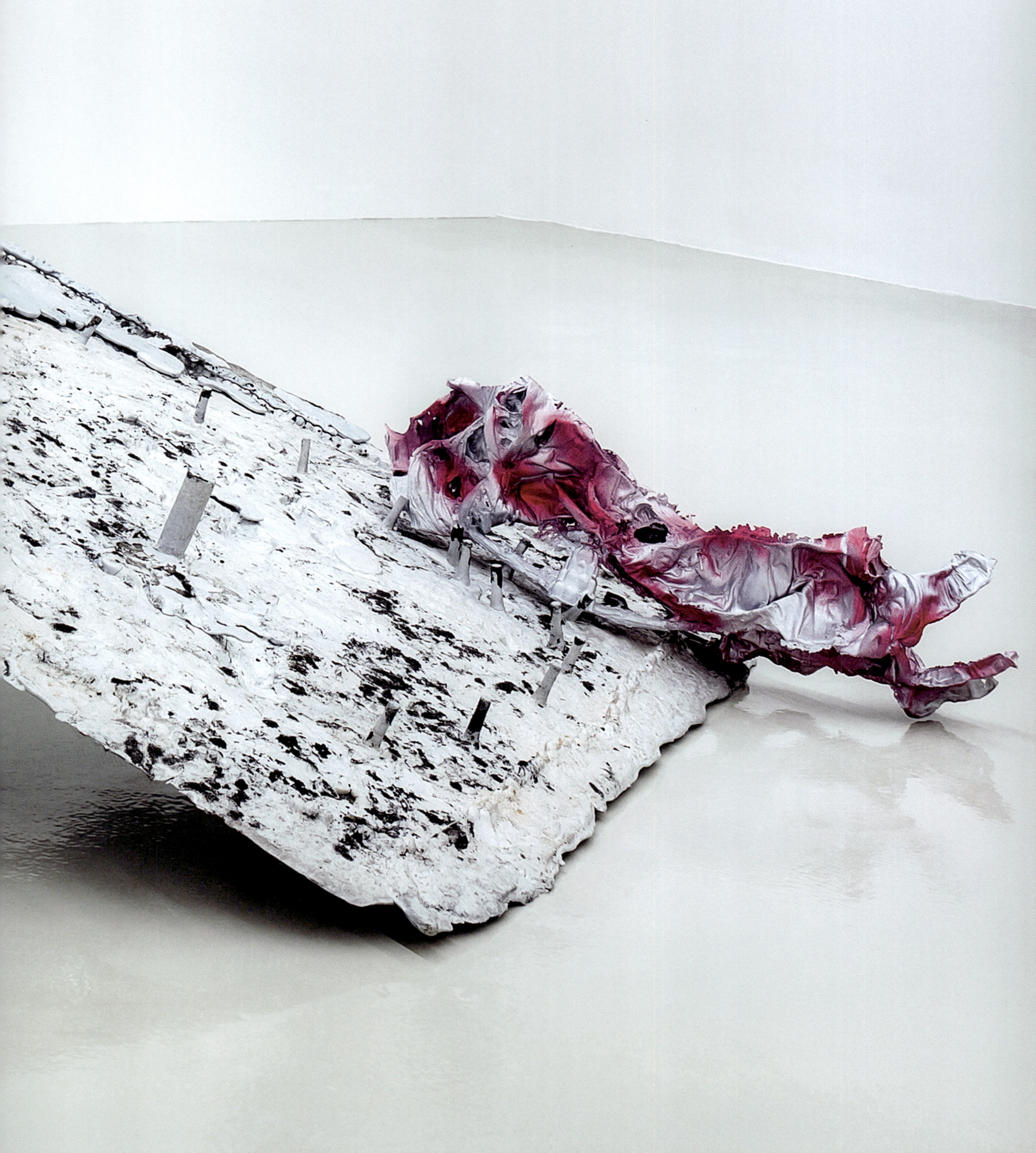

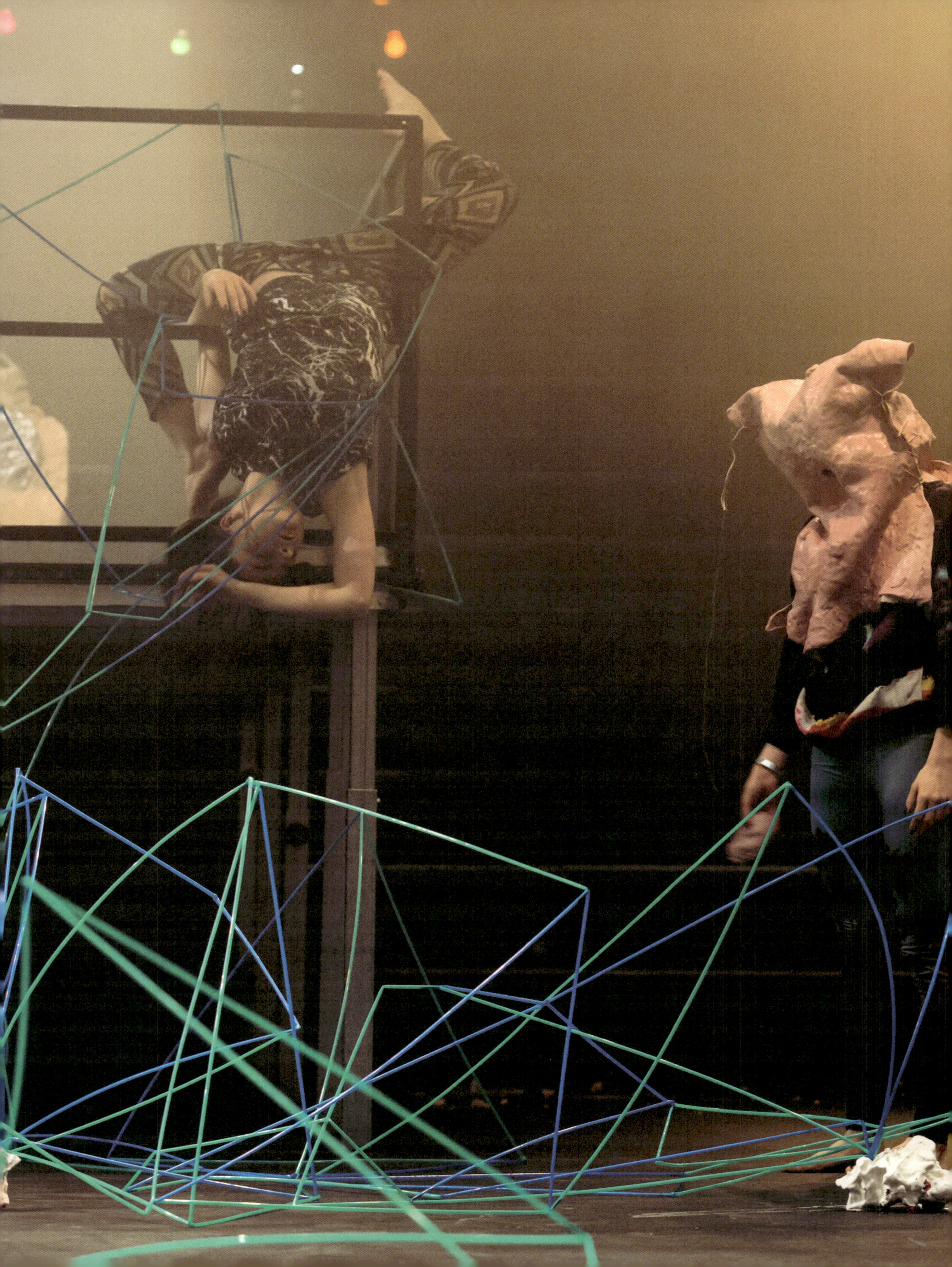

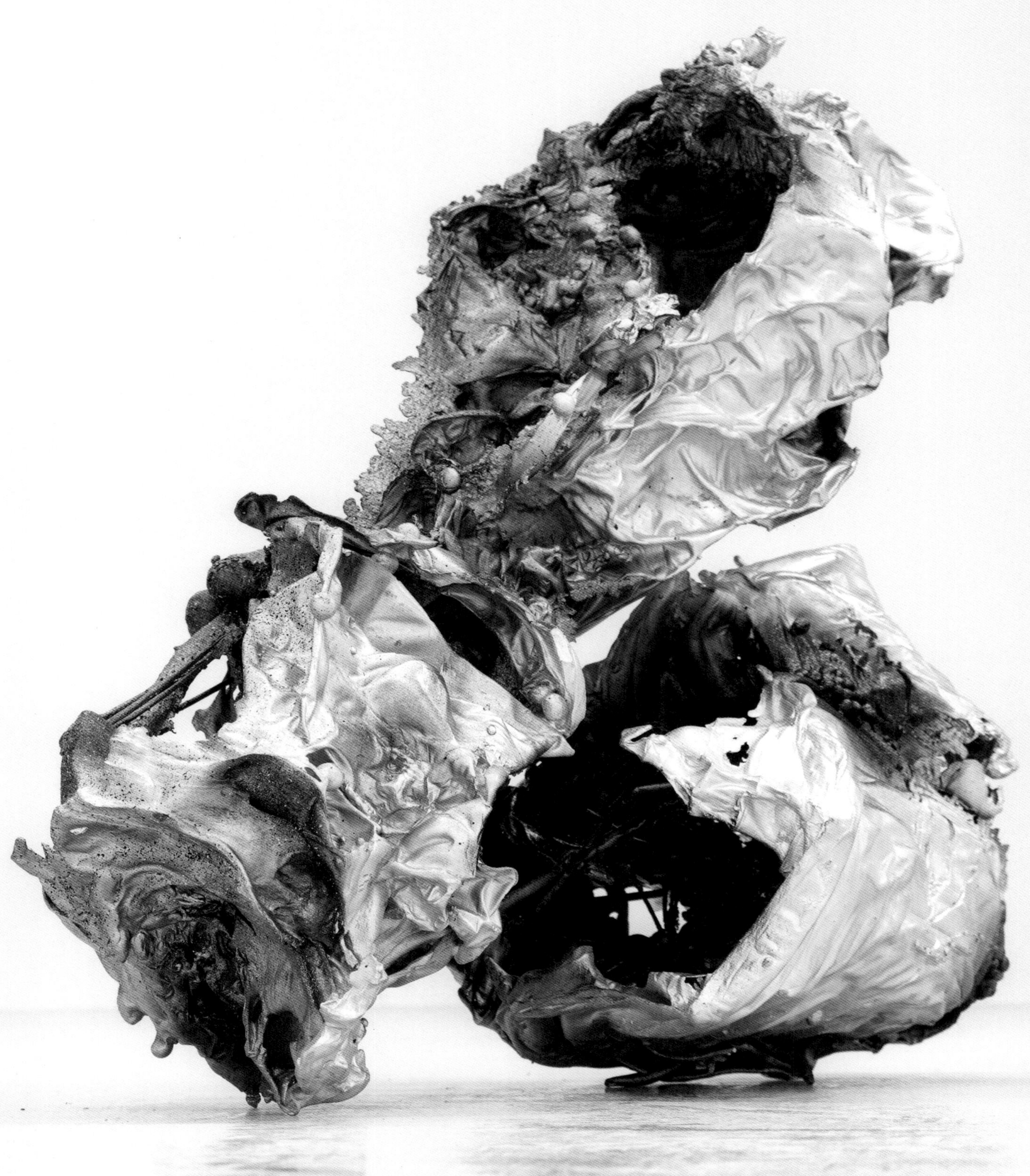

*This page:* KASTANIE, 2016, ALUMINIUM, 62 X 59 X 36 CM. *Previous page:* WÜRFELN, 2015, TQW-HALLE G, VIENNA, IN COOPERATION WITH LINDA SAMARAWEEROVÁ.

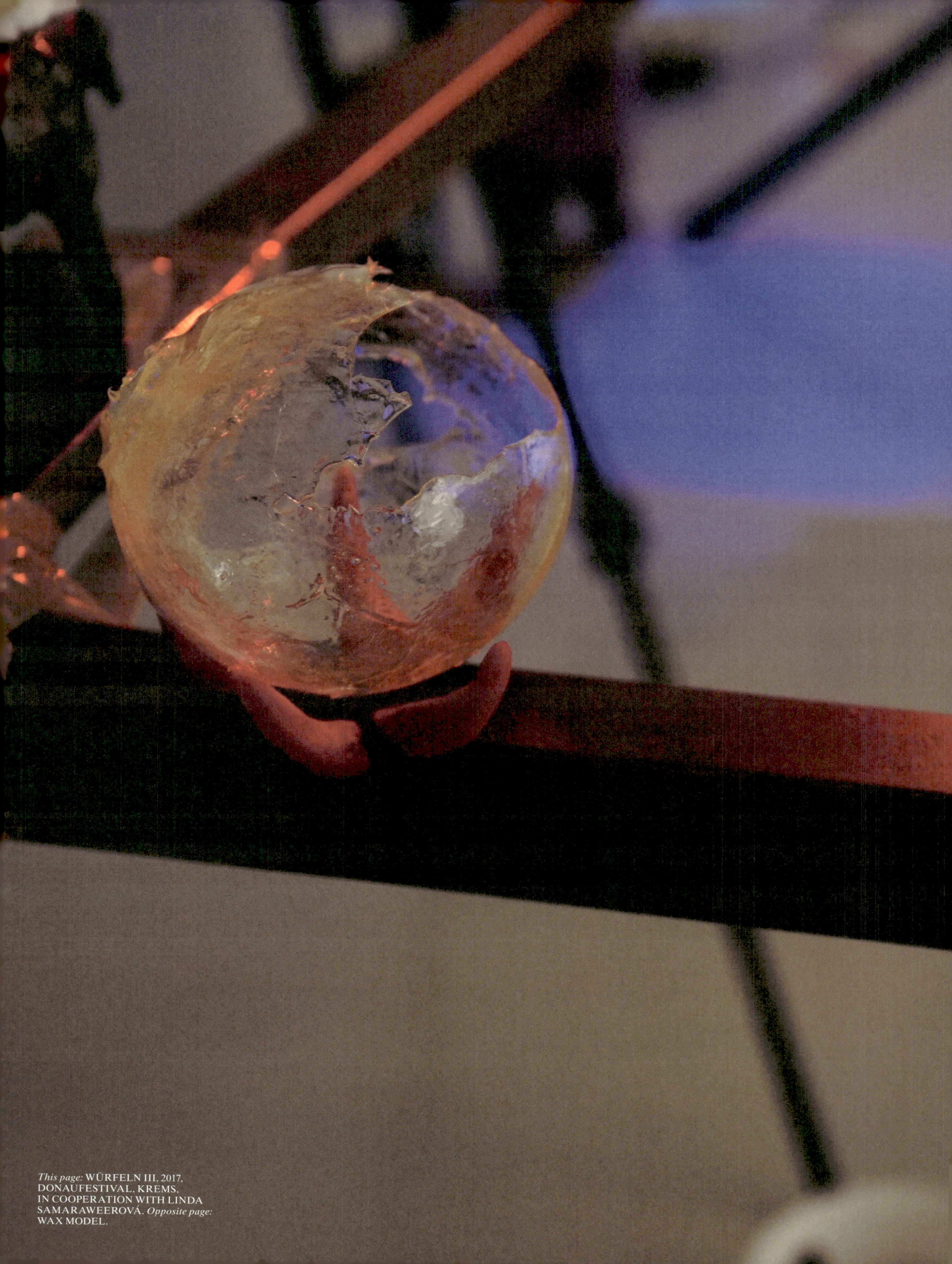

*This page:* WÜRFELN III, 2017, DONAUFESTIVAL, KREMS, IN COOPERATION WITH LINDA SAMARAWEEROVÁ. *Opposite page:* WAX MODEL.

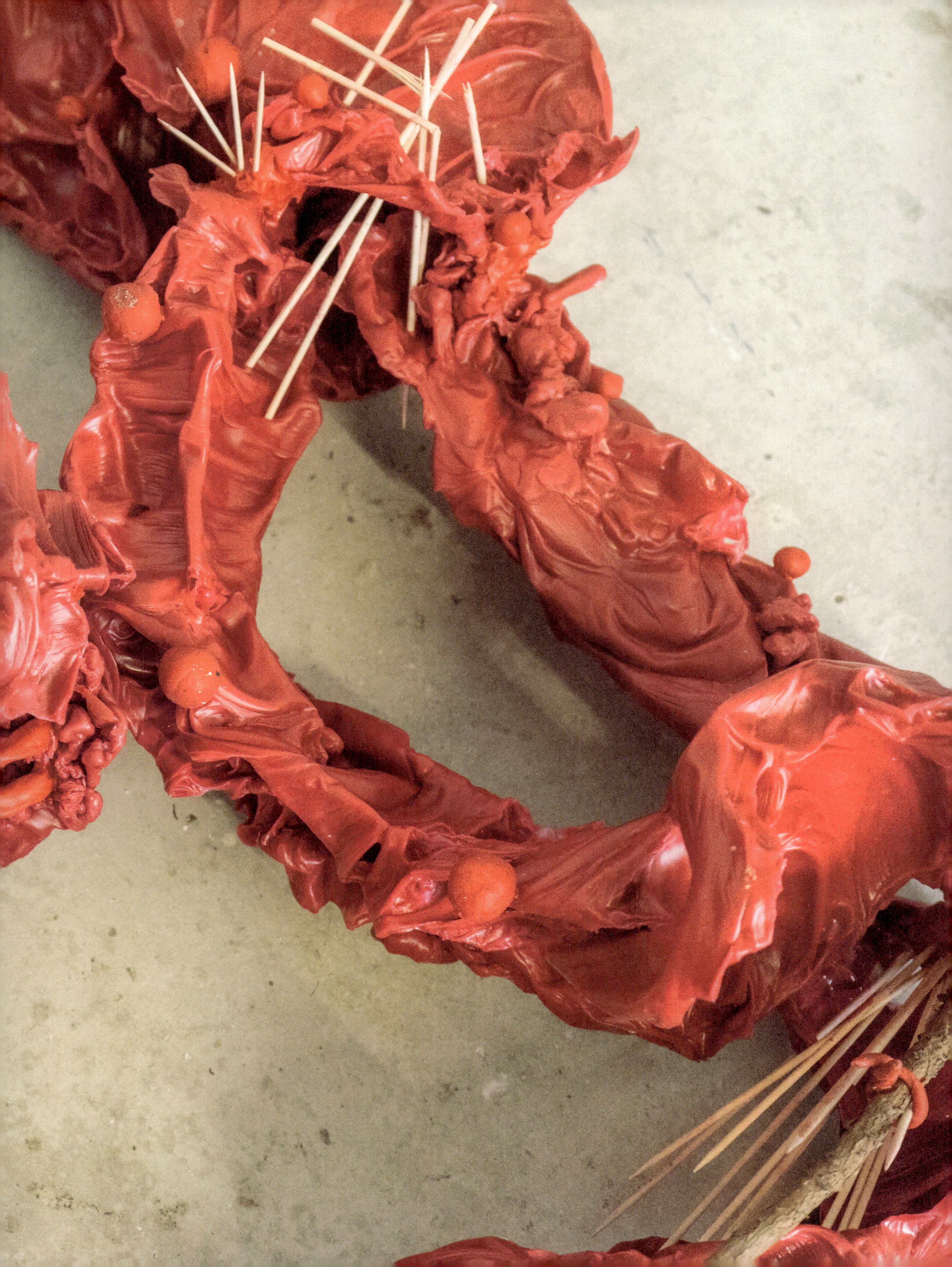

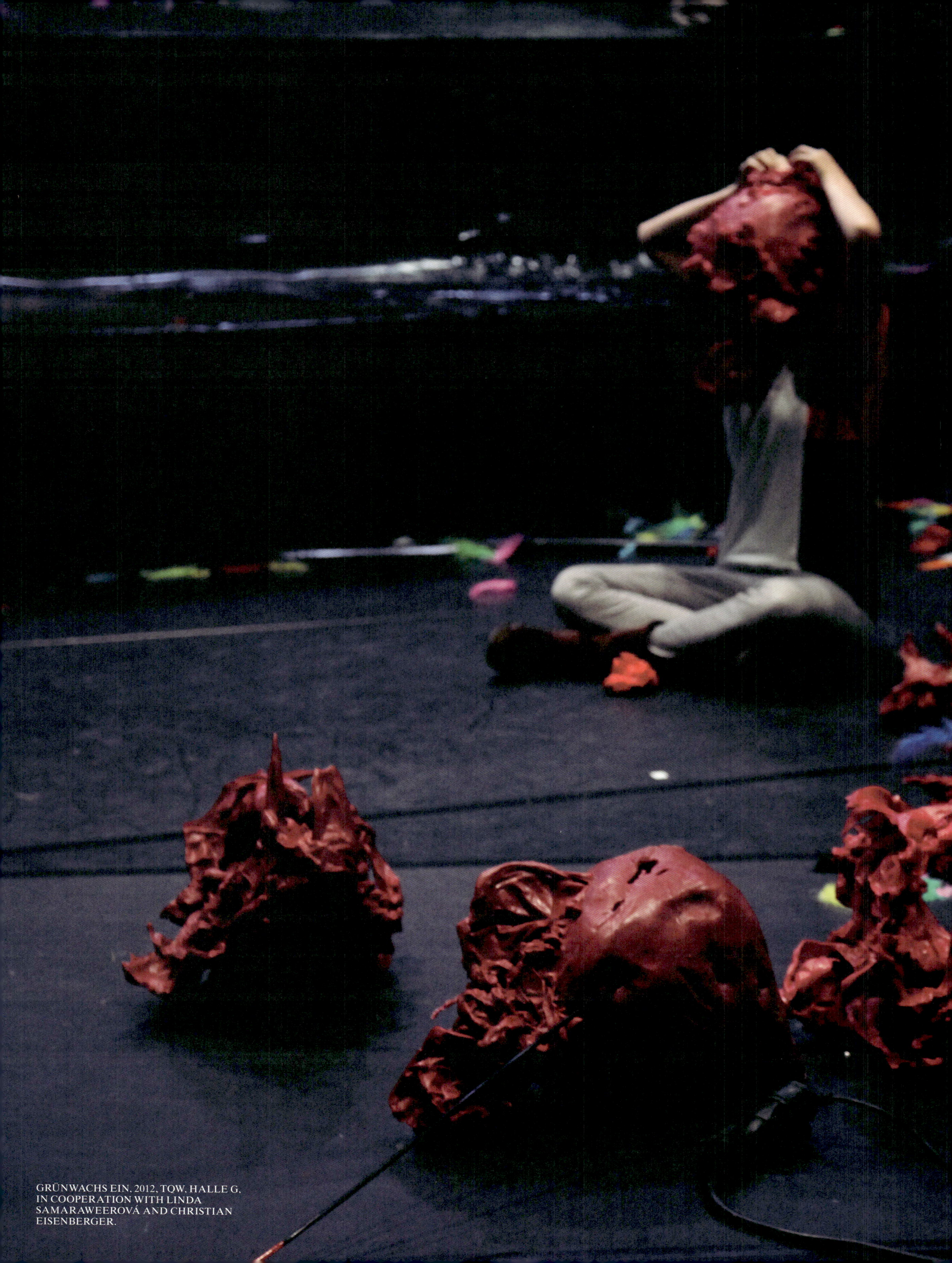

GRÜNWACHS EIN, 2012, TQW, HALLE G,
IN COOPERATION WITH LINDA
SAMARAWEEROVÁ AND CHRISTIAN
EISENBERGER.

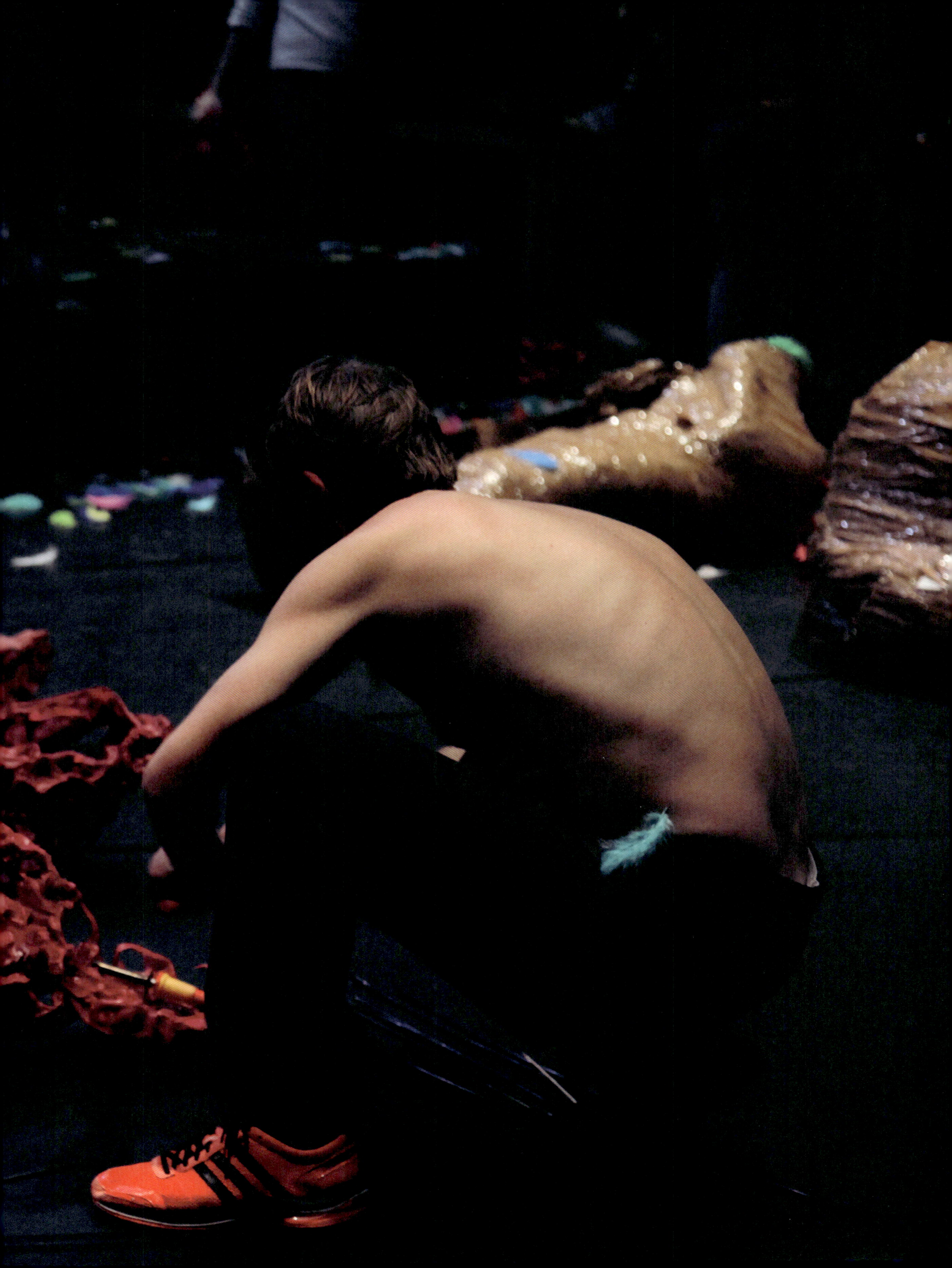

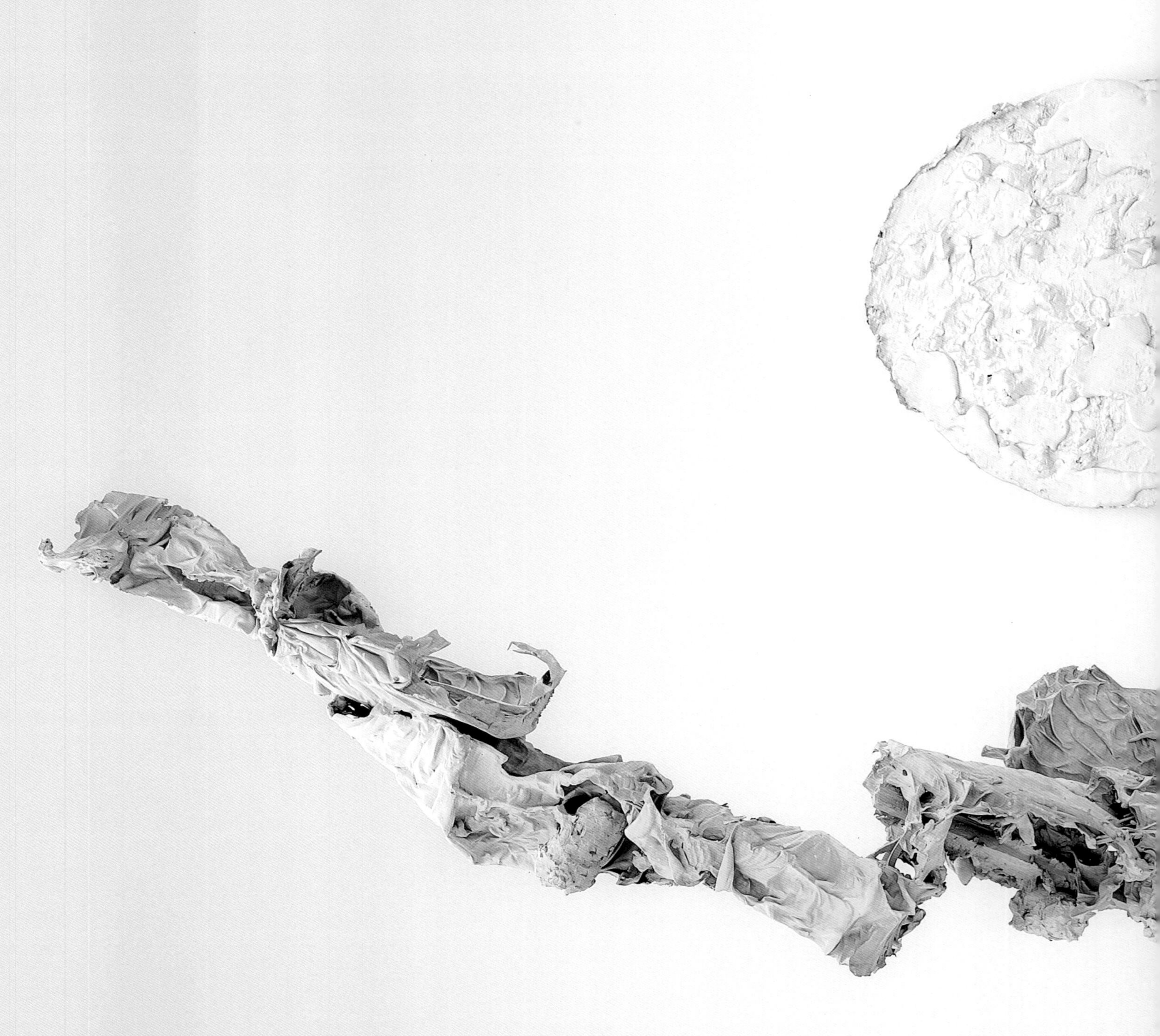

WÜGG, 2016, ALUMINIUM, H 303 CM.
HÖLLENPASS, 2016, ALUMINIUM,
CATALYTIC CONVERTER, 89 X 227 X 3 CM.
GALLERY LISA KANDLHOFER, VIENNA.

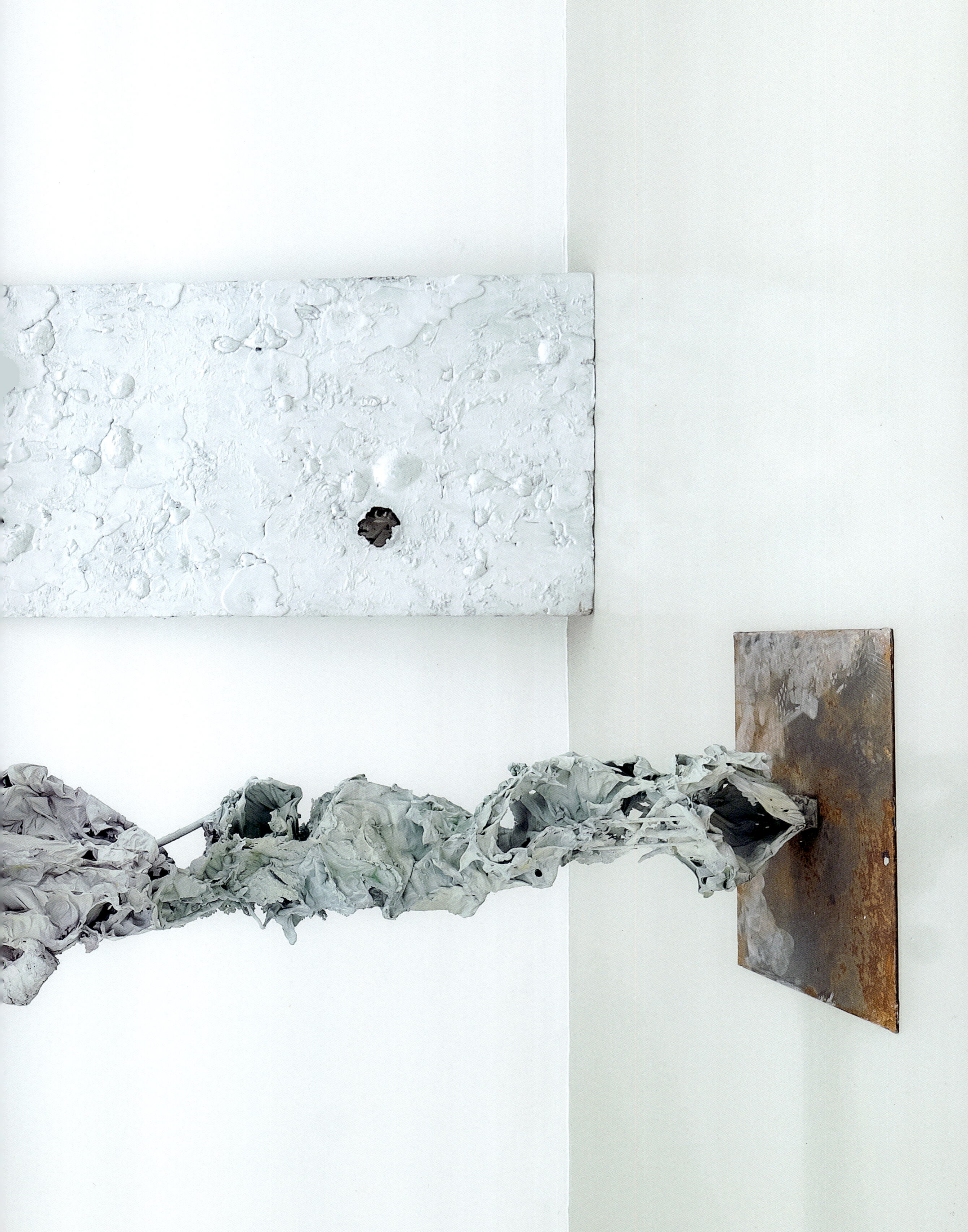

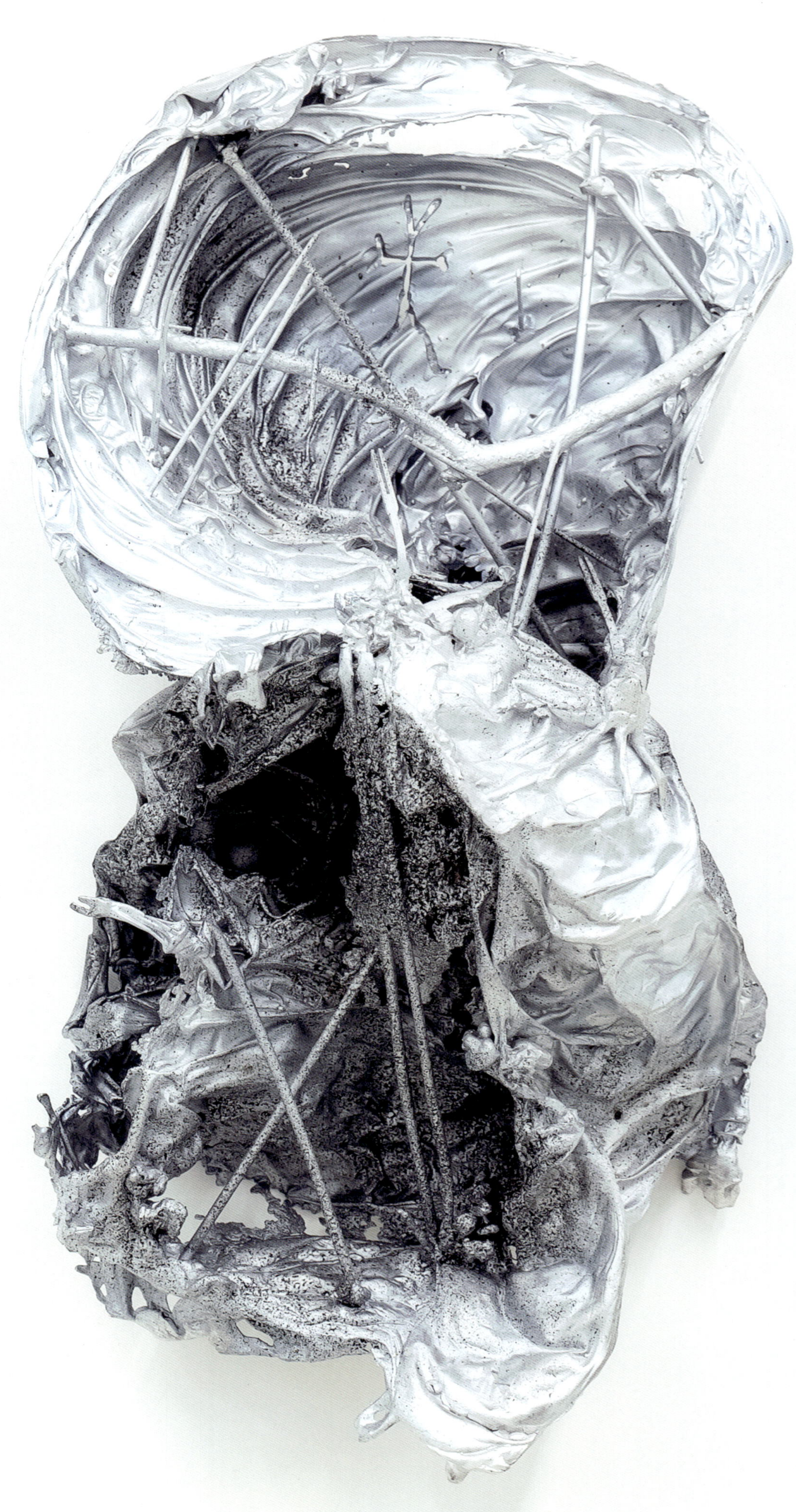

*This page:* K.DREH, 2016, ALUMINIUM, 40 X 25 X 80 CM. *Opposite page:* WÜRFELN, 2015, TQW-HALLE G, VIENNA, IN COOPERATION WITH LINDA SAMARAWEEROVÁ.

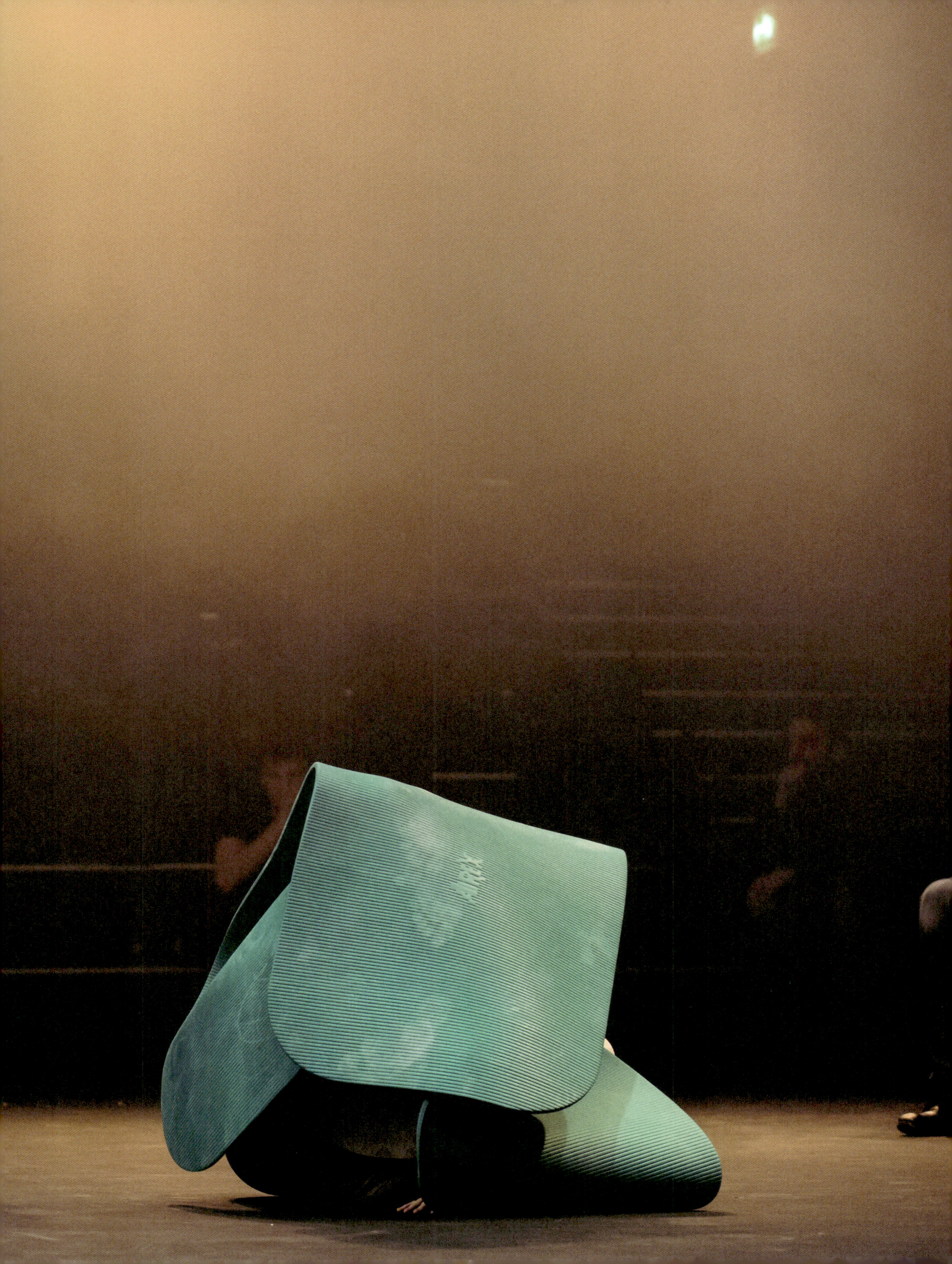

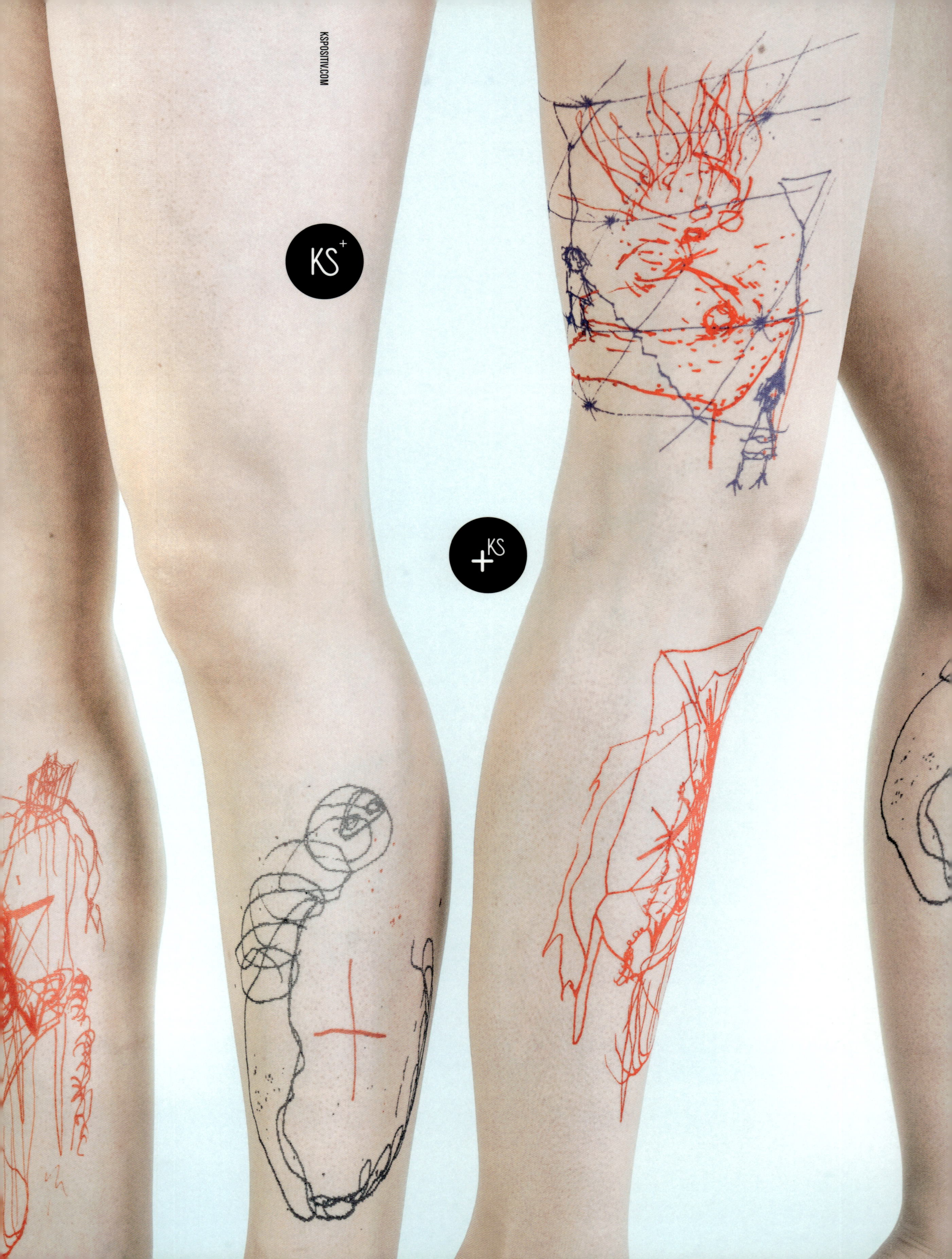
KSPOSITIV.COM
KS+
+KS

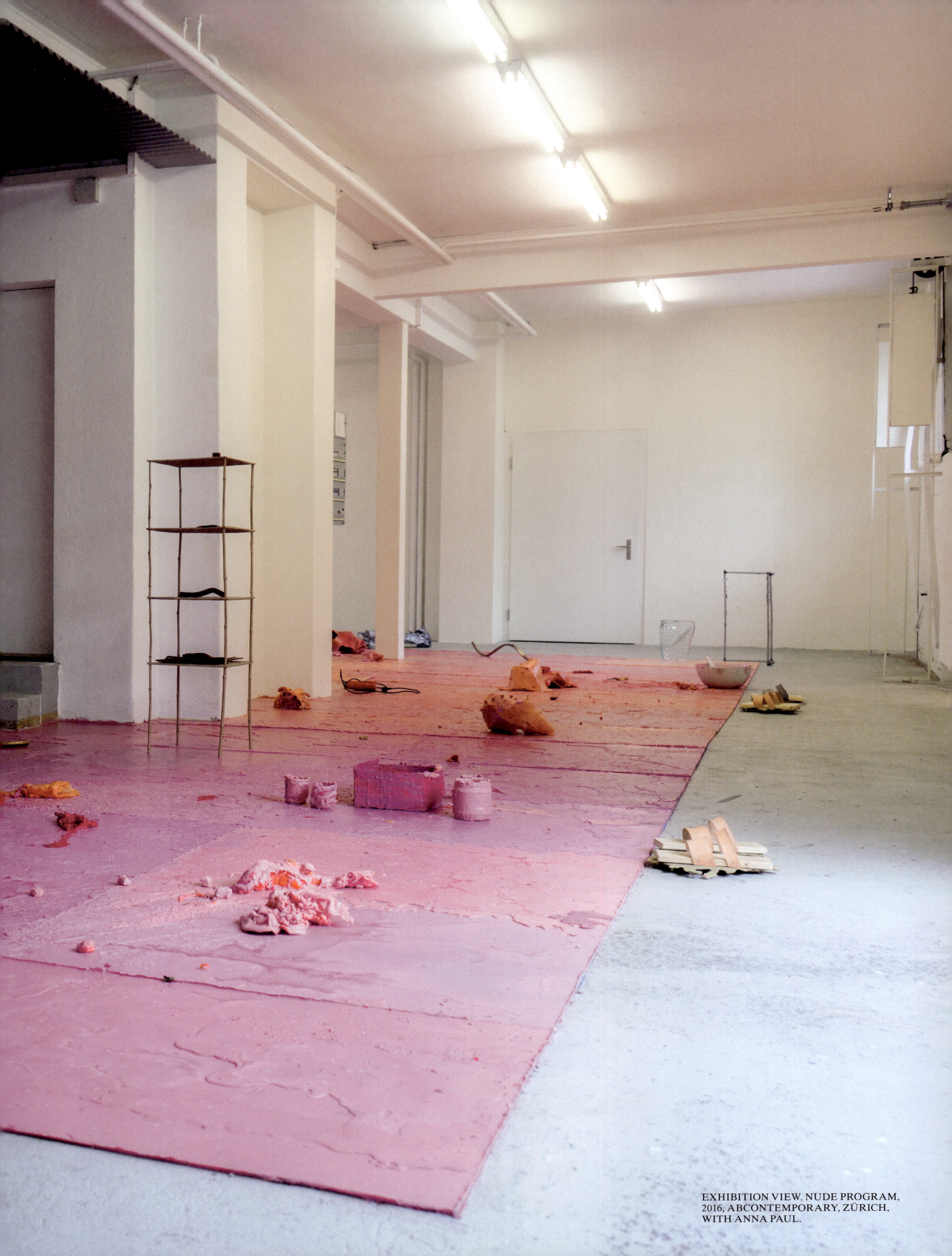

EXHIBITION VIEW, NUDE PROGRAM, 2016, ABCONTEMPORARY, ZÜRICH, WITH ANNA PAUL.

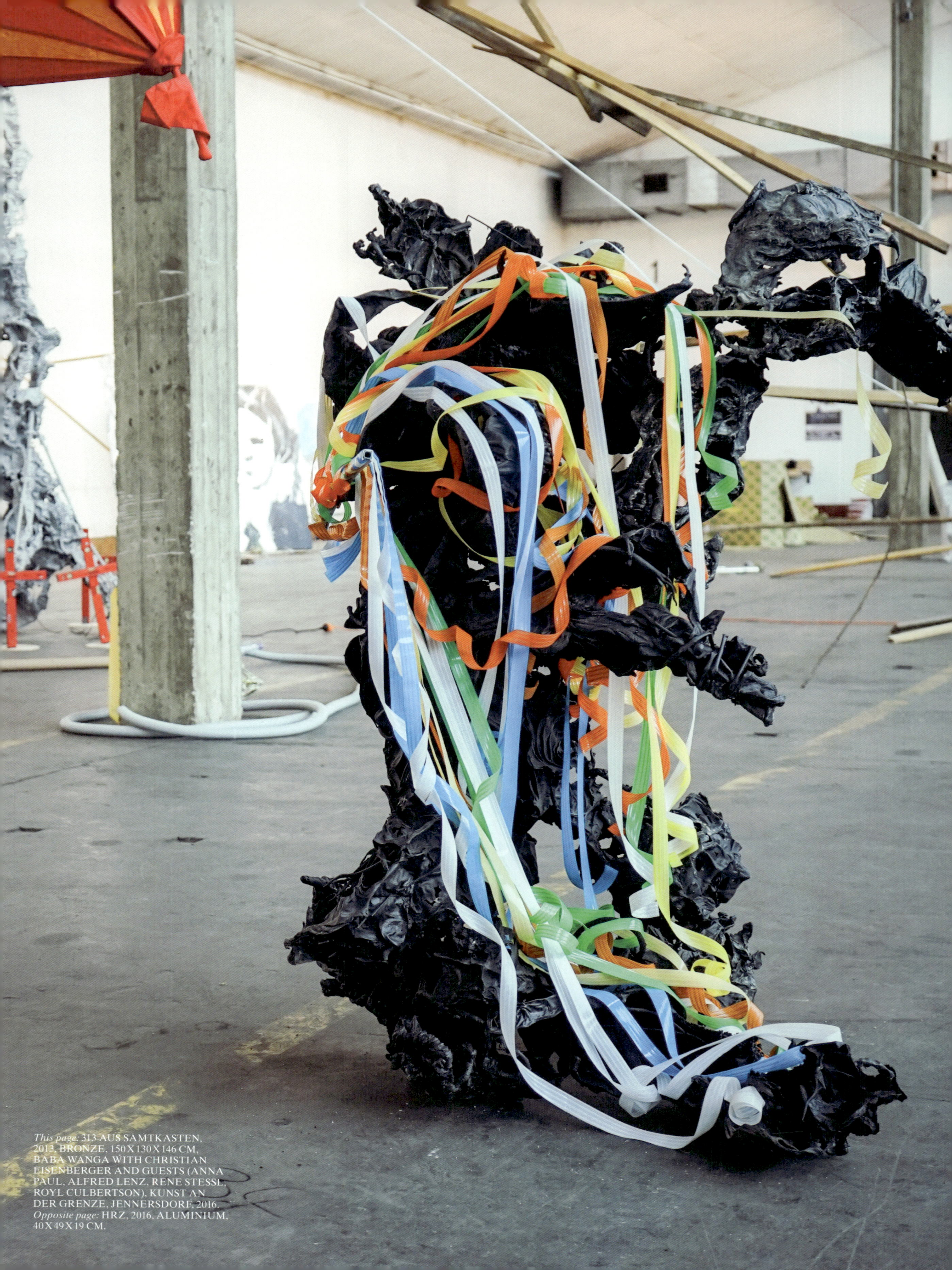

*This page:* 313 AUS SAMTKASTEN, 2013, BRONZE, 150 X 130 X 146 CM, BABA WANGA WITH CHRISTIAN EISENBERGER AND GUESTS (ANNA PAUL, ALFRED LENZ, RENE STESSL, ROYL CULBERTSON), KUNST AN DER GRENZE, JENNERSDORF, 2016. *Opposite page:* HRZ, 2016, ALUMINIUM, 40 X 49 X 19 CM.

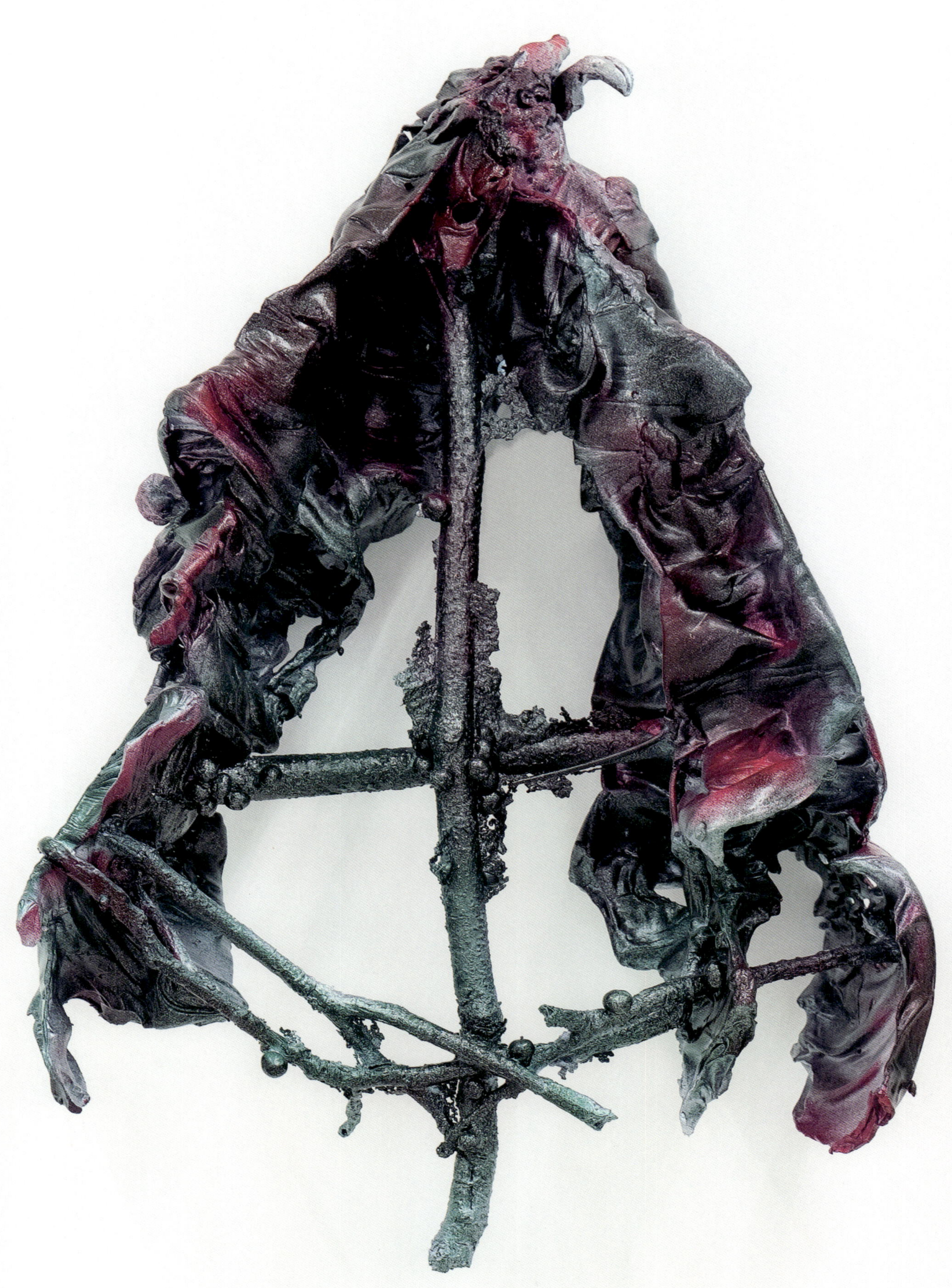

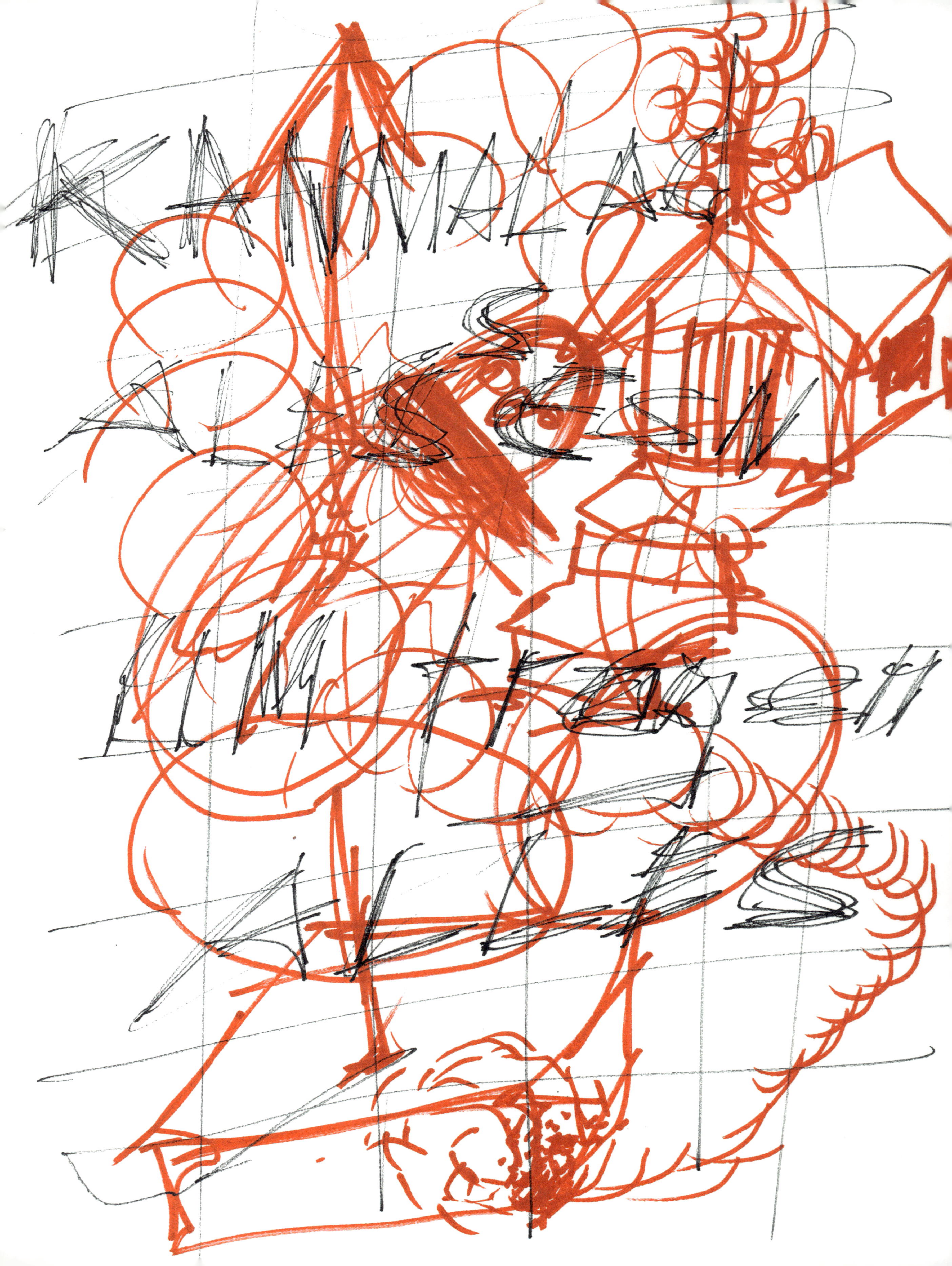
ALLES

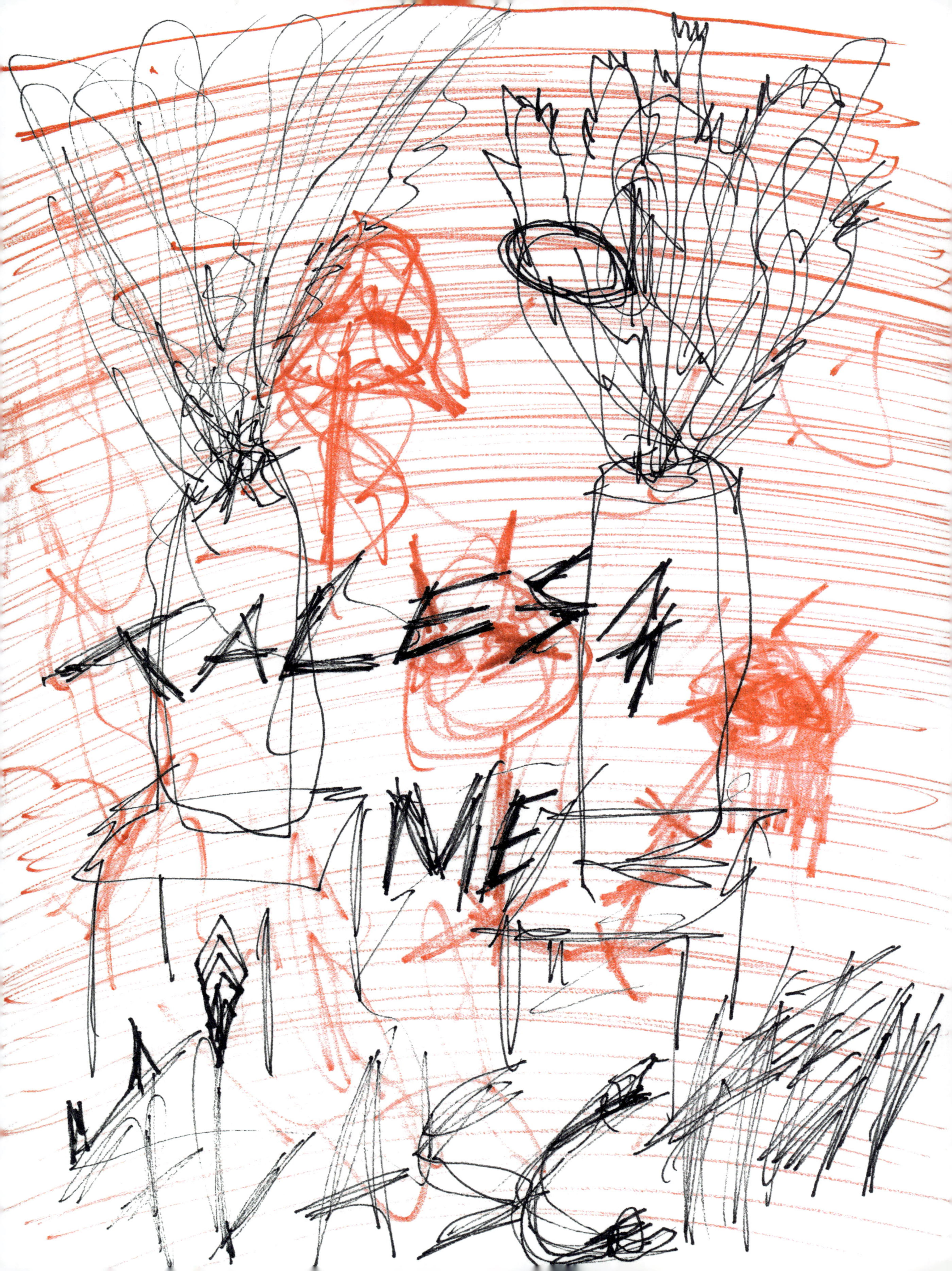
TALES 4
ME

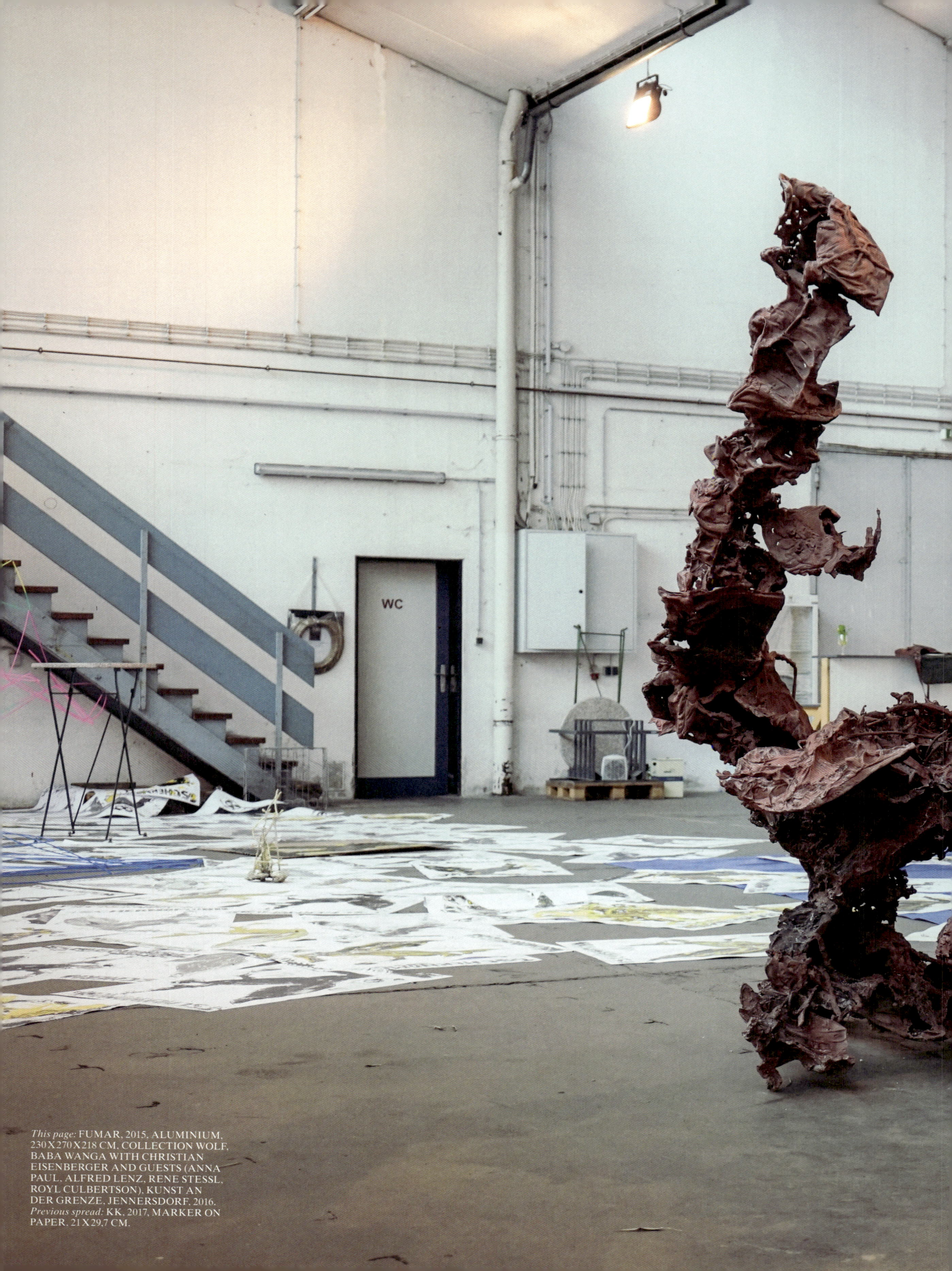


*This page:* FUMAR, 2015, ALUMINIUM, 230 X 270 X 218 CM, COLLECTION WOLF, BABA WANGA WITH CHRISTIAN EISENBERGER AND GUESTS (ANNA PAUL, ALFRED LENZ, RENE STESSL, ROYL CULBERTSON), KUNST AN DER GRENZE, JENNERSDORF, 2016. *Previous spread:* KK, 2017, MARKER ON PAPER, 21 X 29,7 CM.

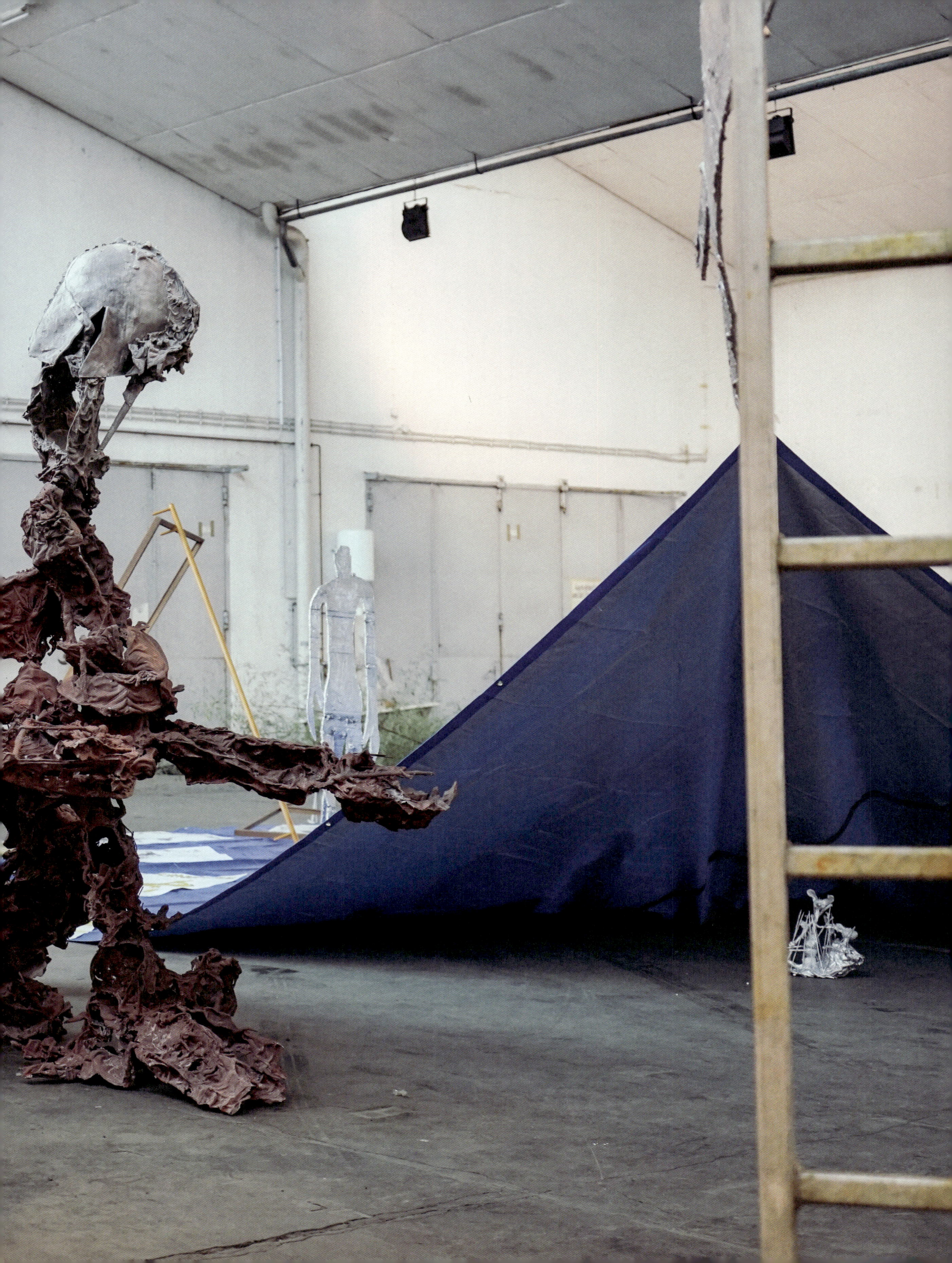

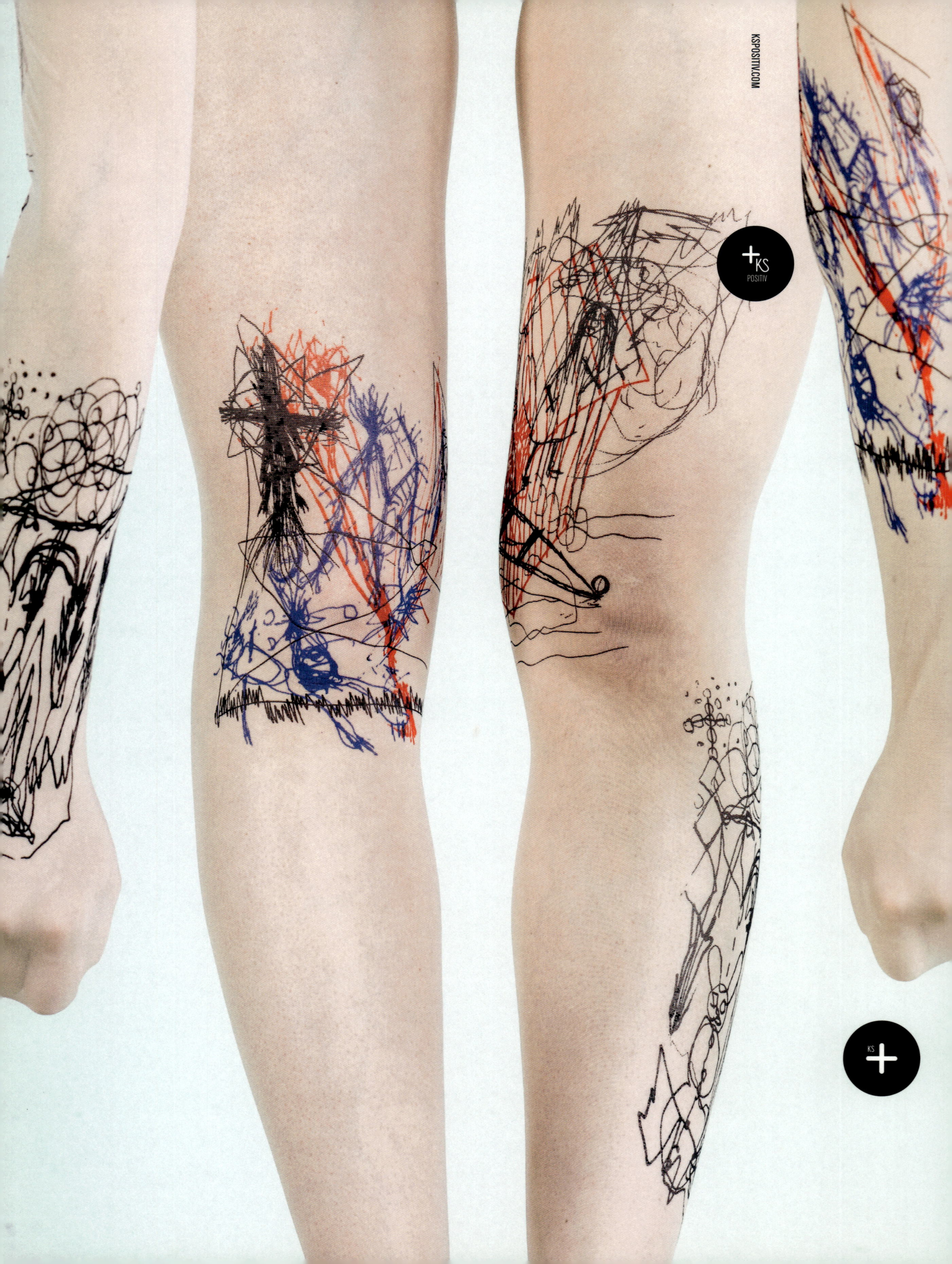
KSPOSITIV.COM
KS
POSITIV
KS

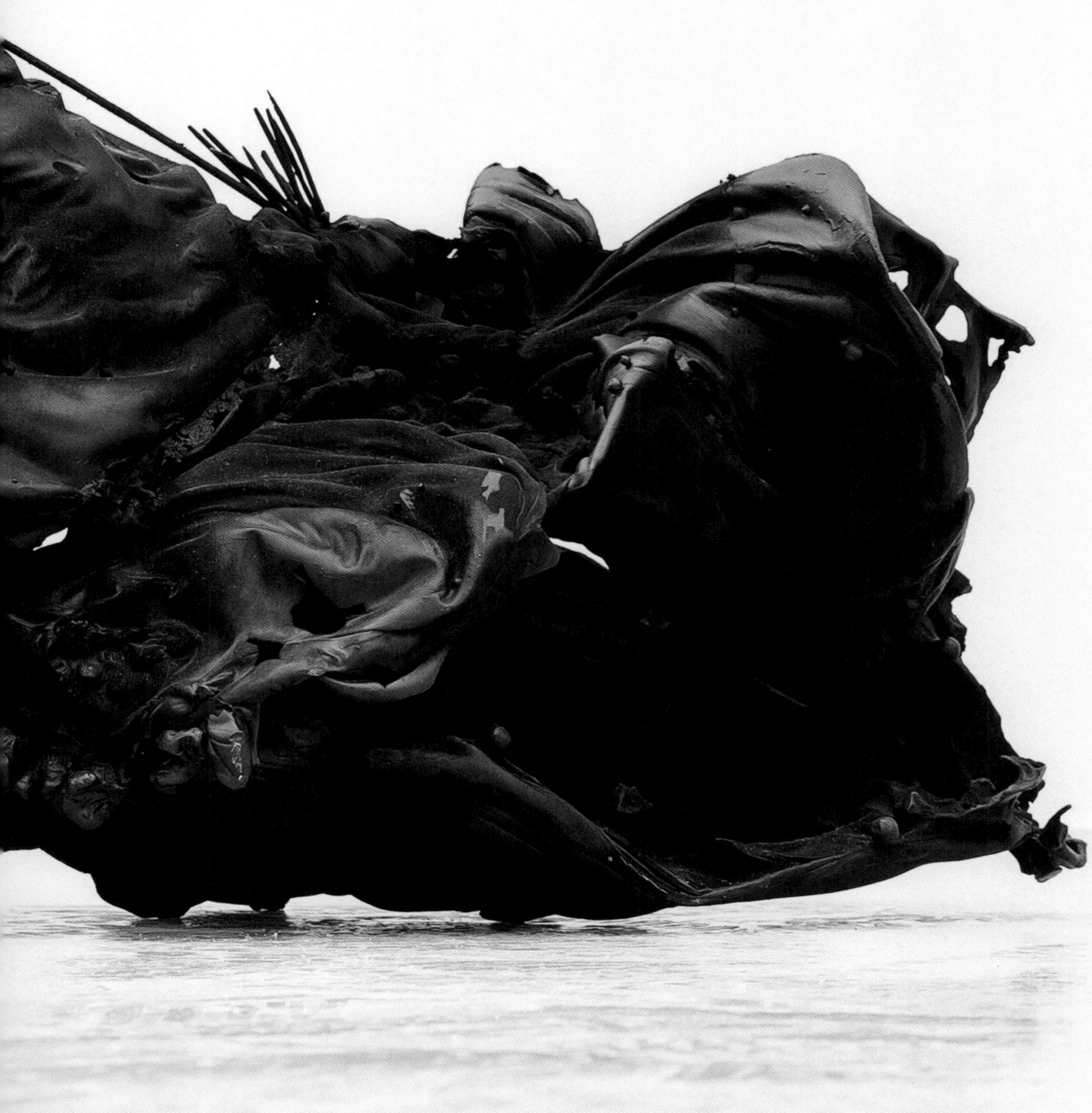

KS SCHWARZ, 2016, ALUMINIUM,
60 X 42 X 29 CM.

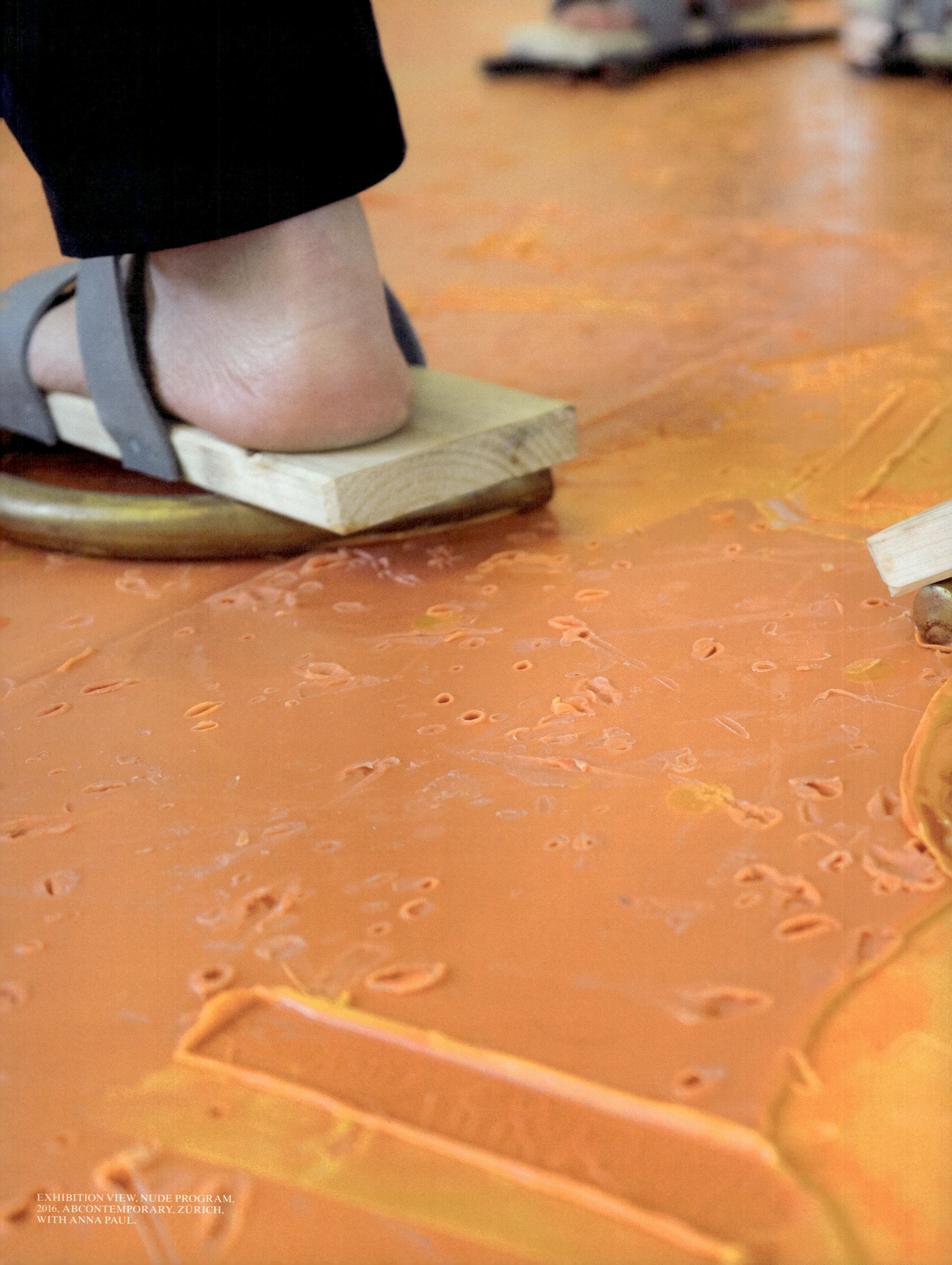

EXHIBITION VIEW, NUDE PROGRAM, 2016, ABCONTEMPORARY, ZÜRICH, WITH ANNA PAUL.

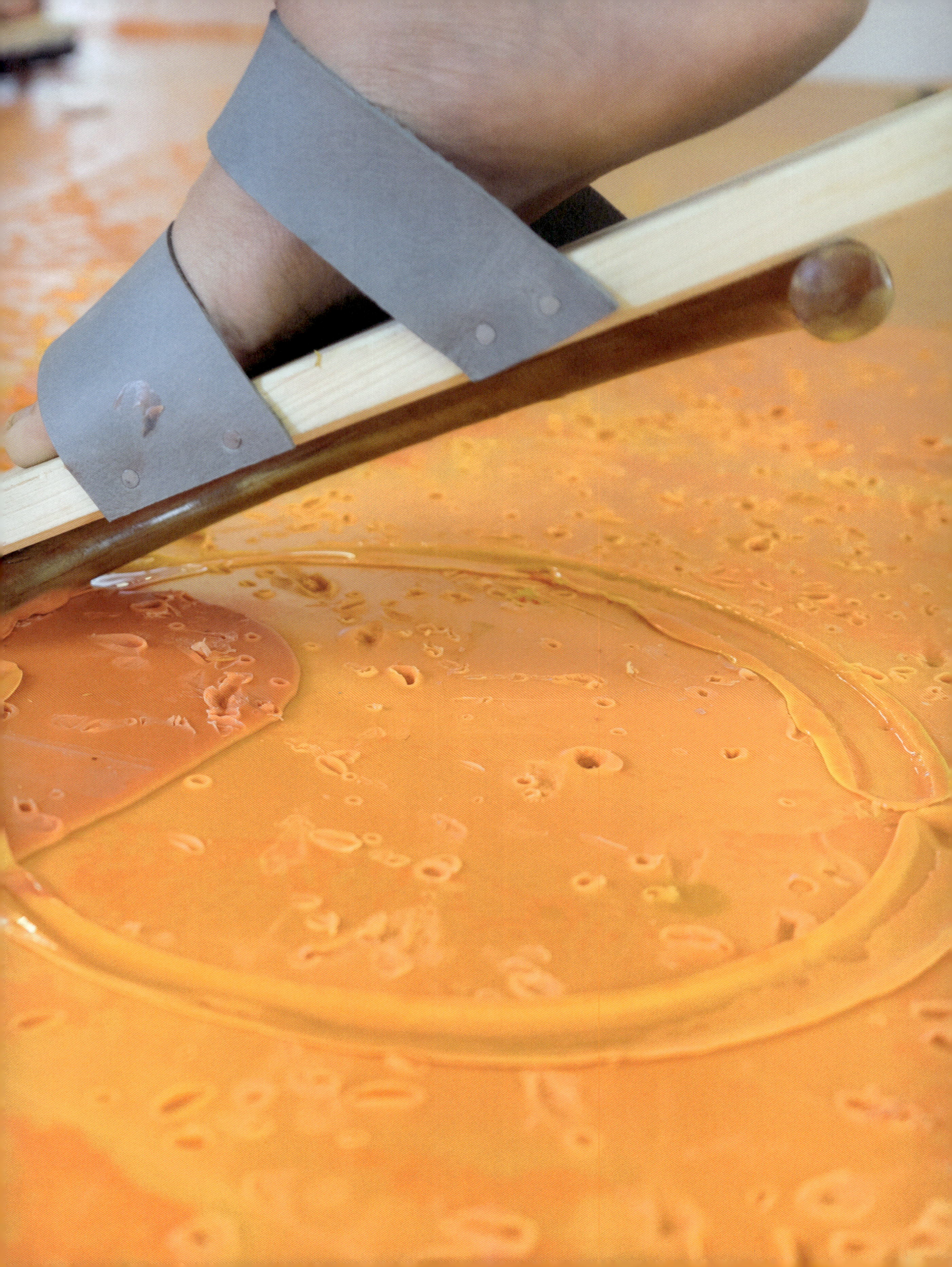

KS SCHWARZ, 2016, ALUMINIUM,
60 X 42 X 29 CM.

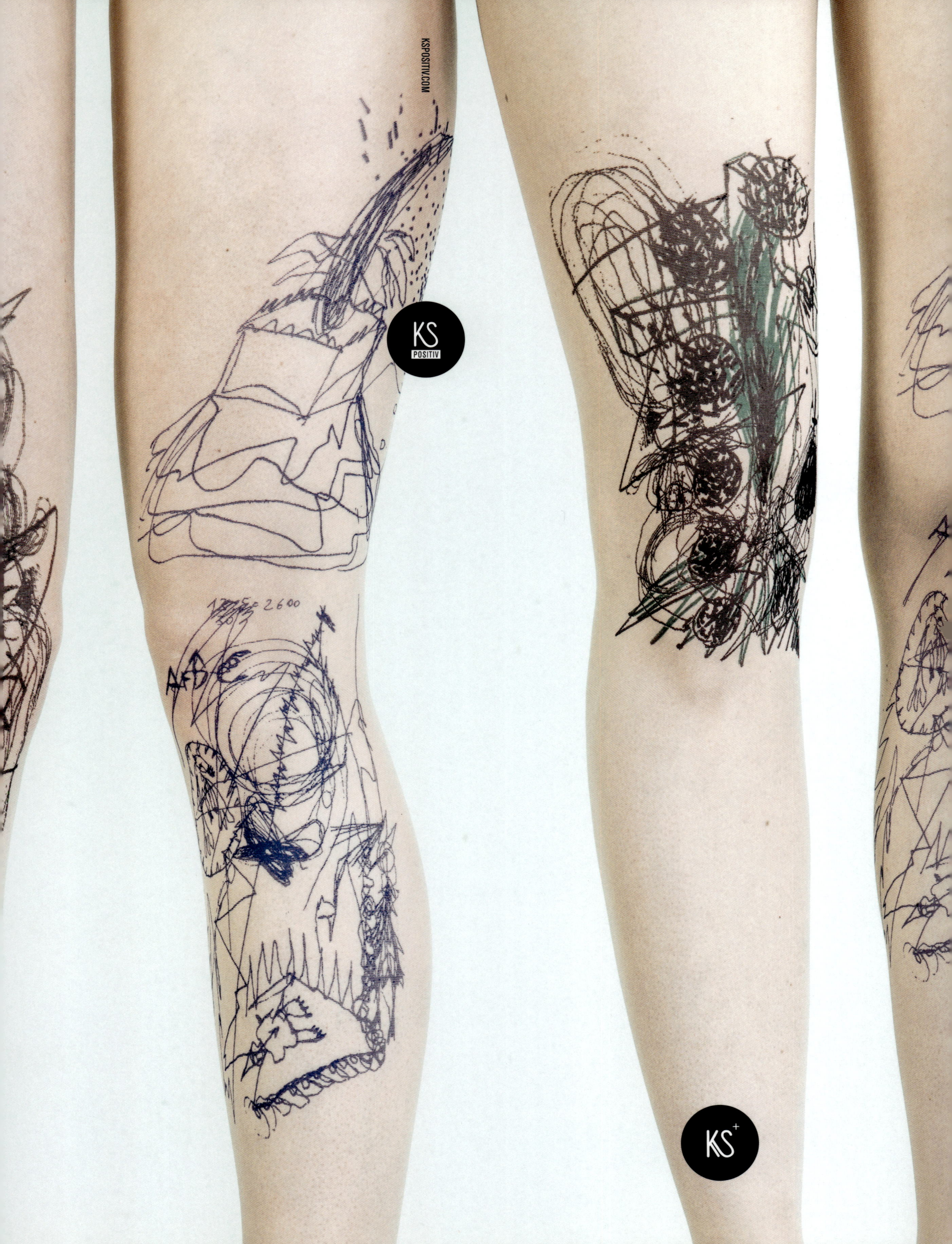
KSPOSITIV.COM
KS
POSITIV
KS+

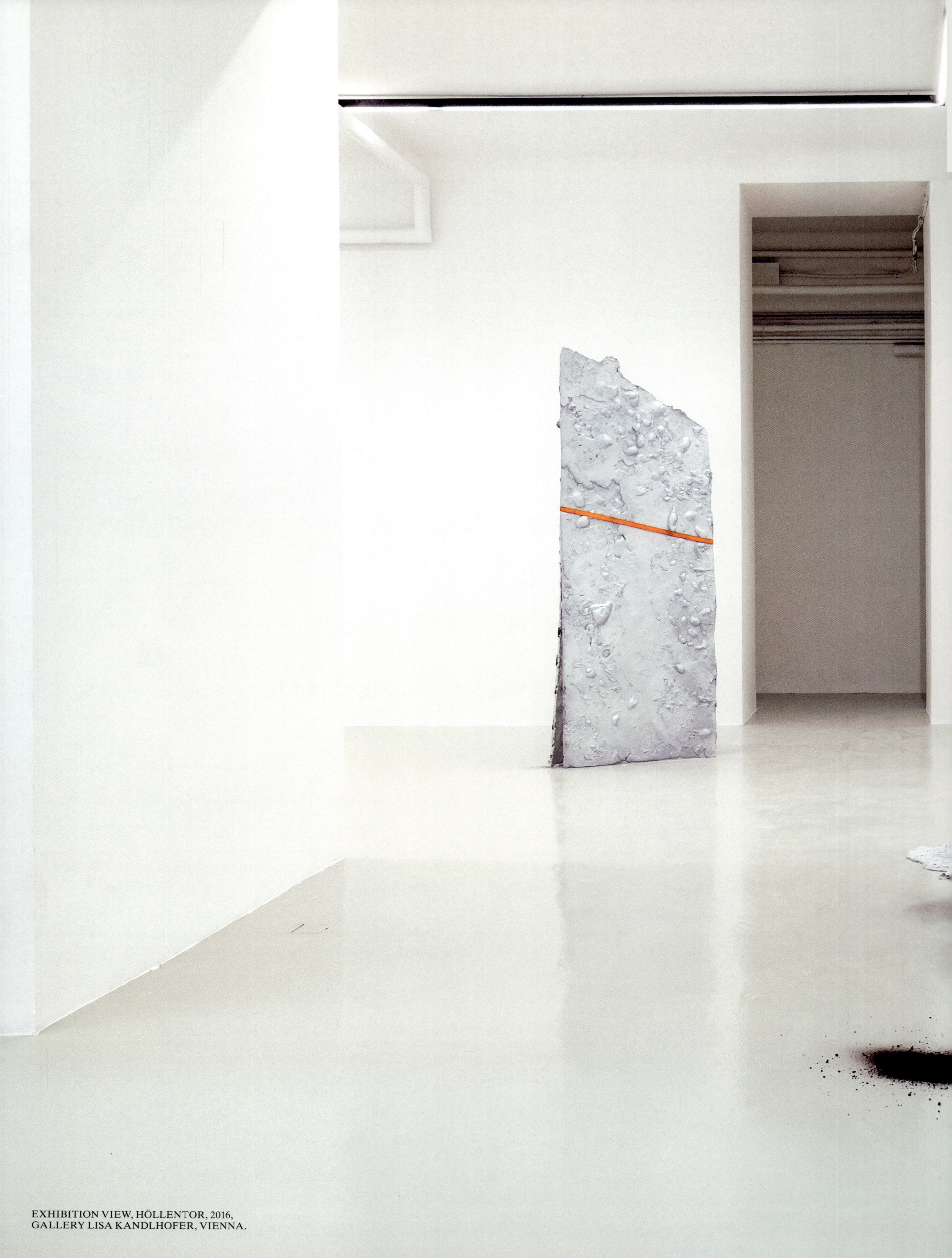

EXHIBITION VIEW, HÖLLENTOR, 2016,
GALLERY LISA KANDLHOFER, VIENNA.

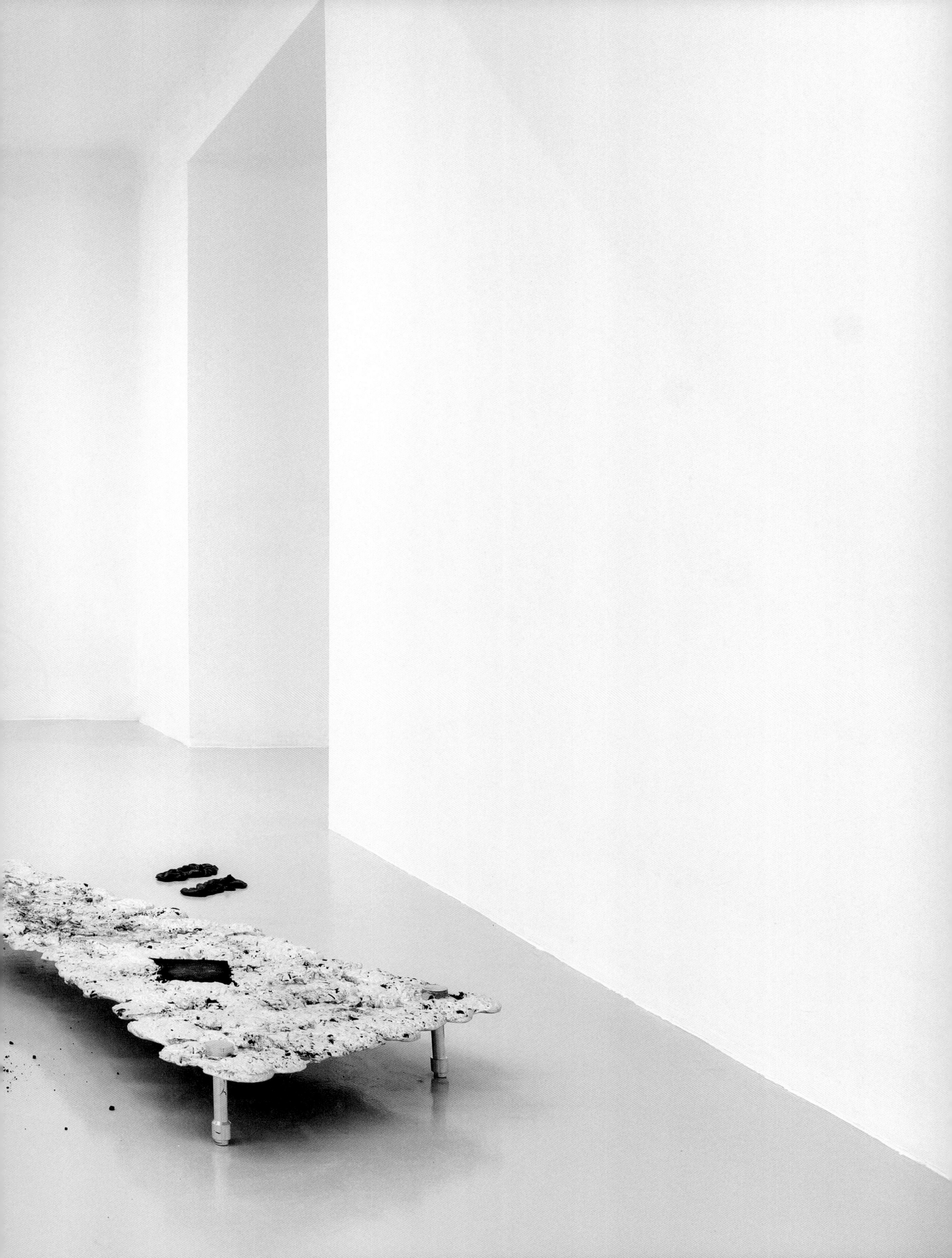

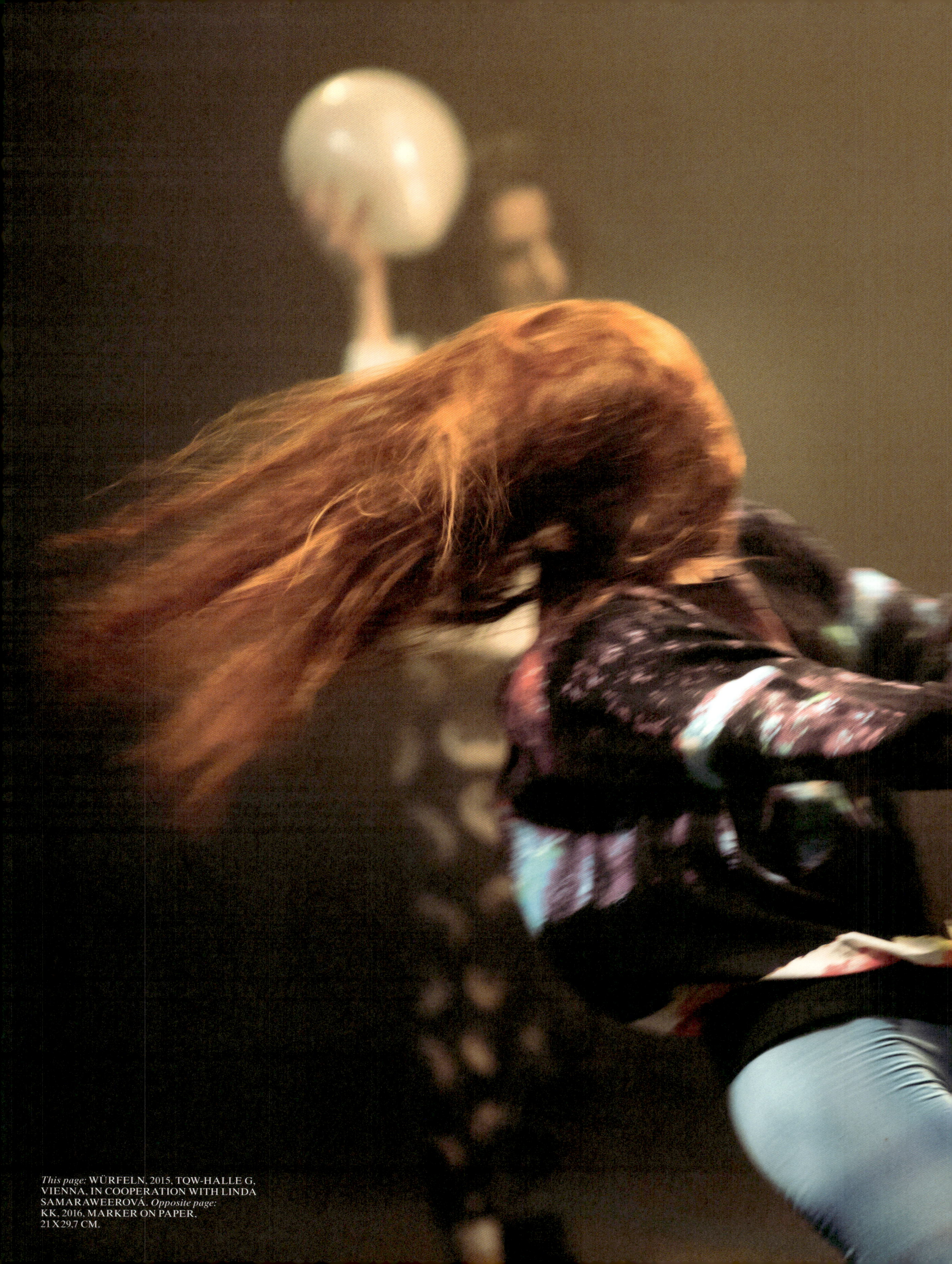

*This page:* WÜRFELN, 2015, TQW-HALLE G, VIENNA, IN COOPERATION WITH LINDA SAMARAWEEROVÁ. *Opposite page:* KK, 2016, MARKER ON PAPER, 21 X 29,7 CM.

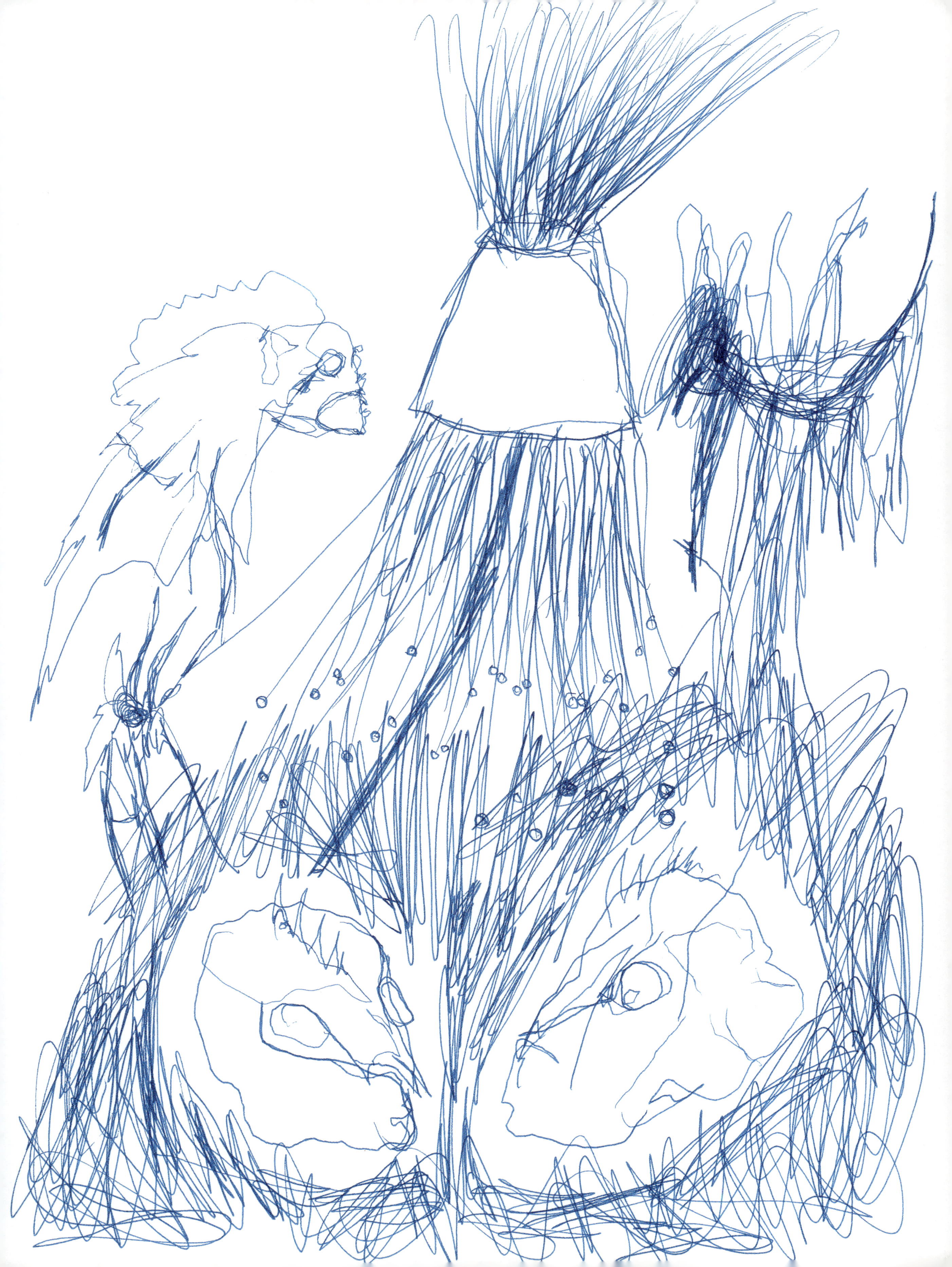

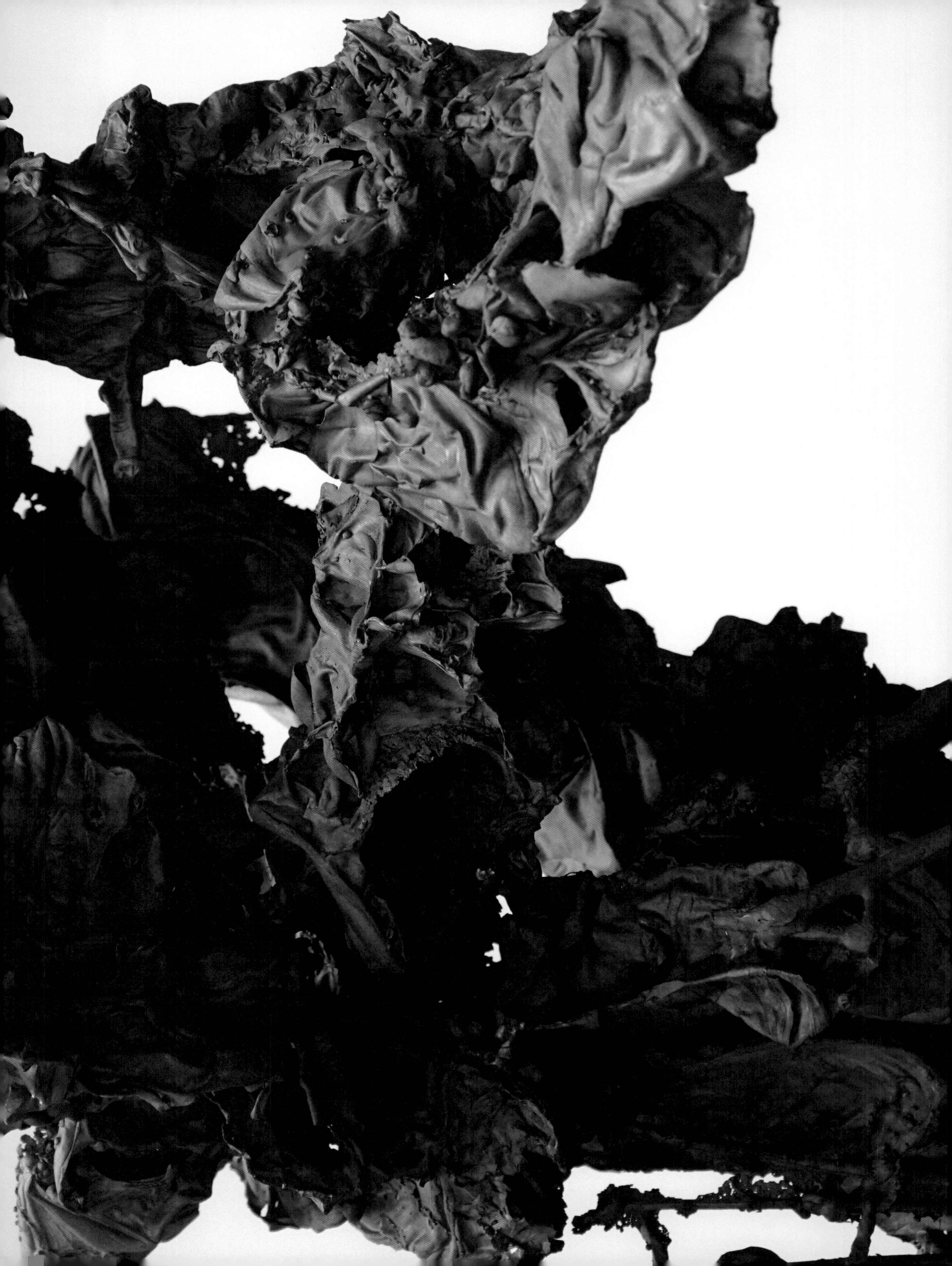

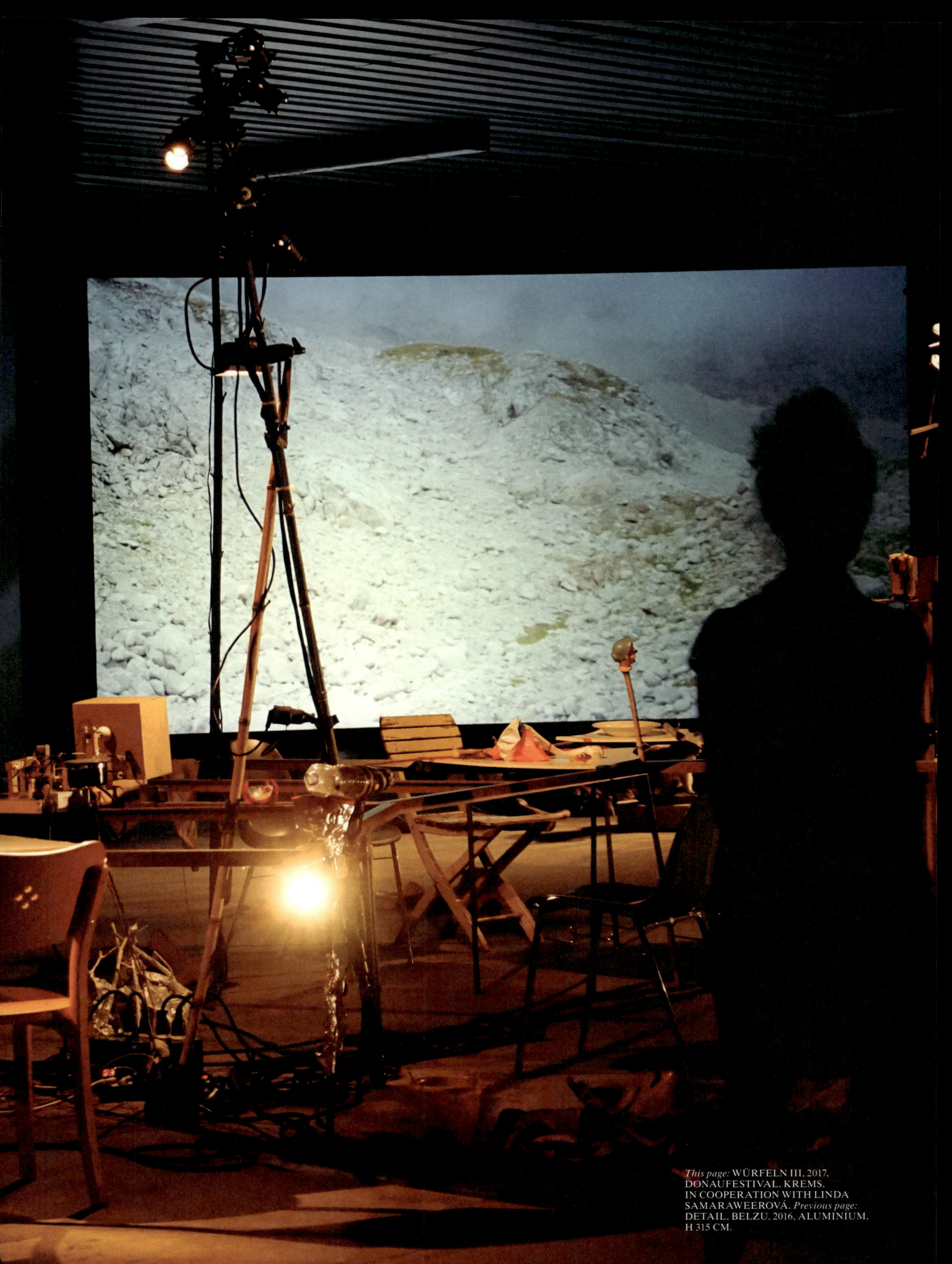

*This page:* WÜRFELN III, 2017, DONAUFESTIVAL, KREMS, IN COOPERATION WITH LINDA SAMARAWEEROVÁ. *Previous page:* DETAIL, BELZU, 2016, ALUMINIUM, H 315 CM.

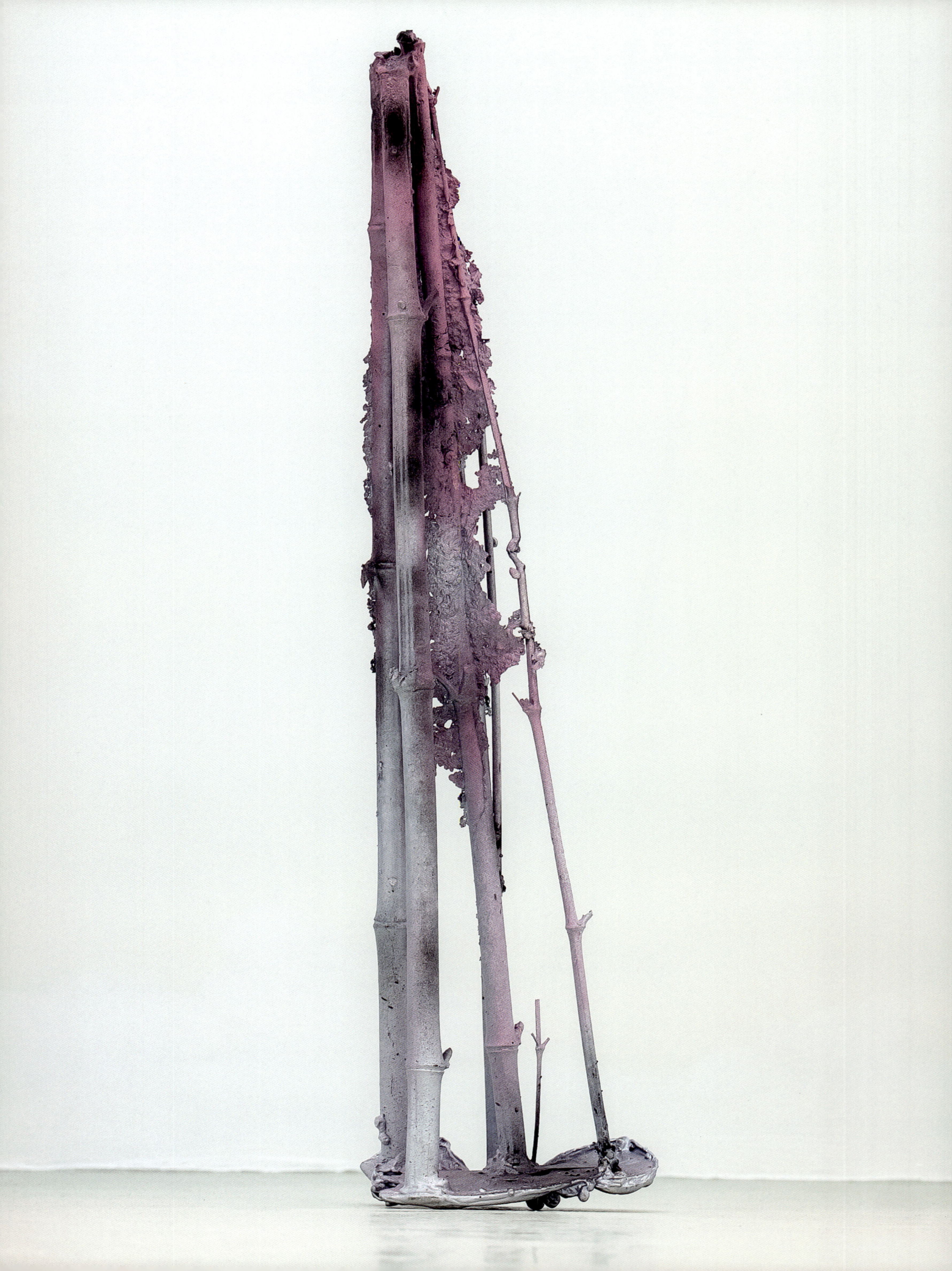

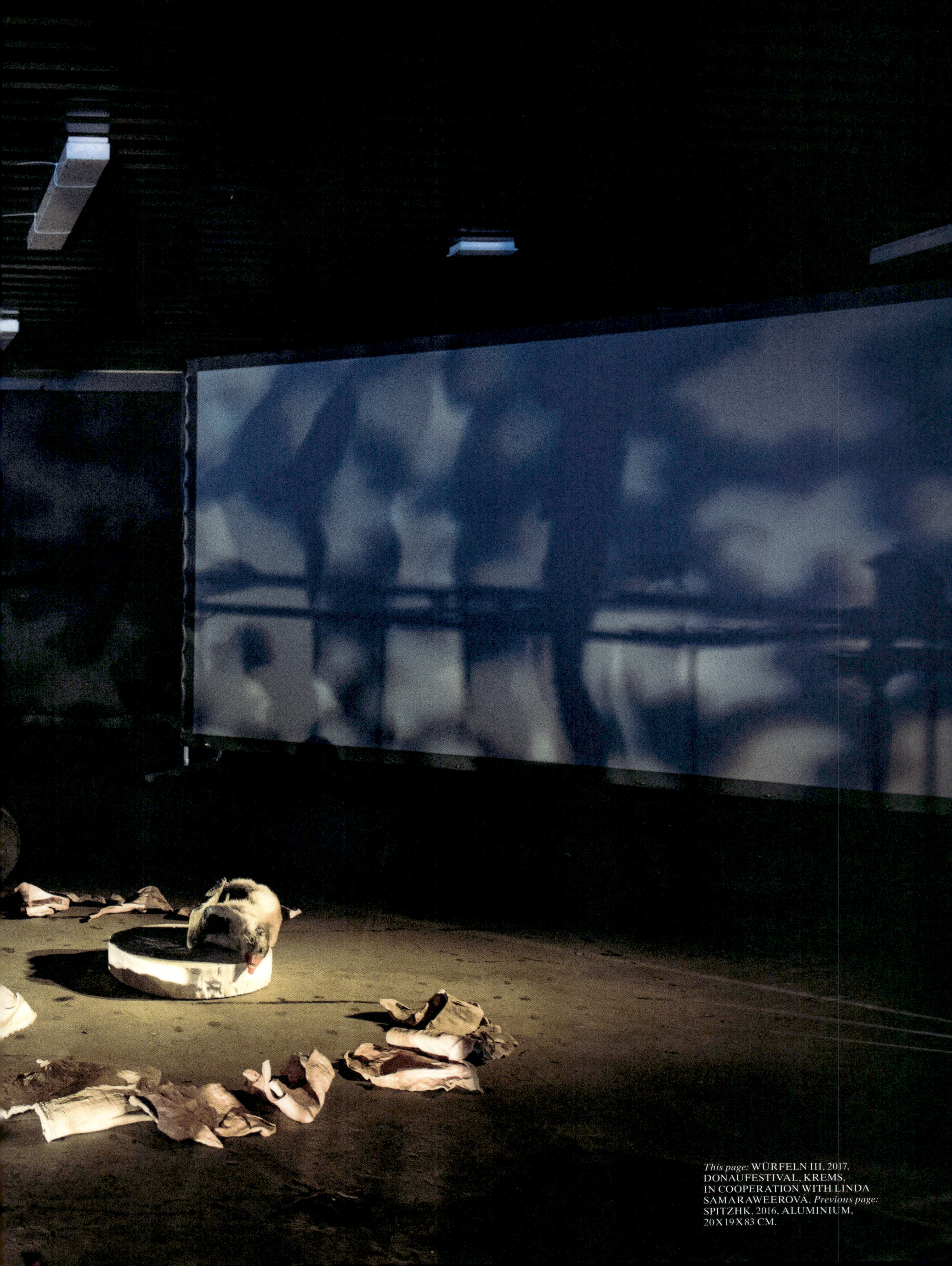

*This page:* WÜRFELN III, 2017, DONAUFESTIVAL, KREMS, IN COOPERATION WITH LINDA SAMARAWEEROVÁ. *Previous page:* SPITZHK, 2016, ALUMINIUM, 20 X 19 X 83 CM.

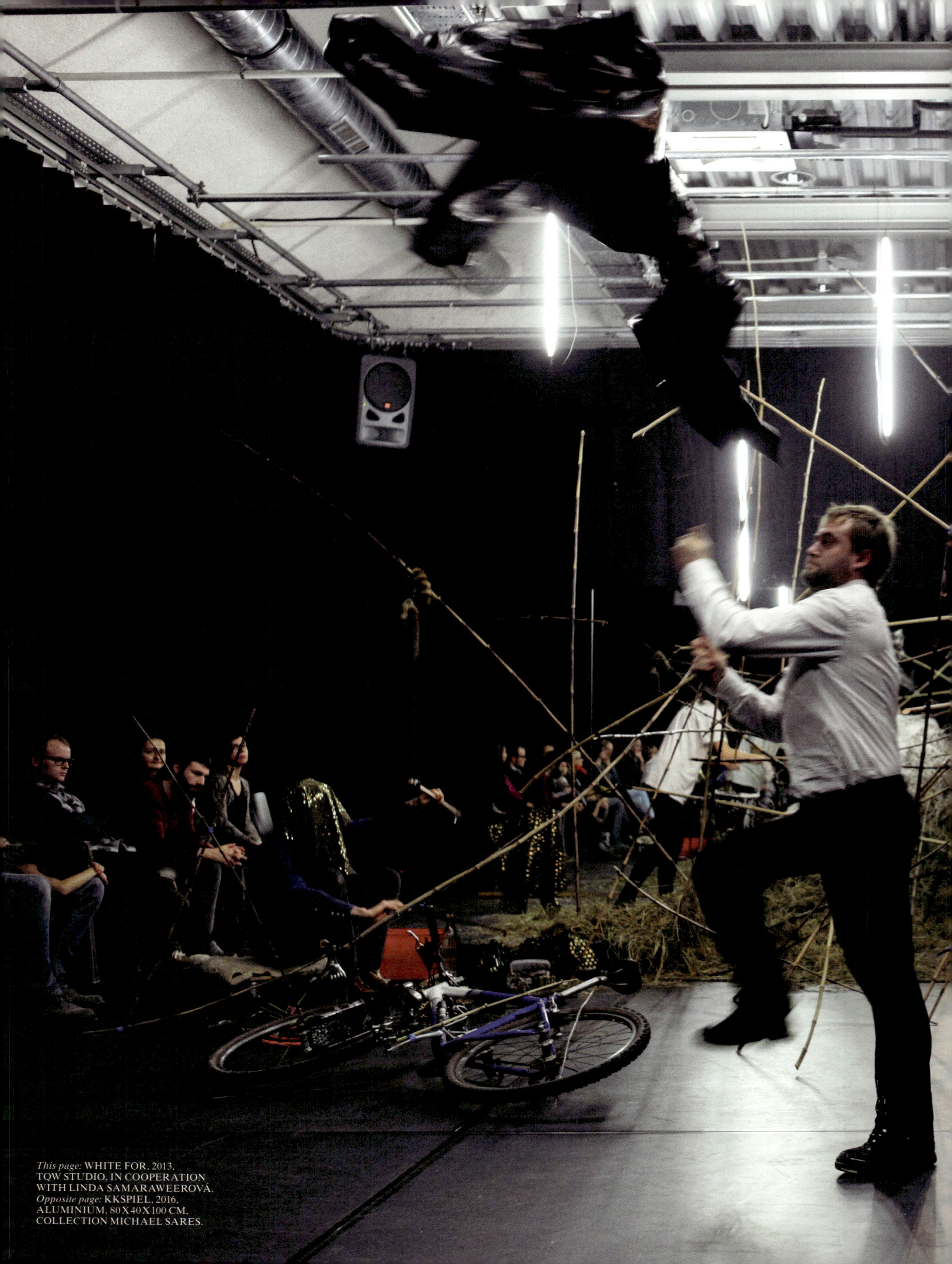

*This page:* WHITE FOR, 2013.
TOW STUDIO, IN COOPERATION
WITH LINDA SAMARAWEEROVÁ.
*Opposite page:* KKSPIEL, 2016,
ALUMINIUM, 80 X 40 X 100 CM,
COLLECTION MICHAEL SARES.

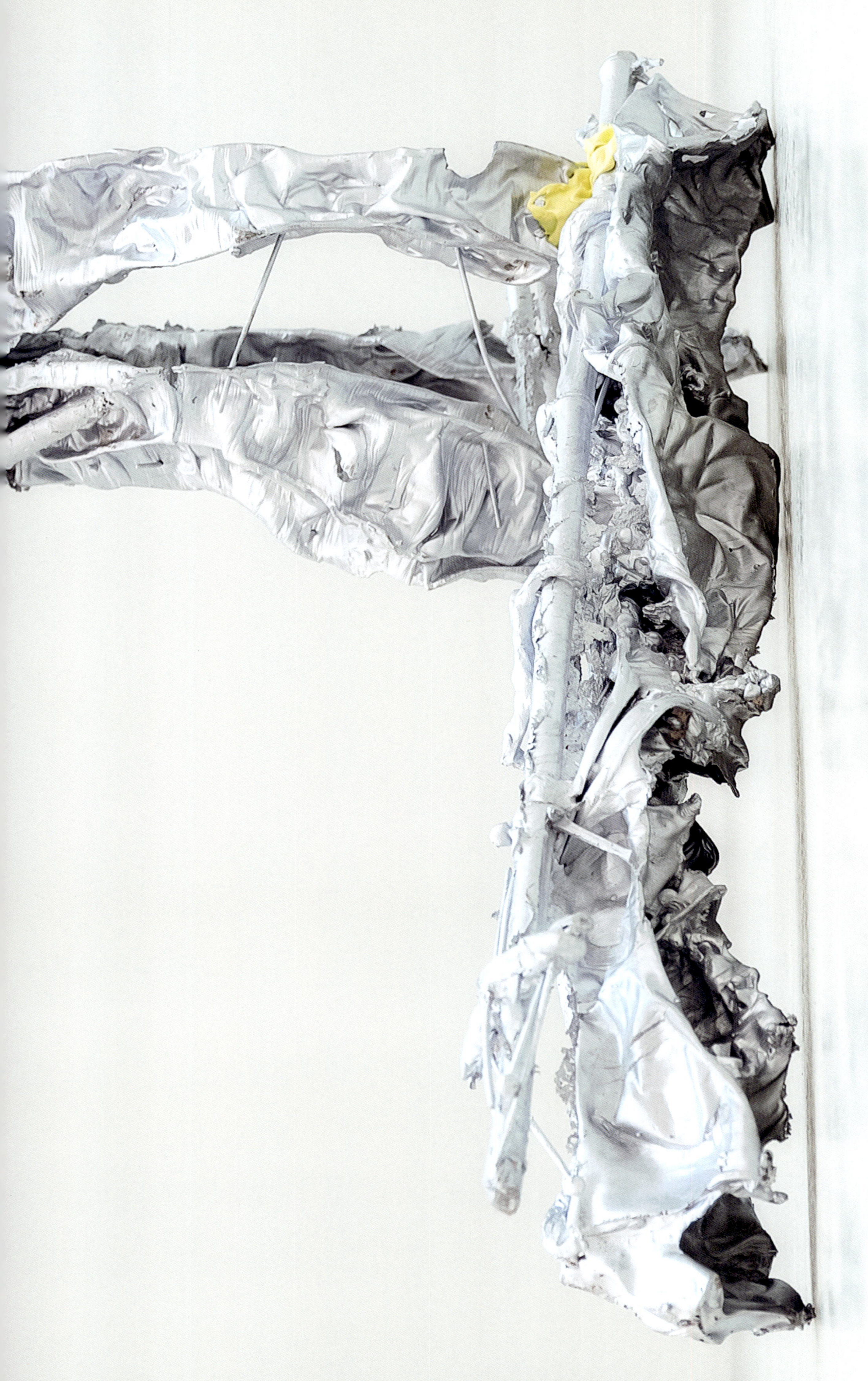

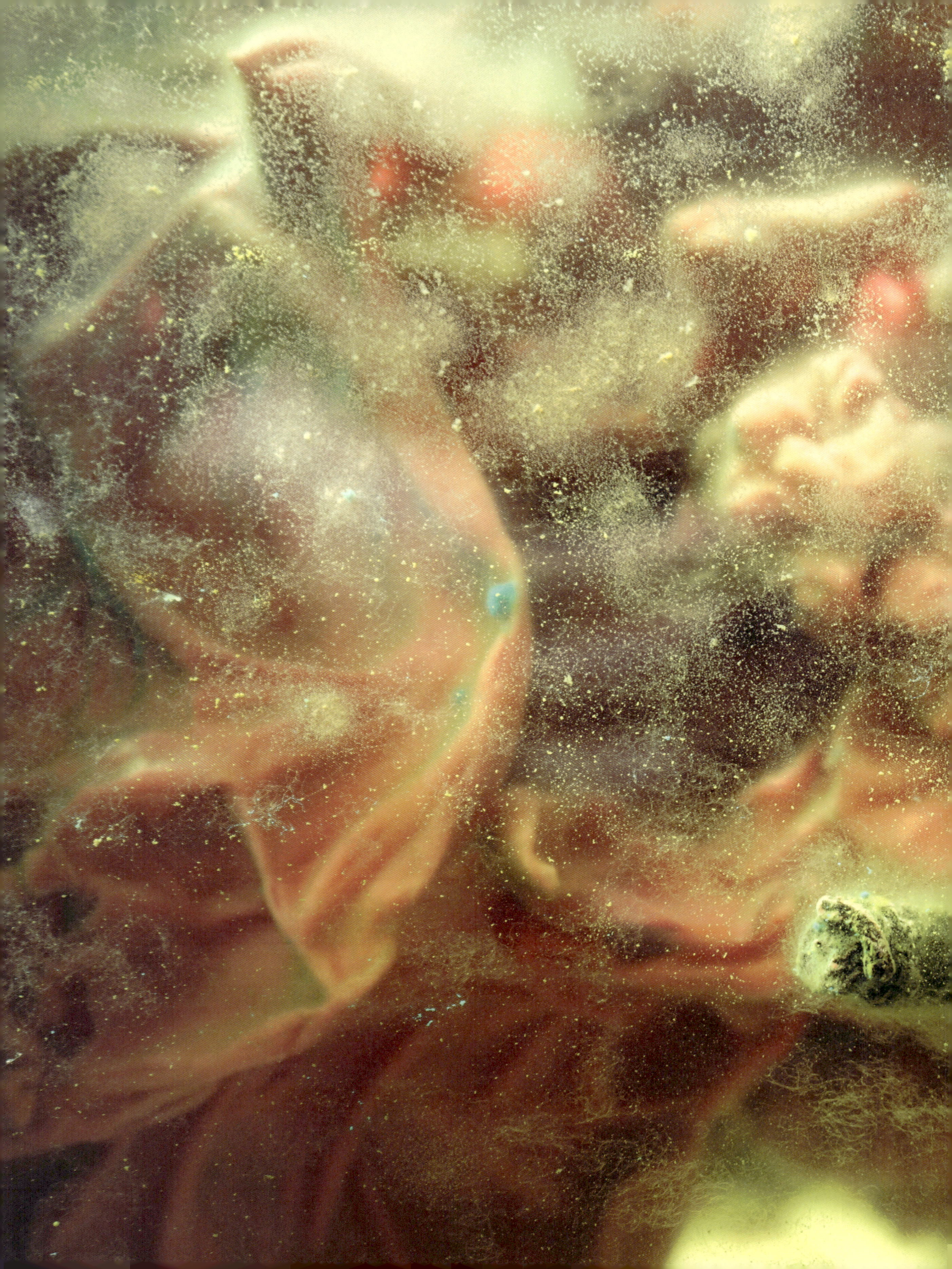

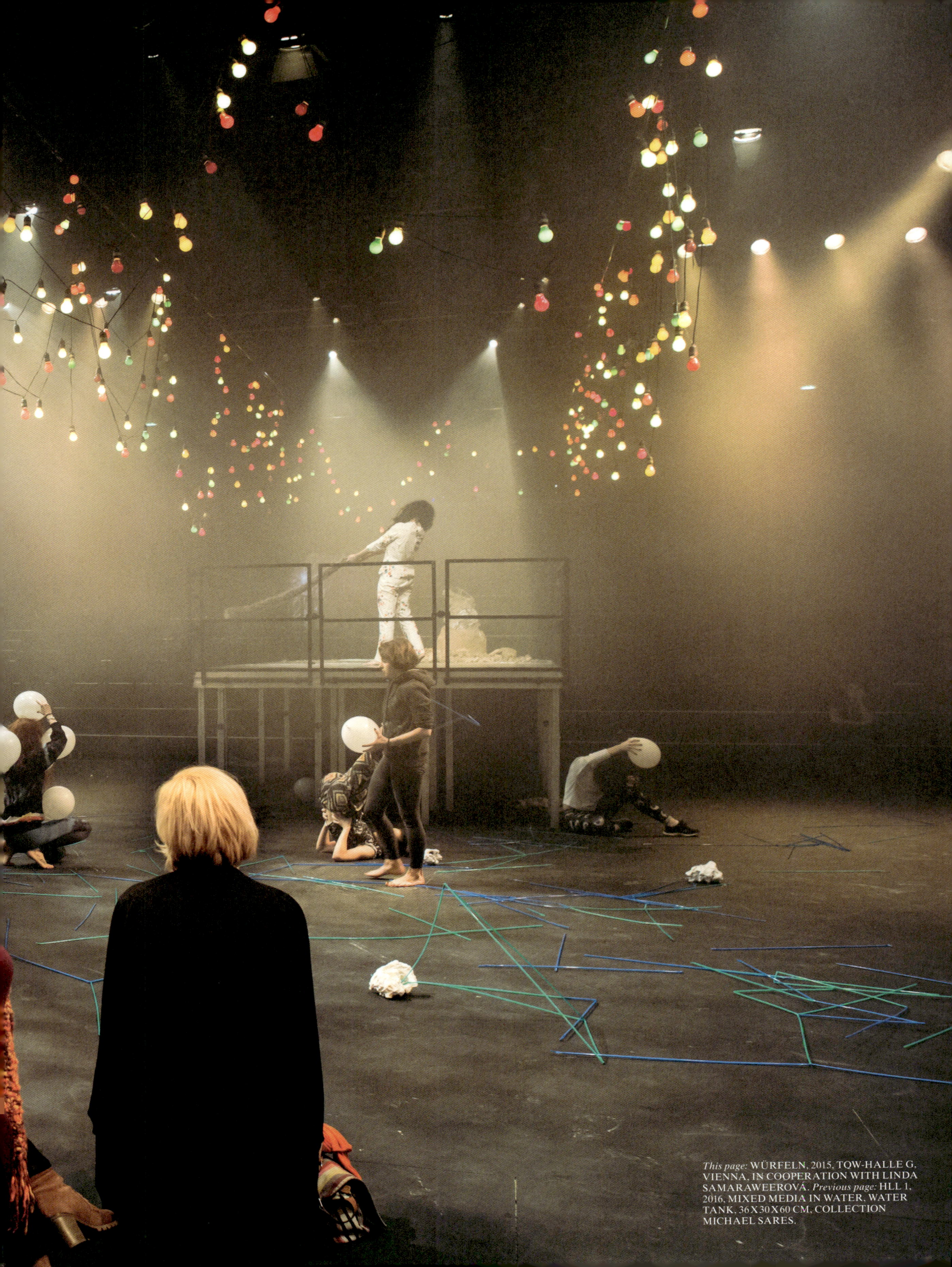

*This page:* WÜRFELN, 2015, TQW-HALLE G, VIENNA, IN COOPERATION WITH LINDA SAMARAWEEROVÁ. *Previous page:* HLL 1, 2016, MIXED MEDIA IN WATER, WATER TANK, 36 X 30 X 60 CM, COLLECTION MICHAEL SARES.

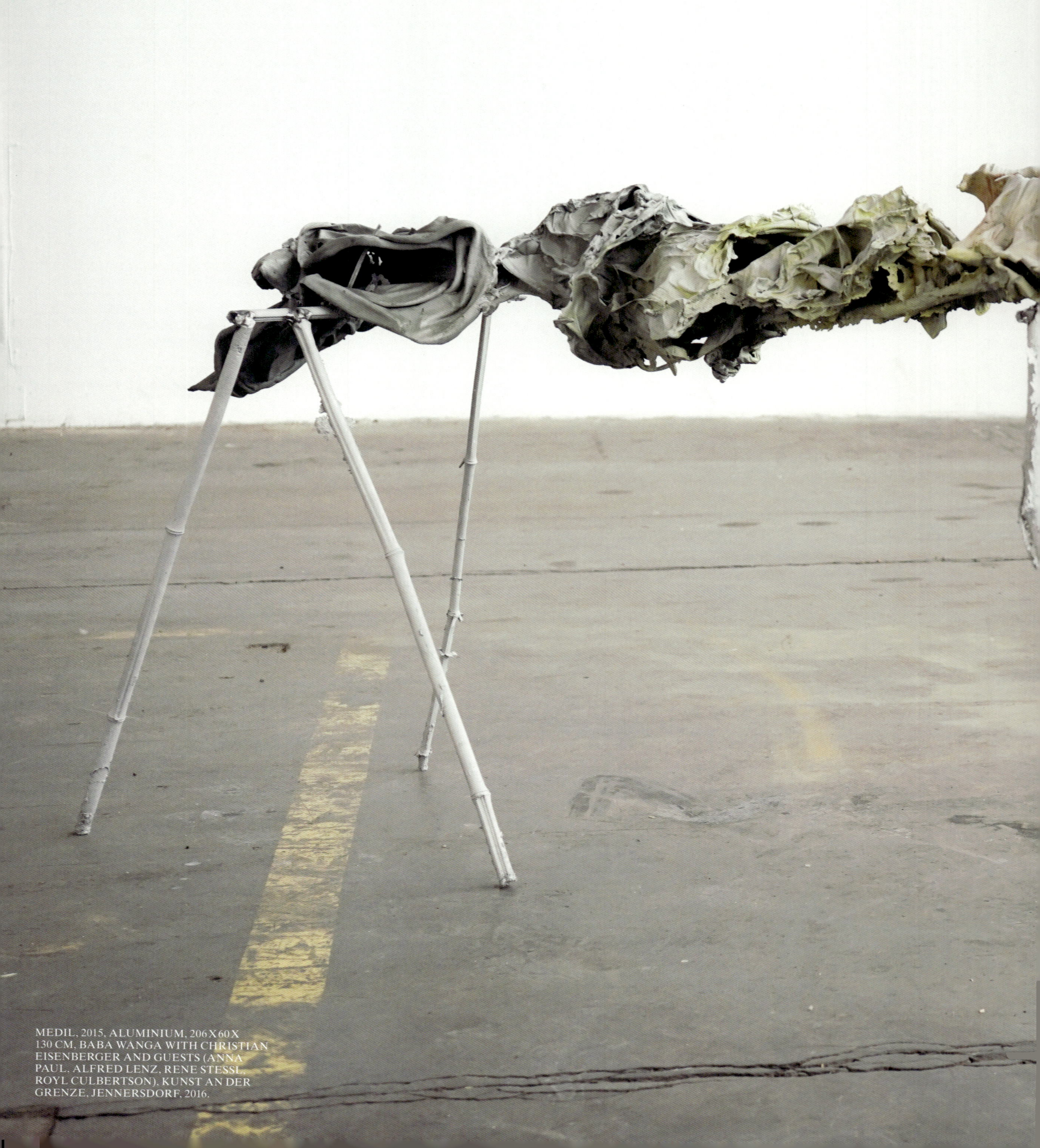

MEDIL, 2015, ALUMINIUM, 206 X 60 X 130 CM, BABA WANGA WITH CHRISTIAN EISENBERGER AND GUESTS (ANNA PAUL, ALFRED LENZ, RENE STESSL, ROYL CULBERTSON), KUNST AN DER GRENZE, JENNERSDORF, 2016.

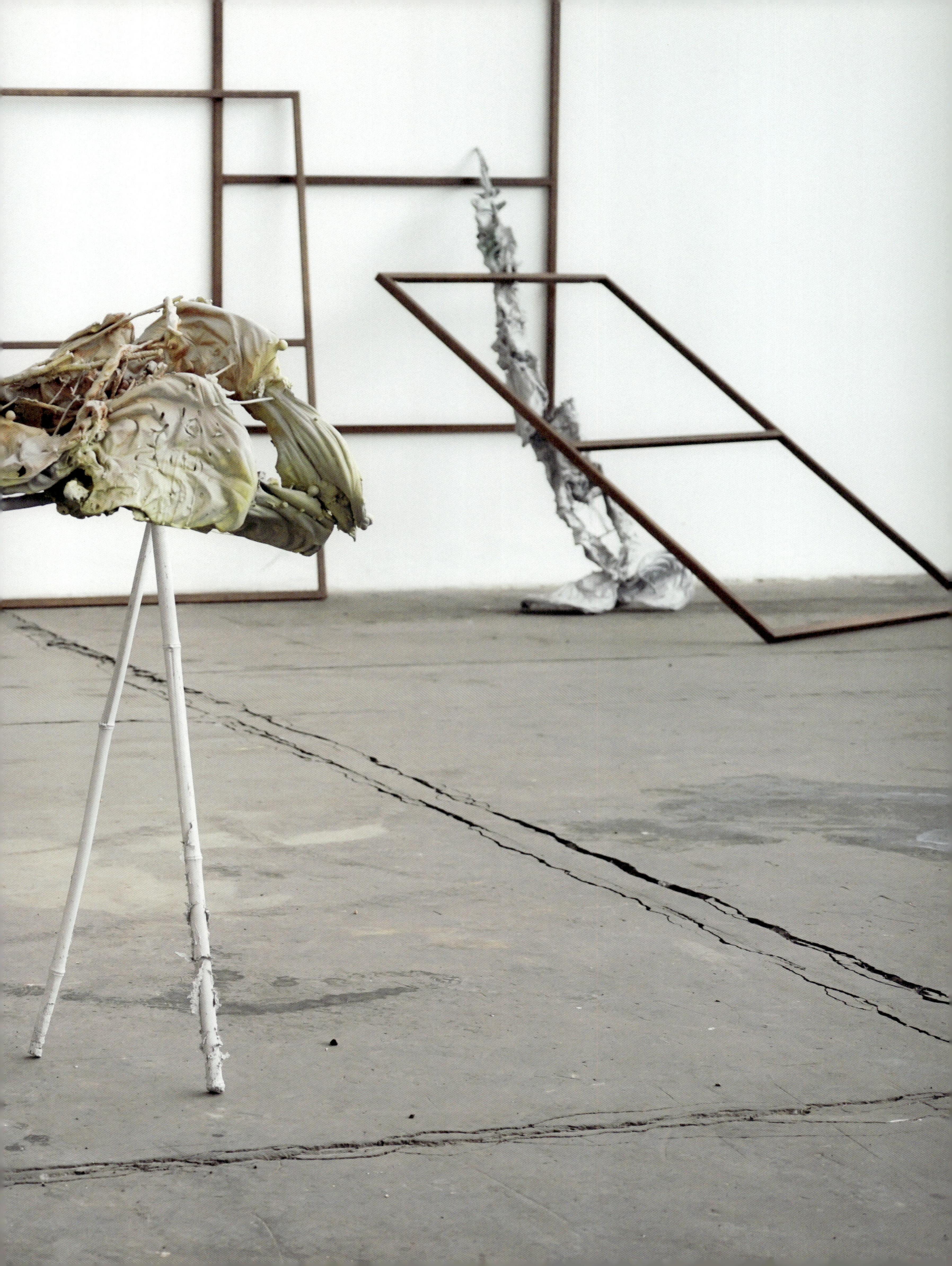

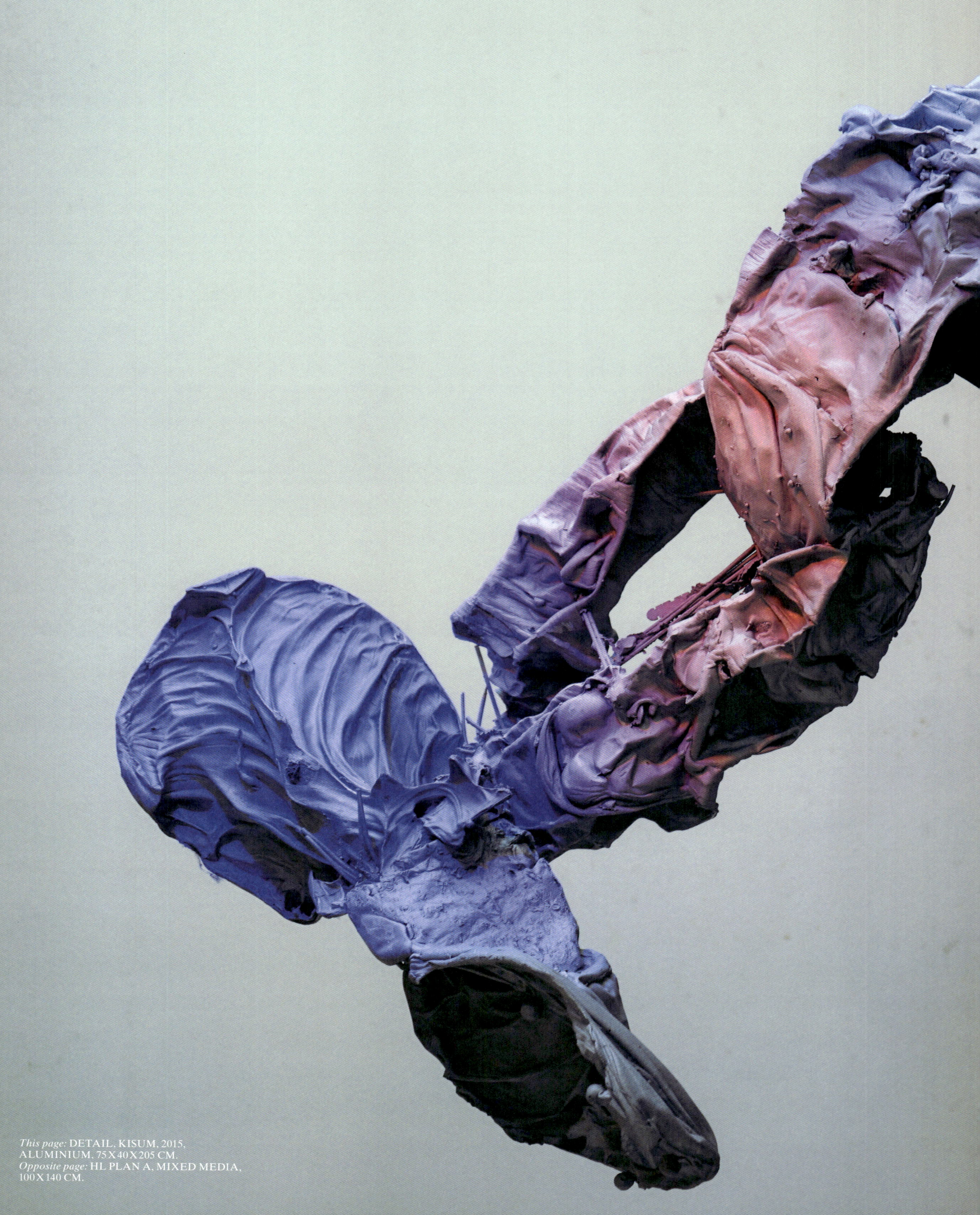

*This page:* DETAIL, KISUM, 2015, ALUMINIUM, 75 X 40 X 205 CM.
*Opposite page:* HL PLAN A, MIXED MEDIA, 100 X 140 CM.

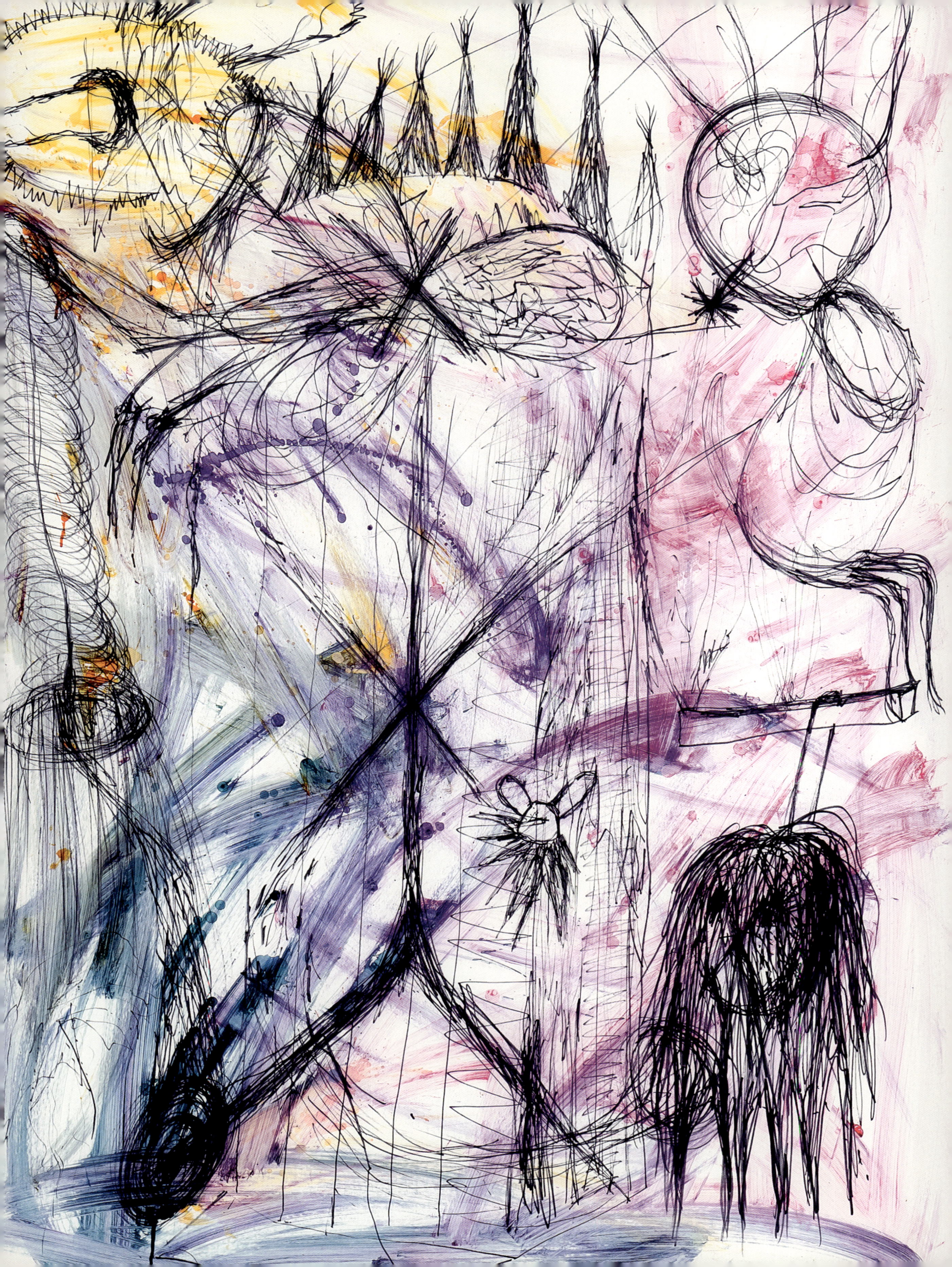

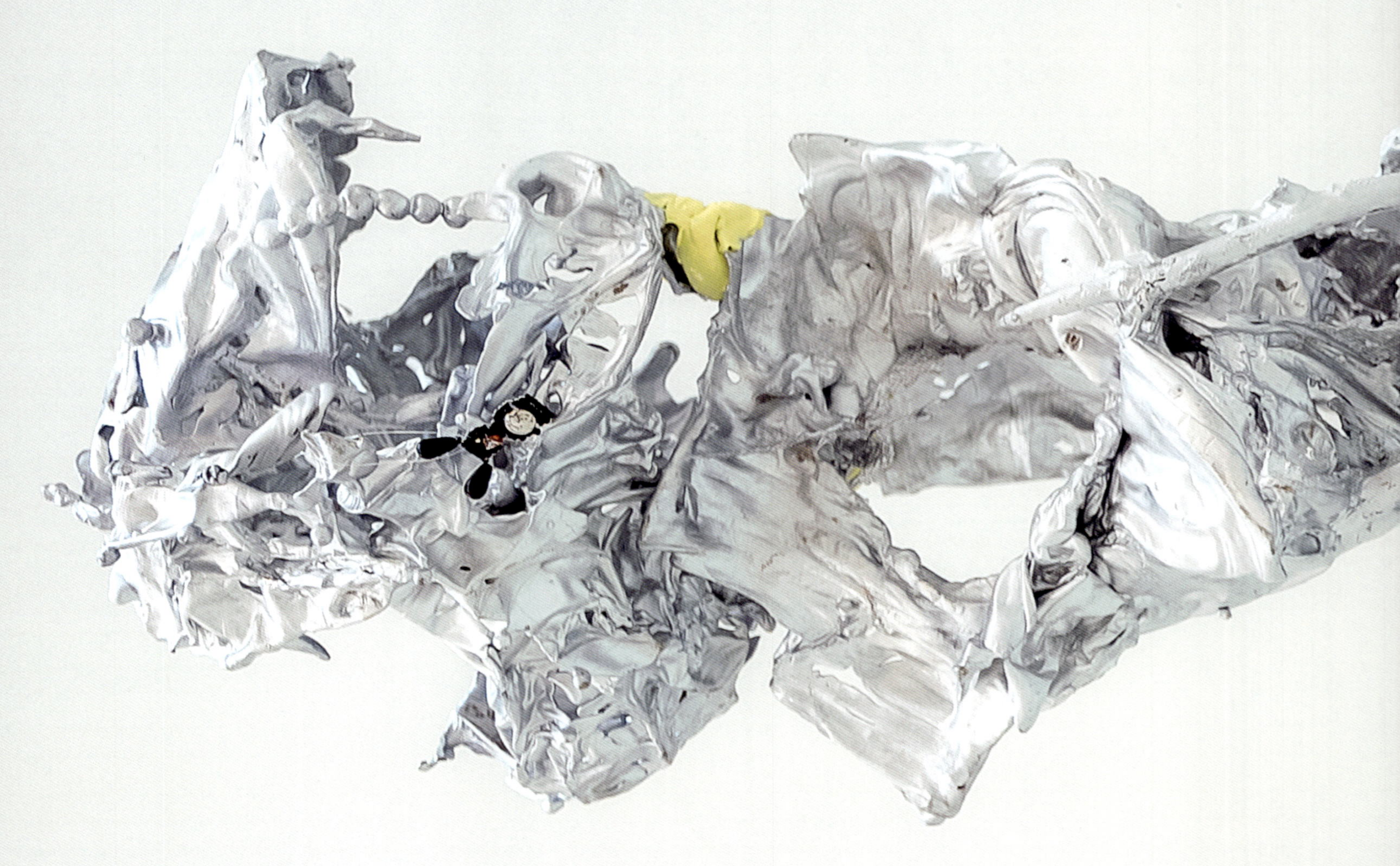

*This page:* KKSPIEL, 2016, ALUMINIUM, 80 X 40 X 100 CM, COLLECTION MICHAEL SARES. *Opposite page:* WÜRFELN III, 2017, DONAUFESTIVAL, KREMS, IN COOPERATION WITH LINDA SAMARAWEEROVÁ.

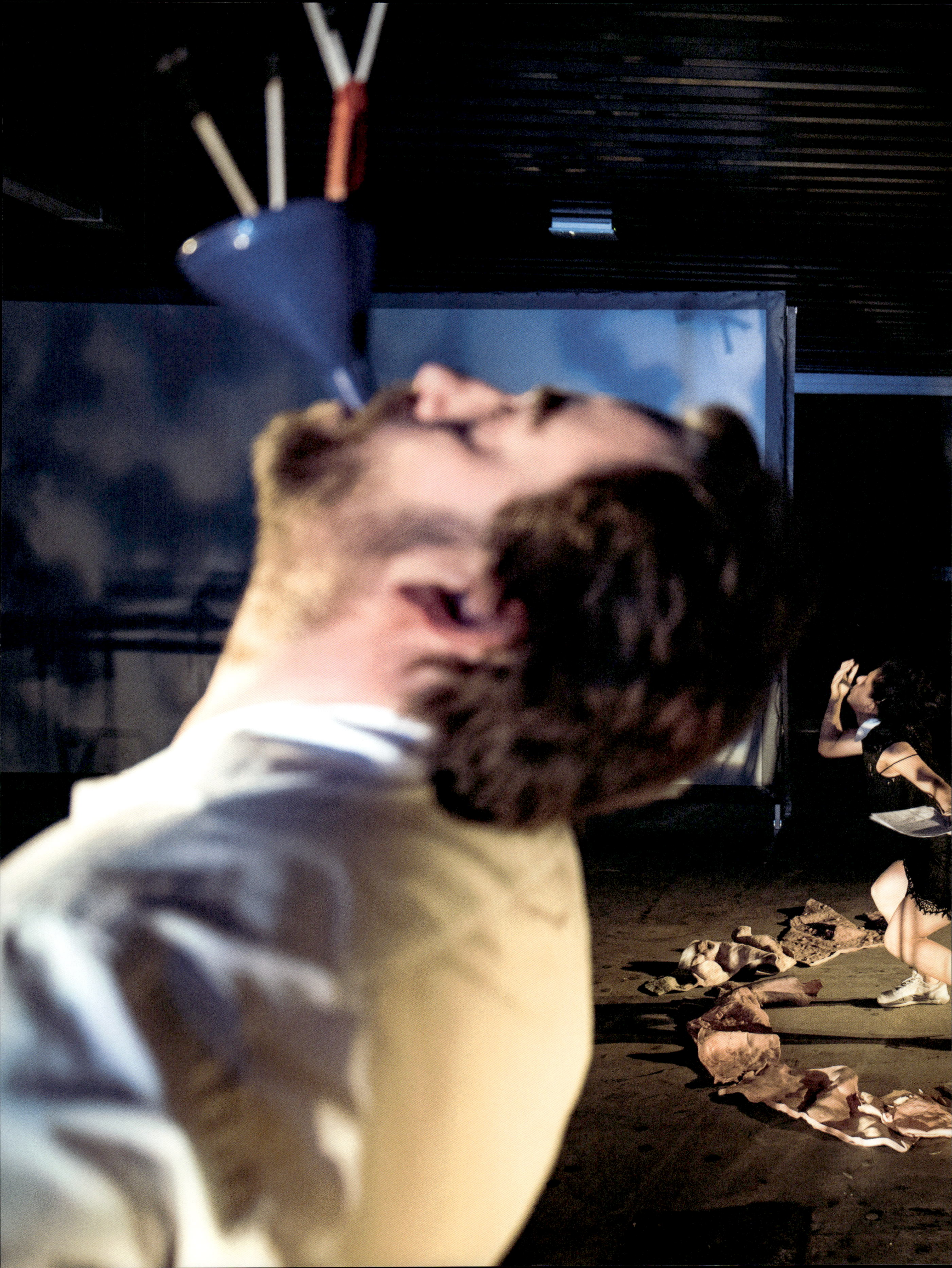

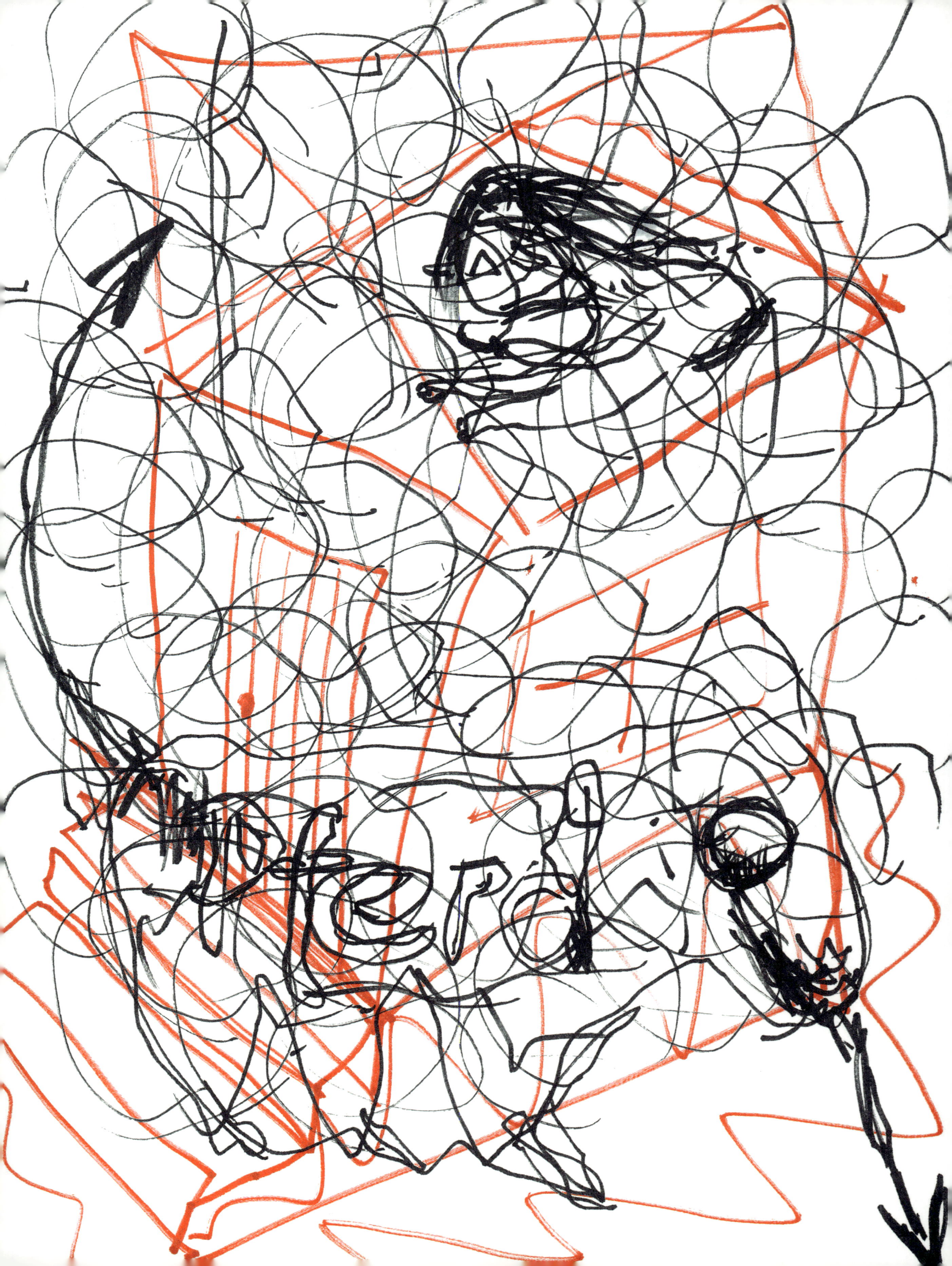

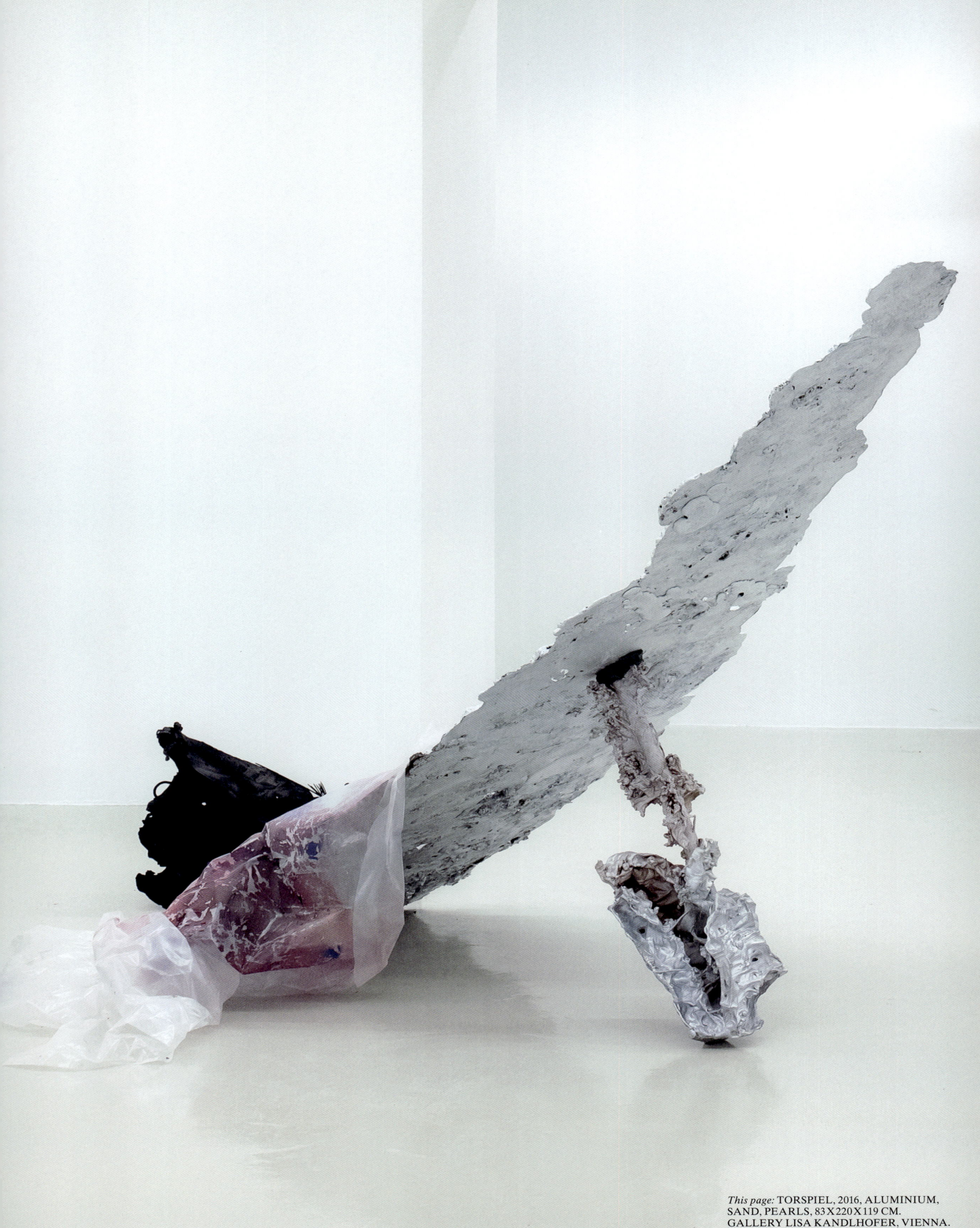

*This page:* TORSPIEL, 2016, ALUMINIUM, SAND, PEARLS, 83 X 220 X 119 CM. GALLERY LISA KANDLHOFER, VIENNA. *Previous page:* KK, 2017, MARKER ON PAPER, 21 X 29,7 CM.

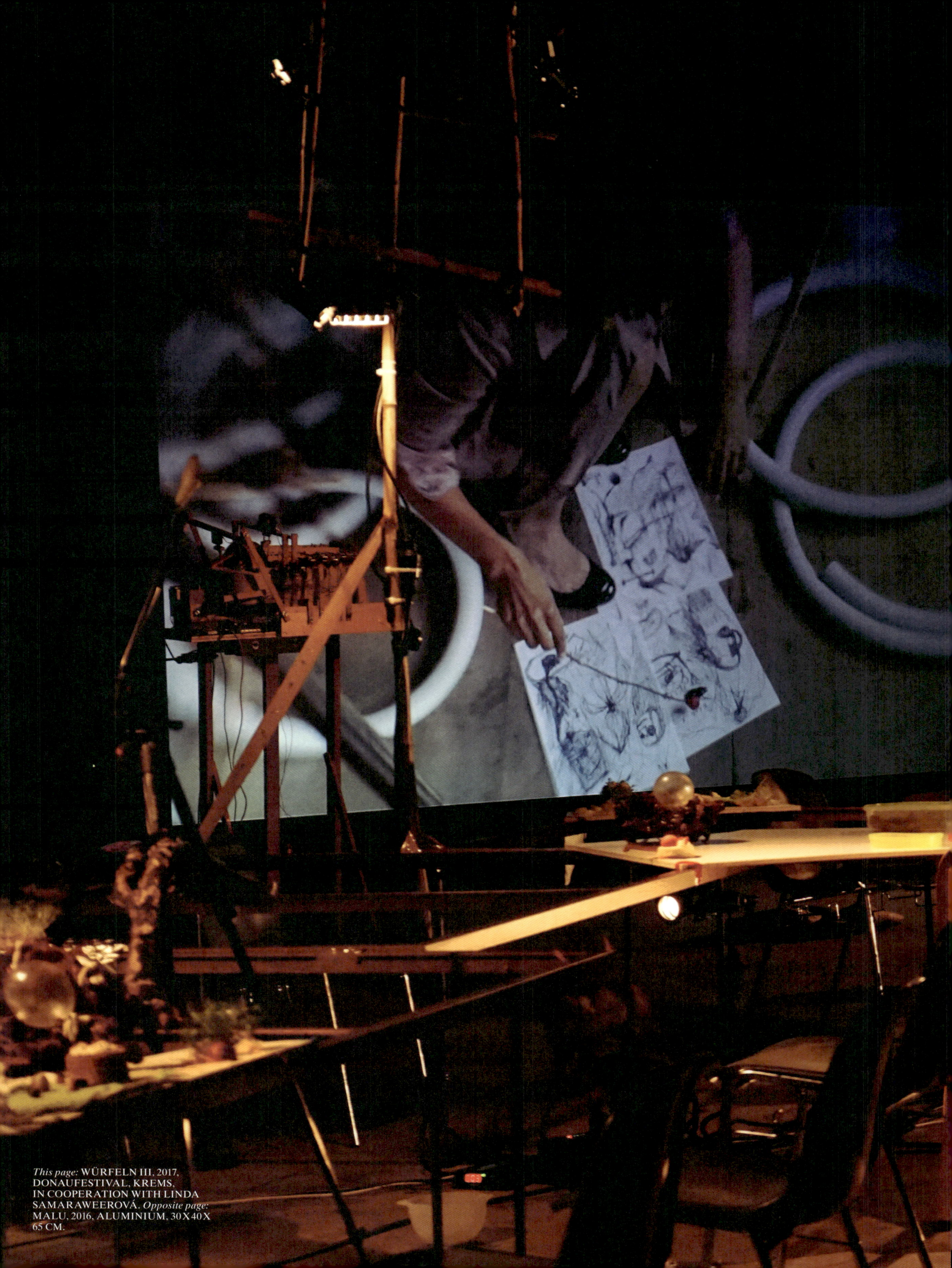

*This page:* WÜRFELN III, 2017, DONAUFESTIVAL, KREMS, IN COOPERATION WITH LINDA SAMARAWEEROVÁ. *Opposite page:* MALU, 2016, ALUMINIUM, 30X40X 65 CM.

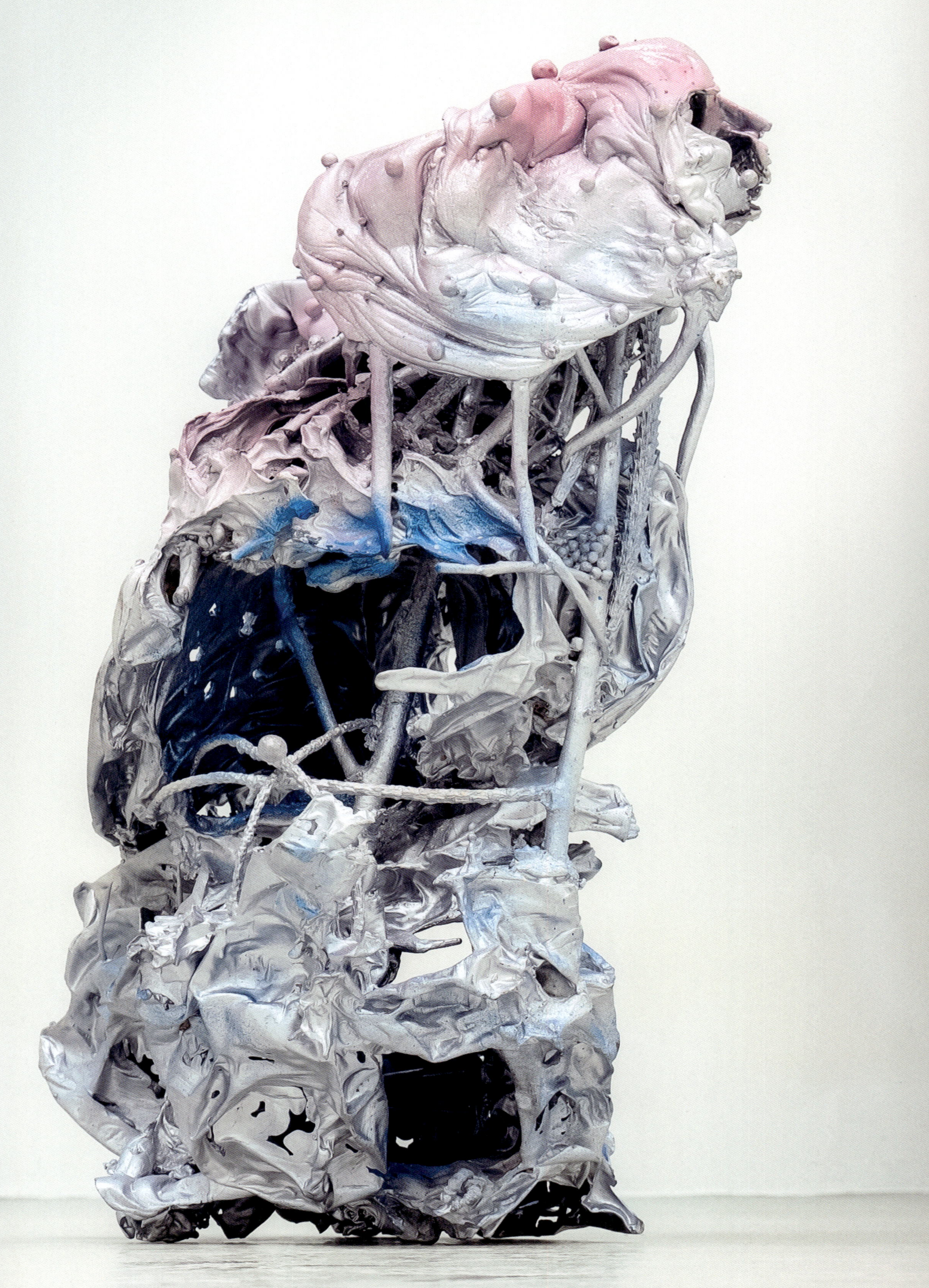

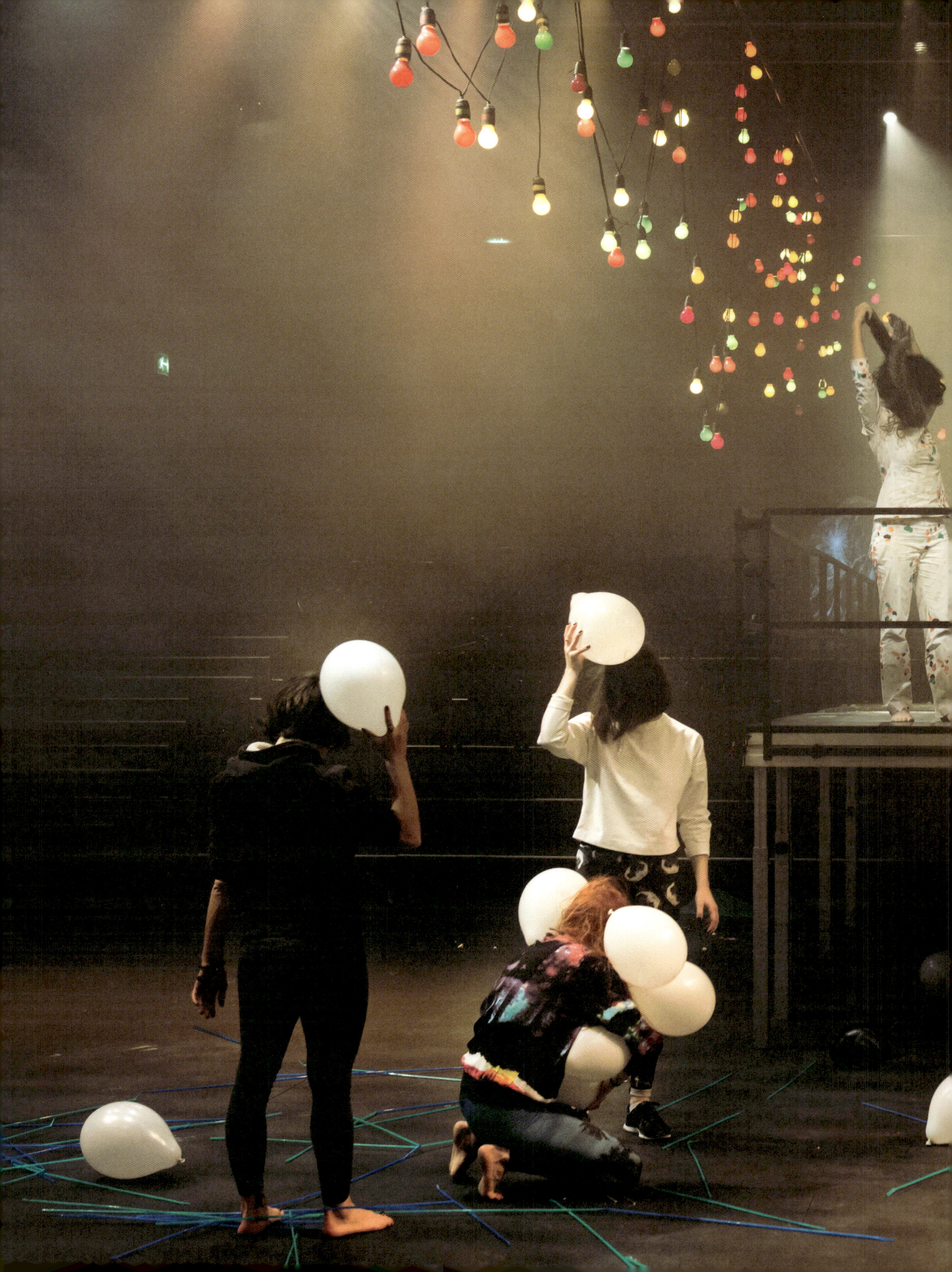

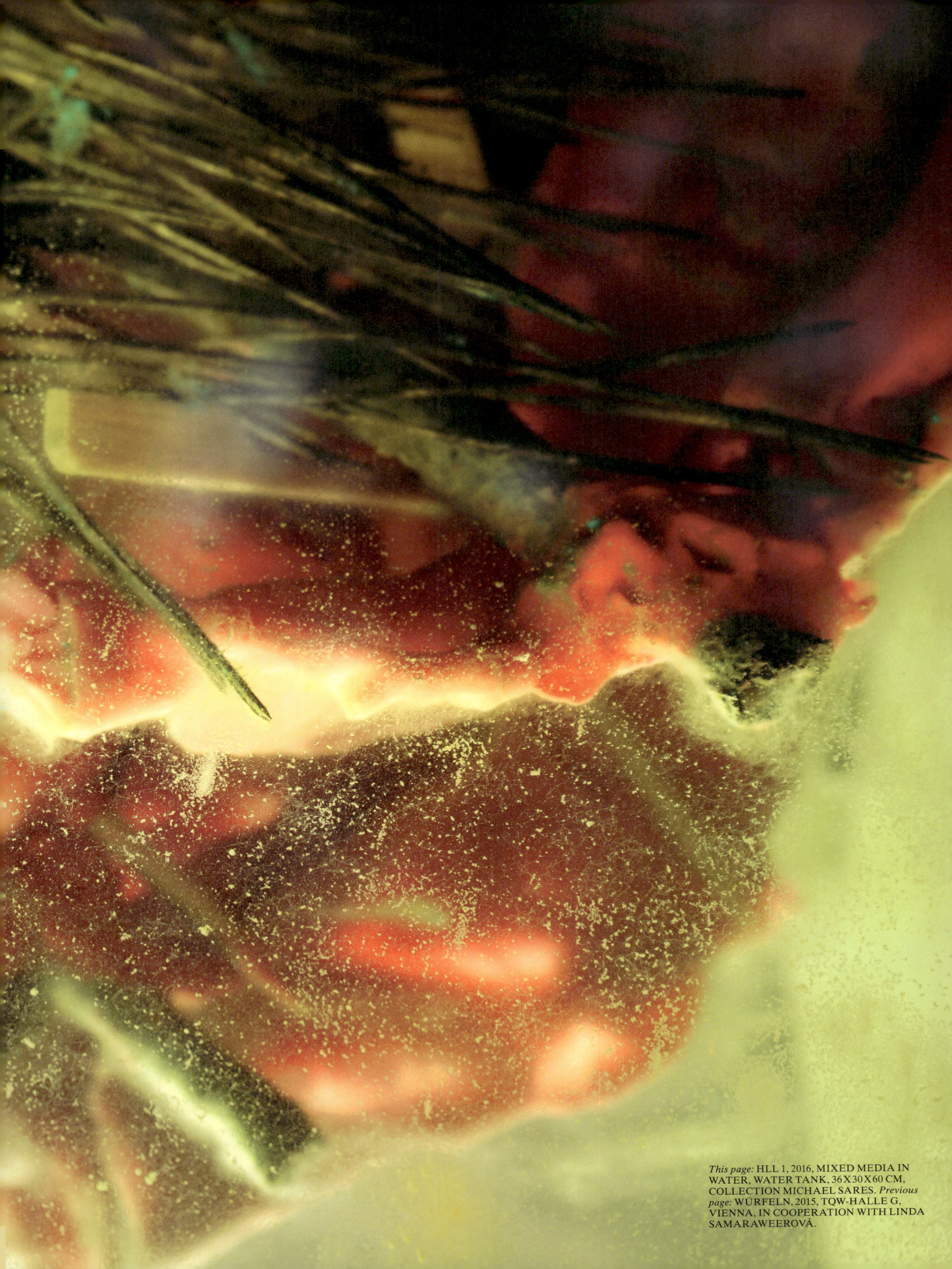

*This page:* HLL 1, 2016, MIXED MEDIA IN WATER, WATER TANK, 36 X 30 X 60 CM, COLLECTION MICHAEL SARES. *Previous page:* WÜRFELN, 2015, TQW-HALLE G, VIENNA, IN COOPERATION WITH LINDA SAMARAWEEROVÁ.

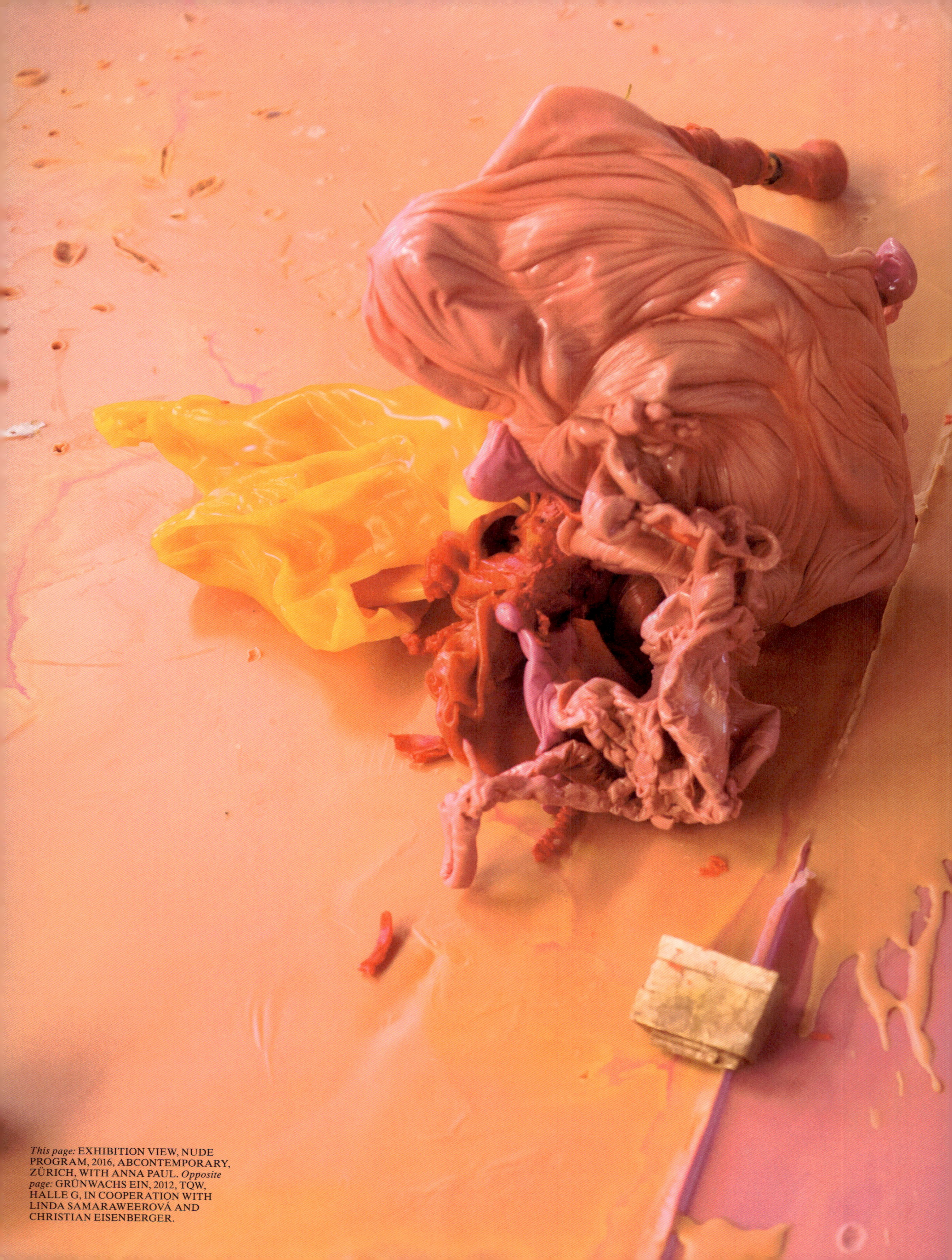

*This page:* EXHIBITION VIEW, NUDE PROGRAM, 2016, ABCONTEMPORARY, ZÜRICH, WITH ANNA PAUL. *Opposite page:* GRÜNWACHS EIN, 2012, TQW, HALLE G, IN COOPERATION WITH LINDA SAMARAWEEROVÁ AND CHRISTIAN EISENBERGER.

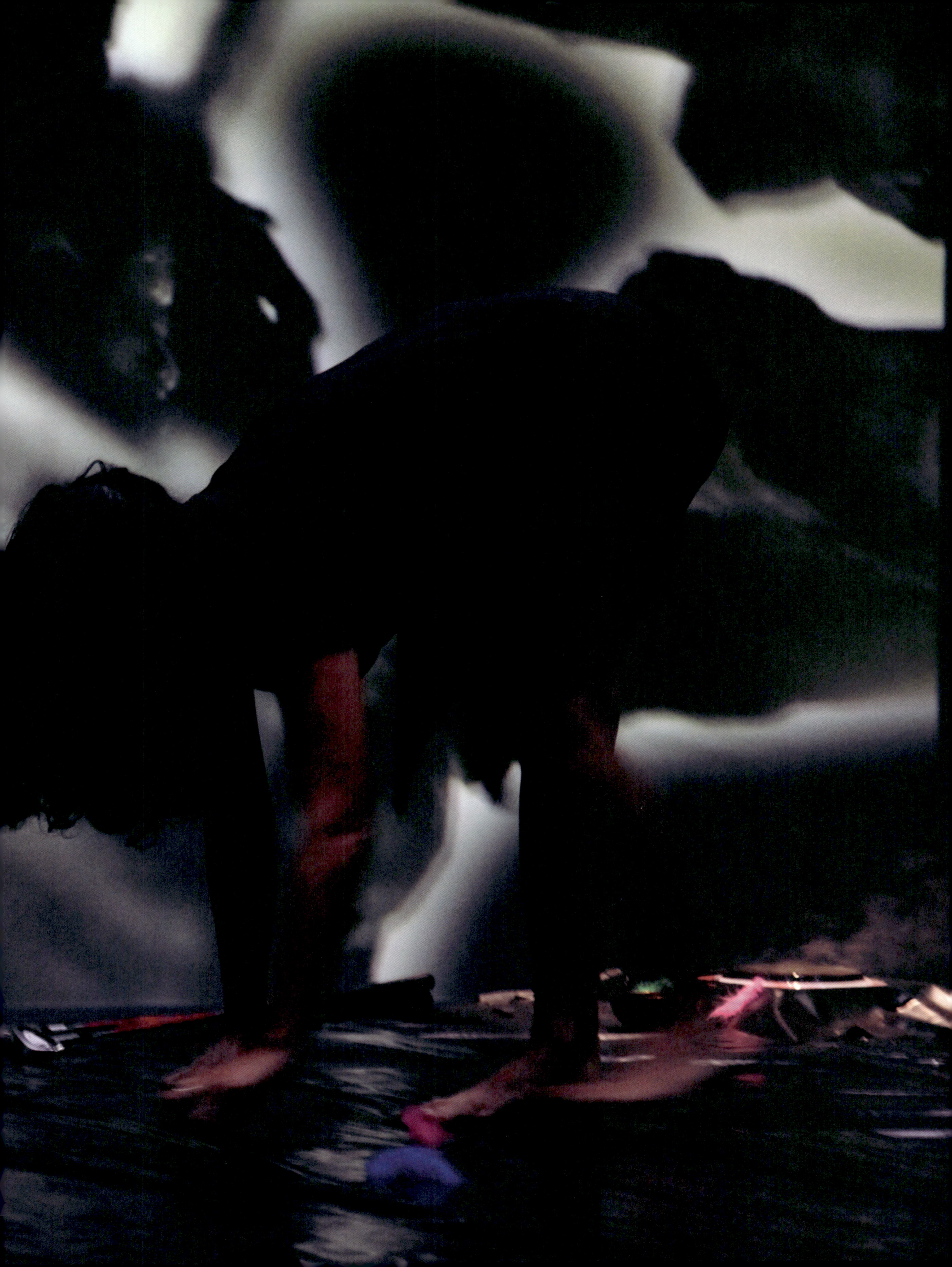

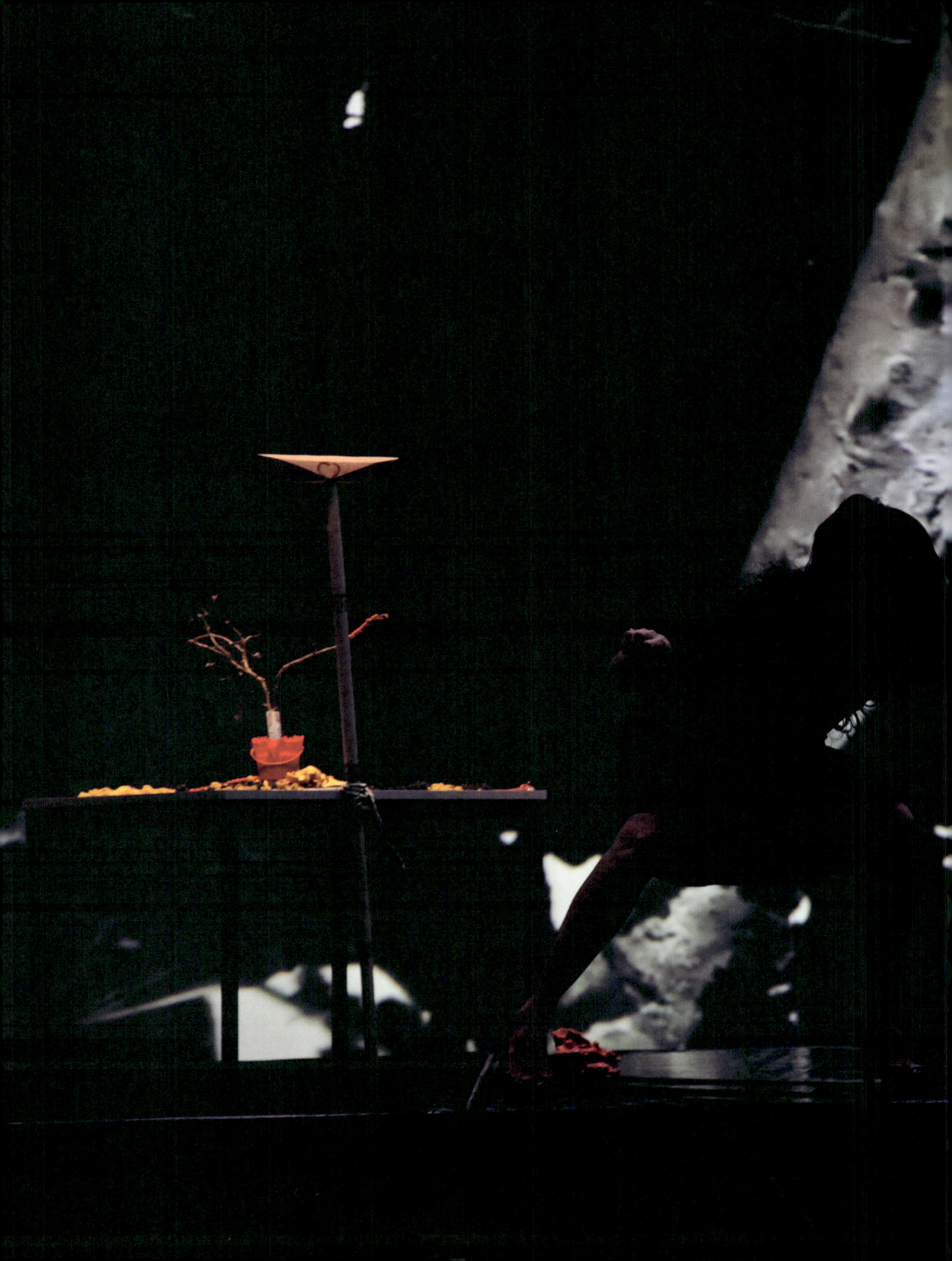

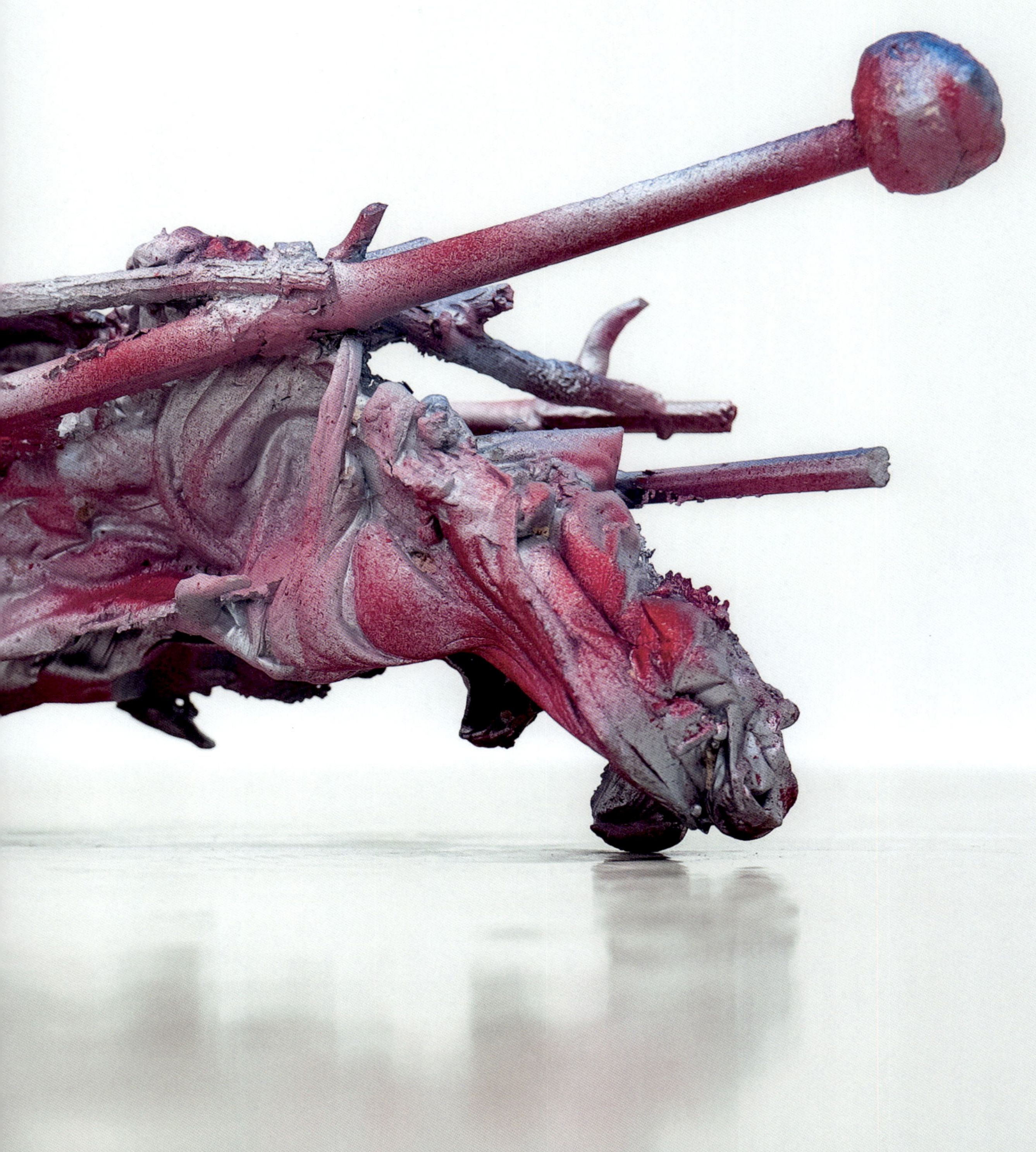

*This page:* SCHLAGZEUG, 2016, SPRAY PAINT ON ALUMINIUM, 86 X 20 X 24 CM. *Previous page:* GRÜNWACHS EIN, 2012, TQW, HALLE G, IN COOPERATION WITH LINDA SAMARAWEEROVÁ AND CHRISTIAN EISENBERGER.

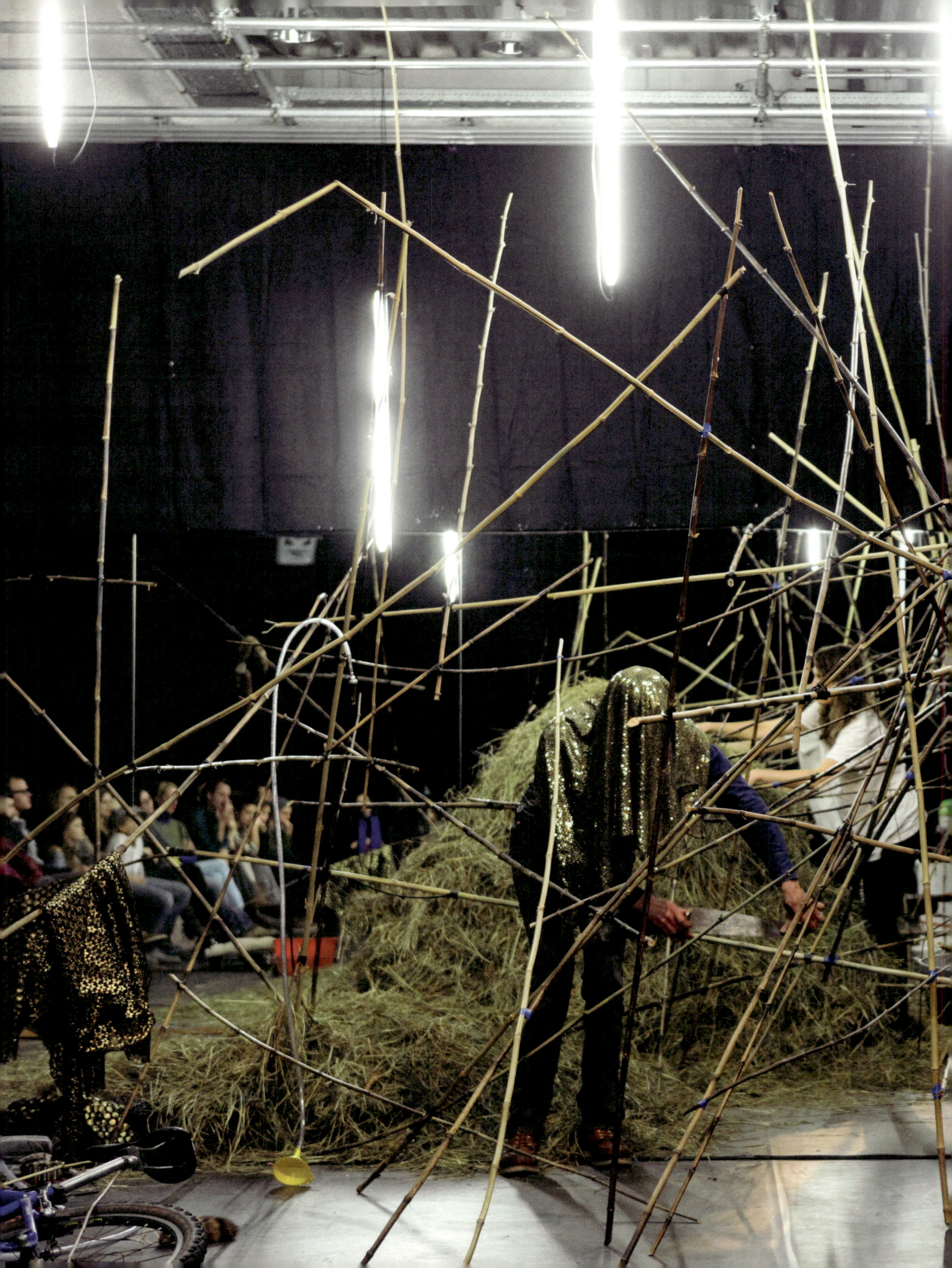

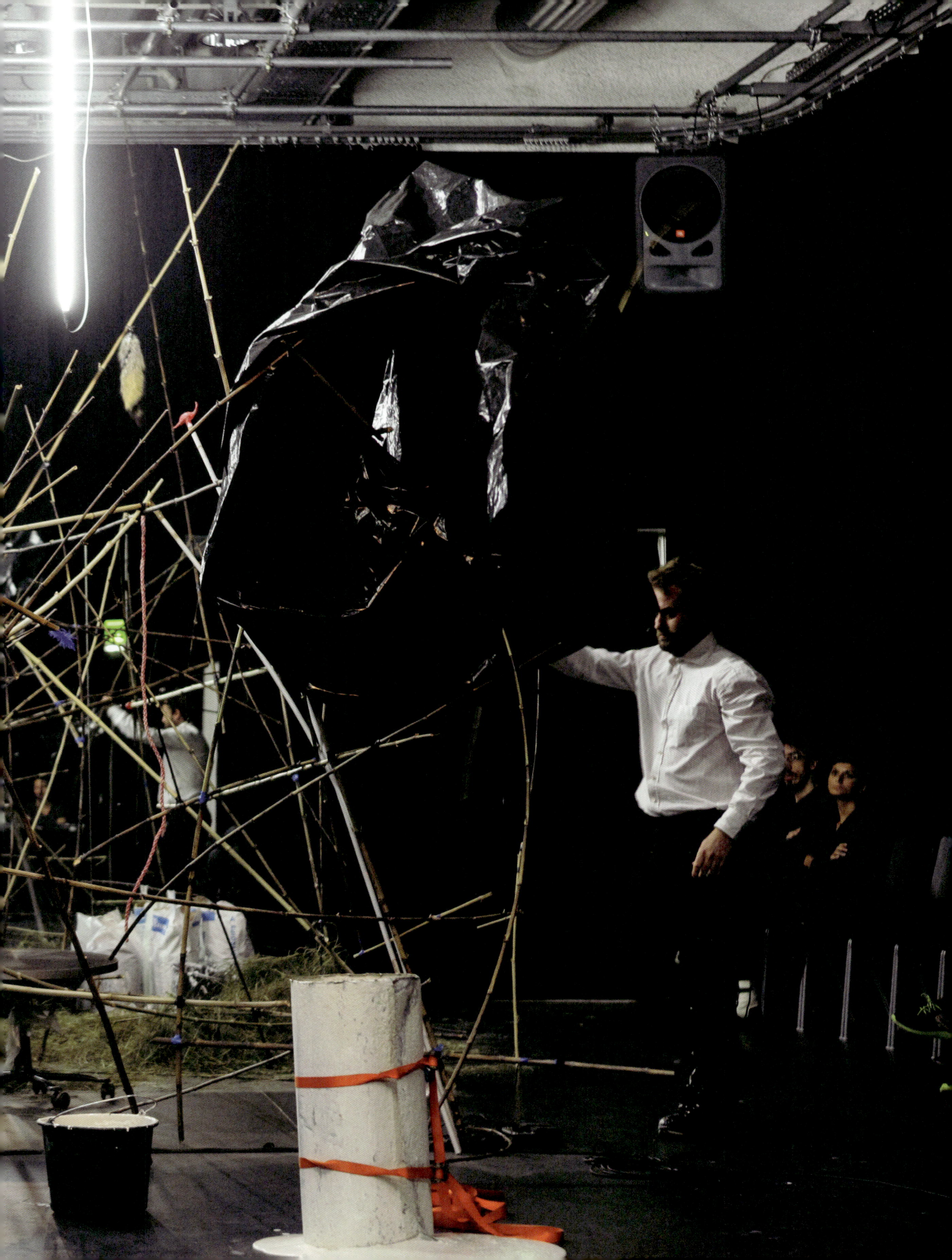

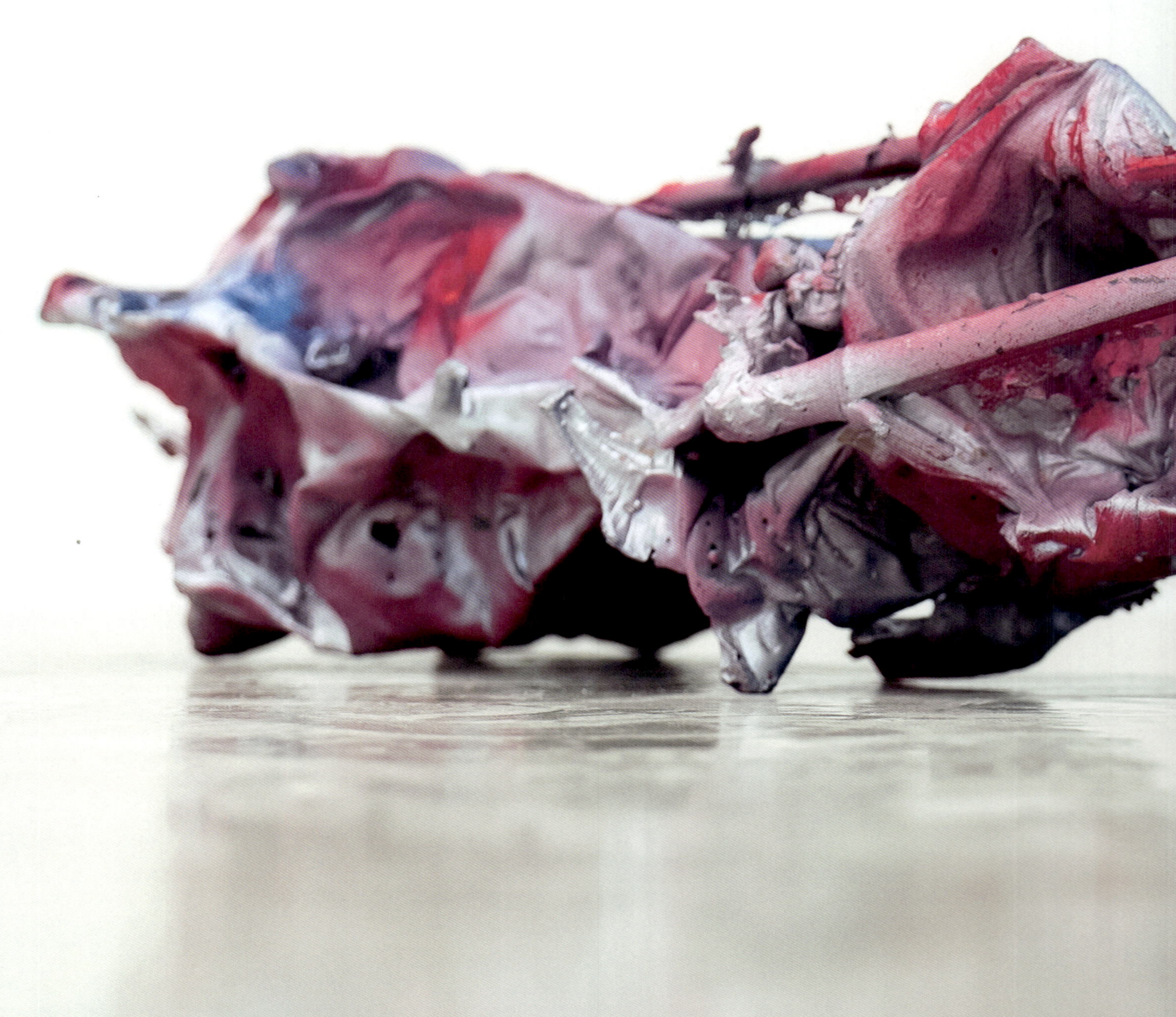

*This page:* SCHLAGZEUG, 2016, SPRAY PAINT ON ALUMINIUM, 86 X 20 X 24 CM. *Opposite page:* GRÜNWACHS EIN, 2012, TQW, HALLE G, IN COOPERATION WITH LINDA SAMARAWEEROVÁ AND CHRISTIAN EISENBERGER.

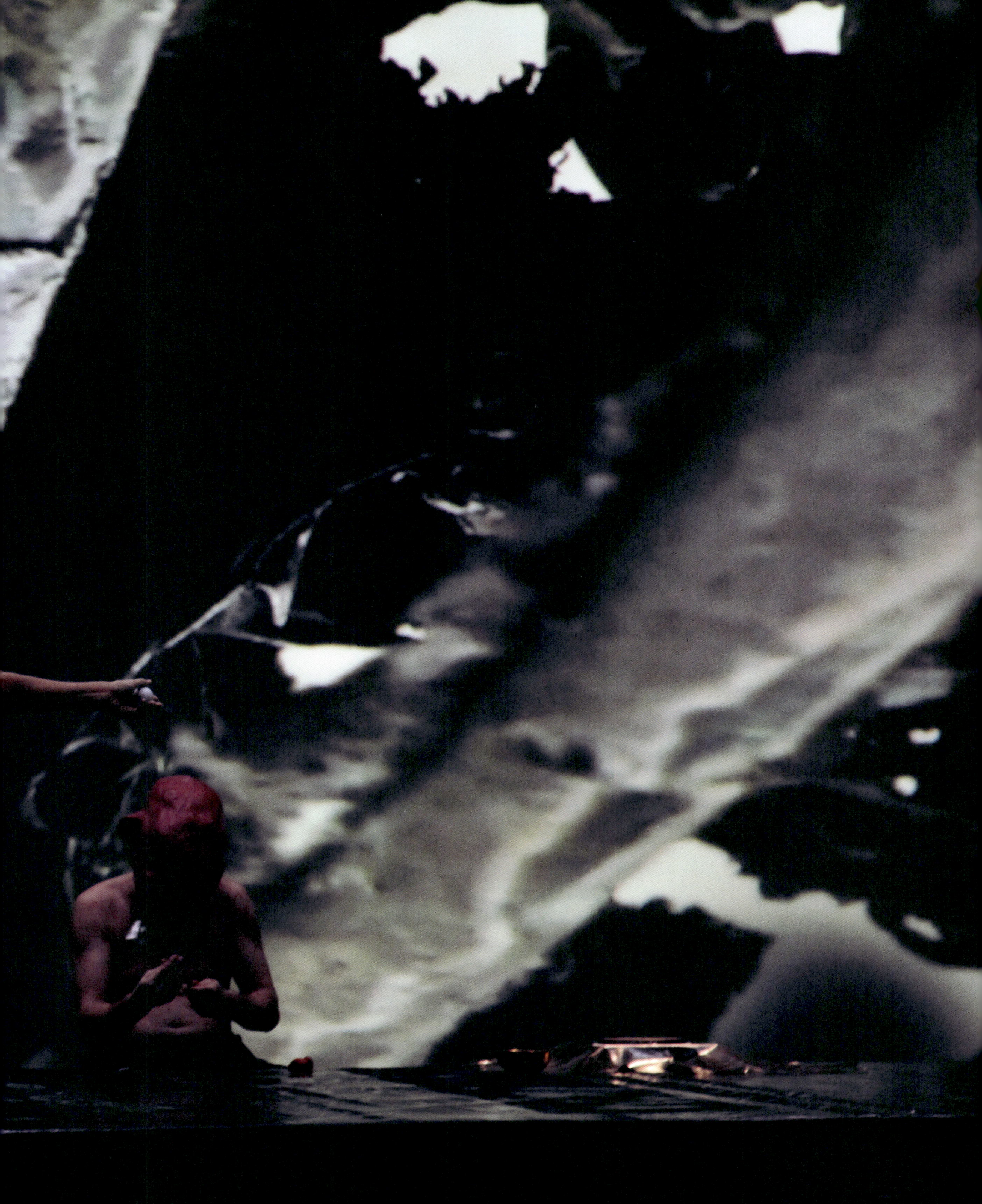

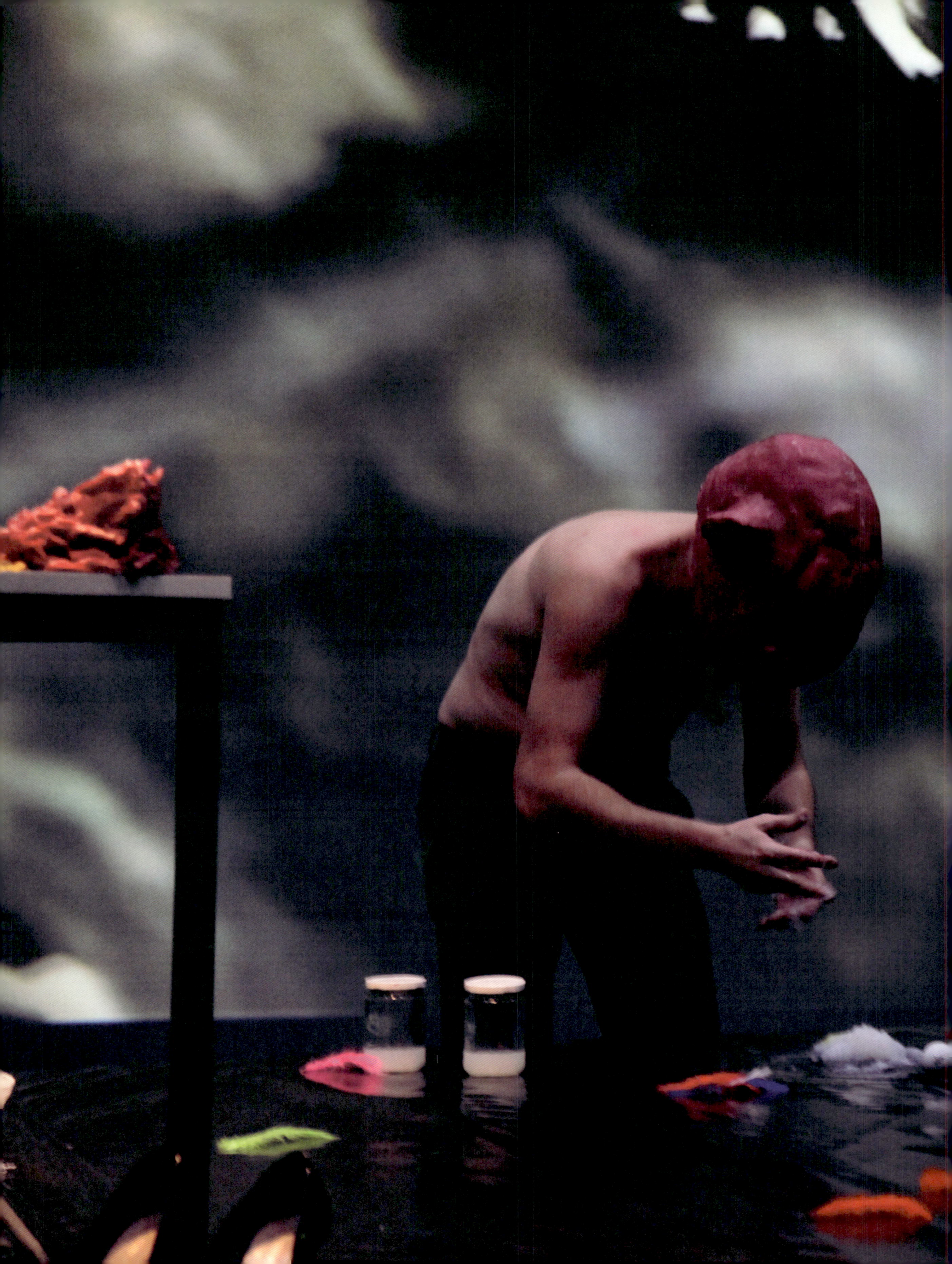

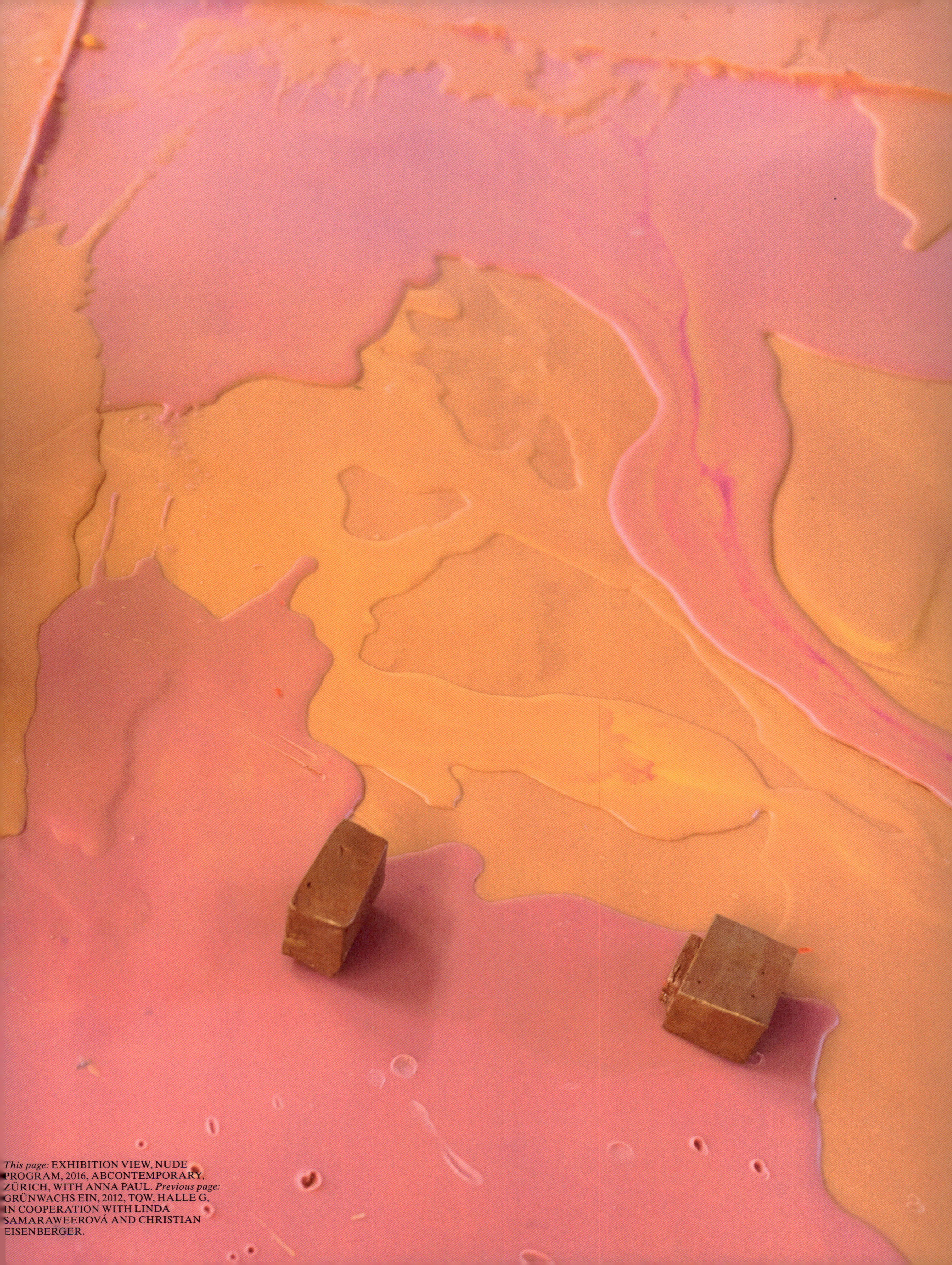

*This page:* EXHIBITION VIEW, NUDE PROGRAM, 2016, ABCONTEMPORARY, ZÜRICH, WITH ANNA PAUL. *Previous page:* GRÜNWACHS EIN, 2012, TQW, HALLE G, IN COOPERATION WITH LINDA SAMARAWEEROVÁ AND CHRISTIAN EISENBERGER.

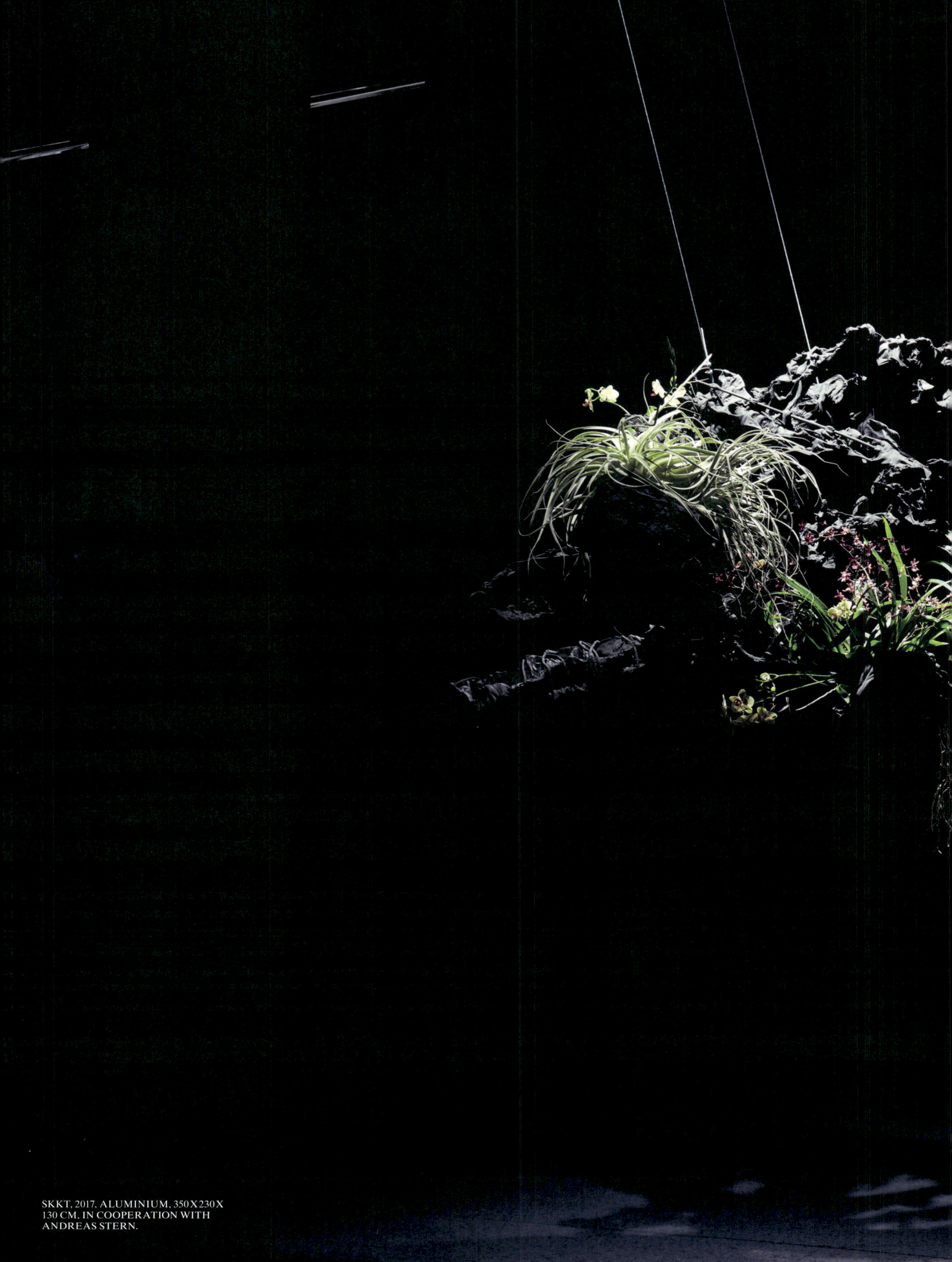

SKKT, 2017, ALUMINIUM, 350 X 230 X 130 CM, IN COOPERATION WITH ANDREAS STERN.

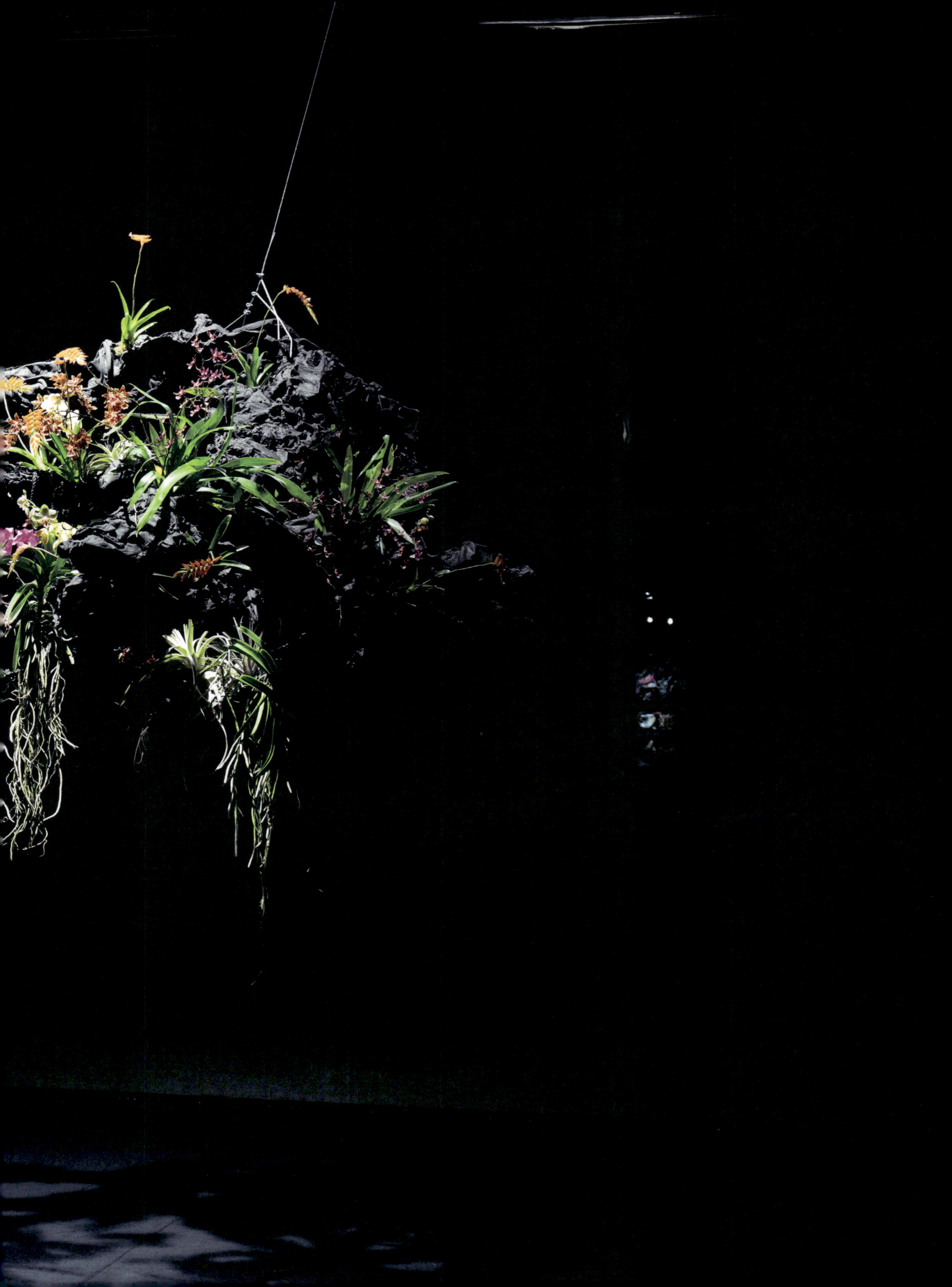

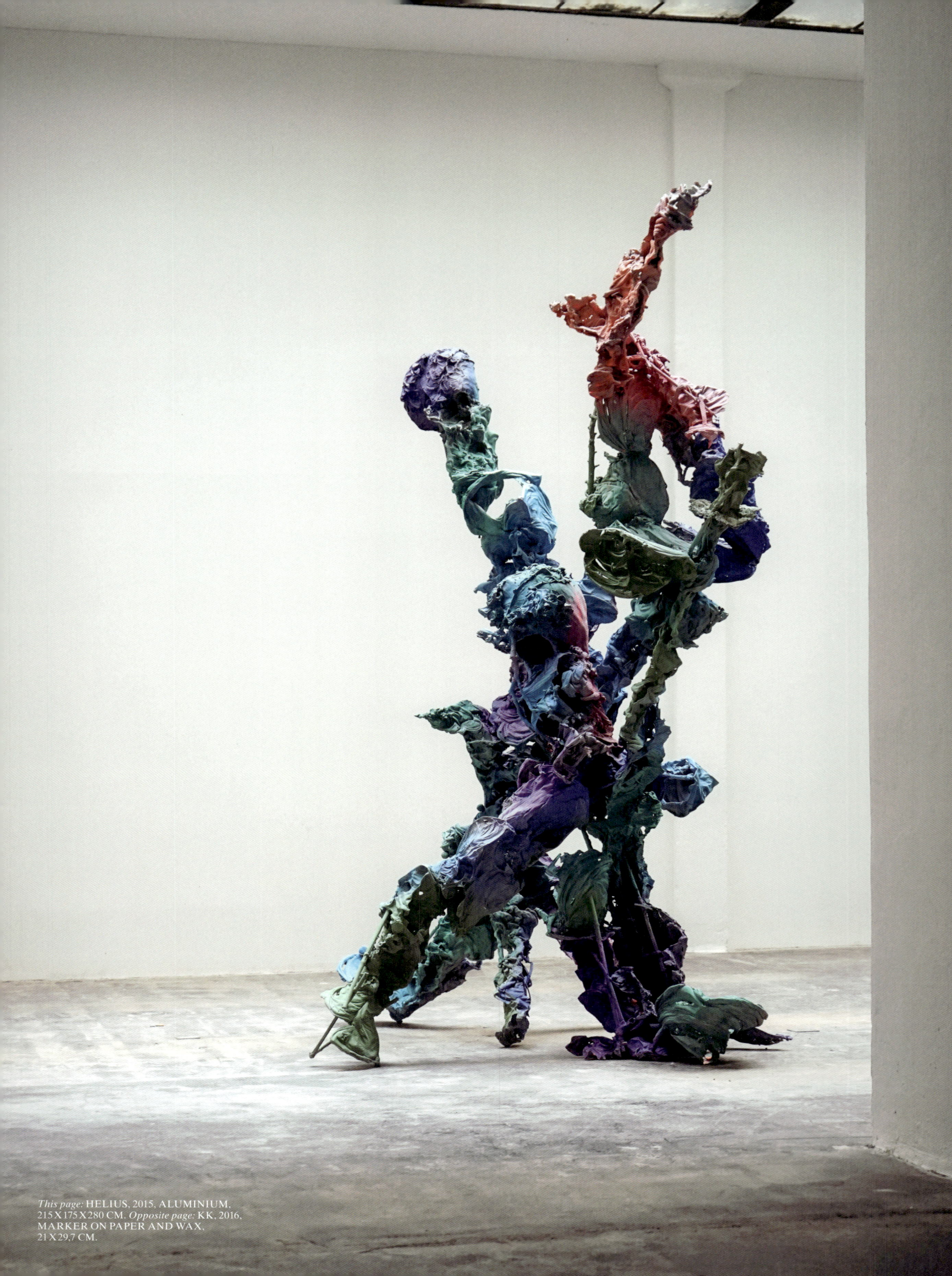

*This page:* HELIUS, 2015, ALUMINIUM, 215 X 175 X 280 CM. *Opposite page:* KK, 2016, MARKER ON PAPER AND WAX, 21 X 29,7 CM.

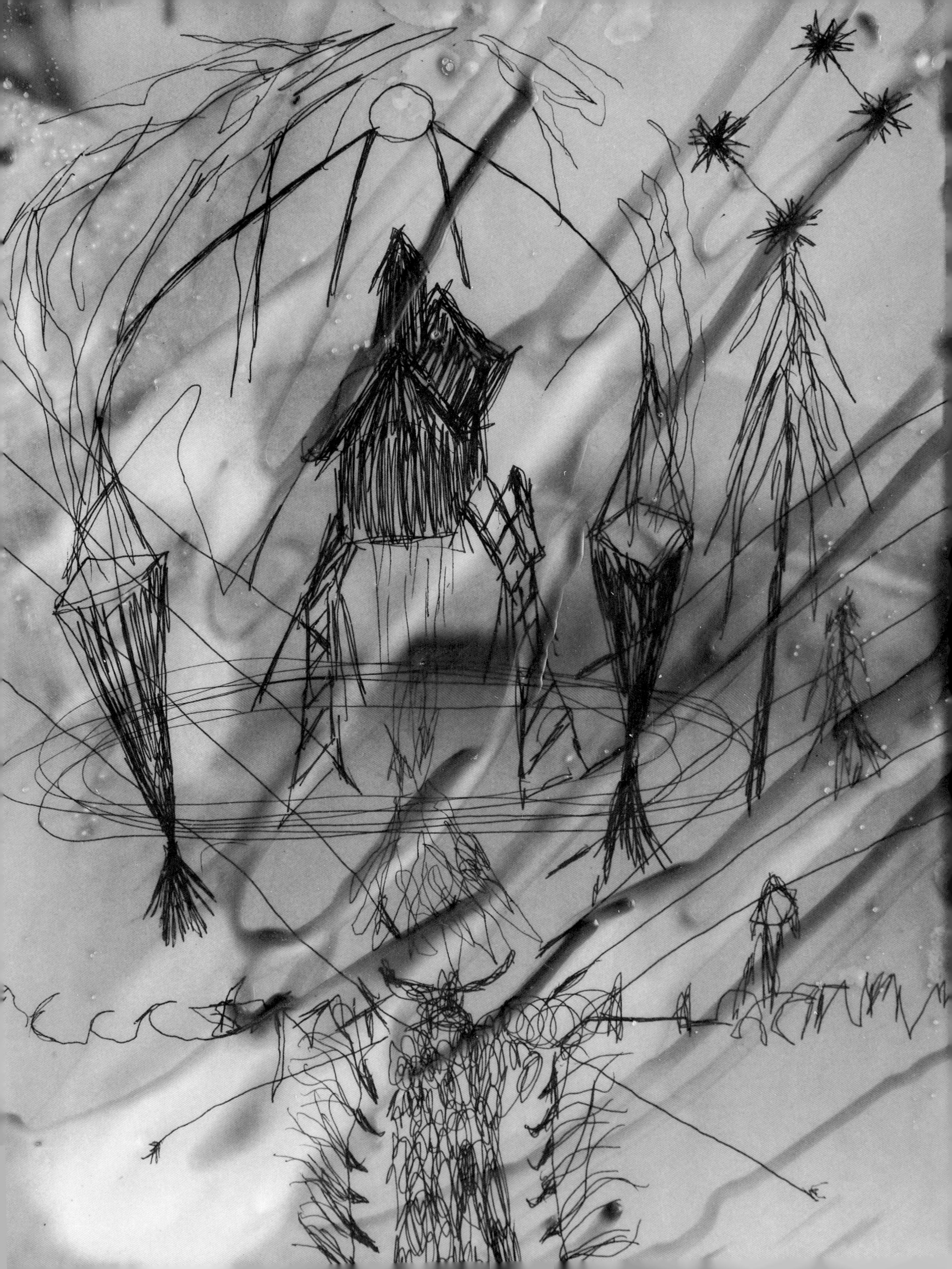

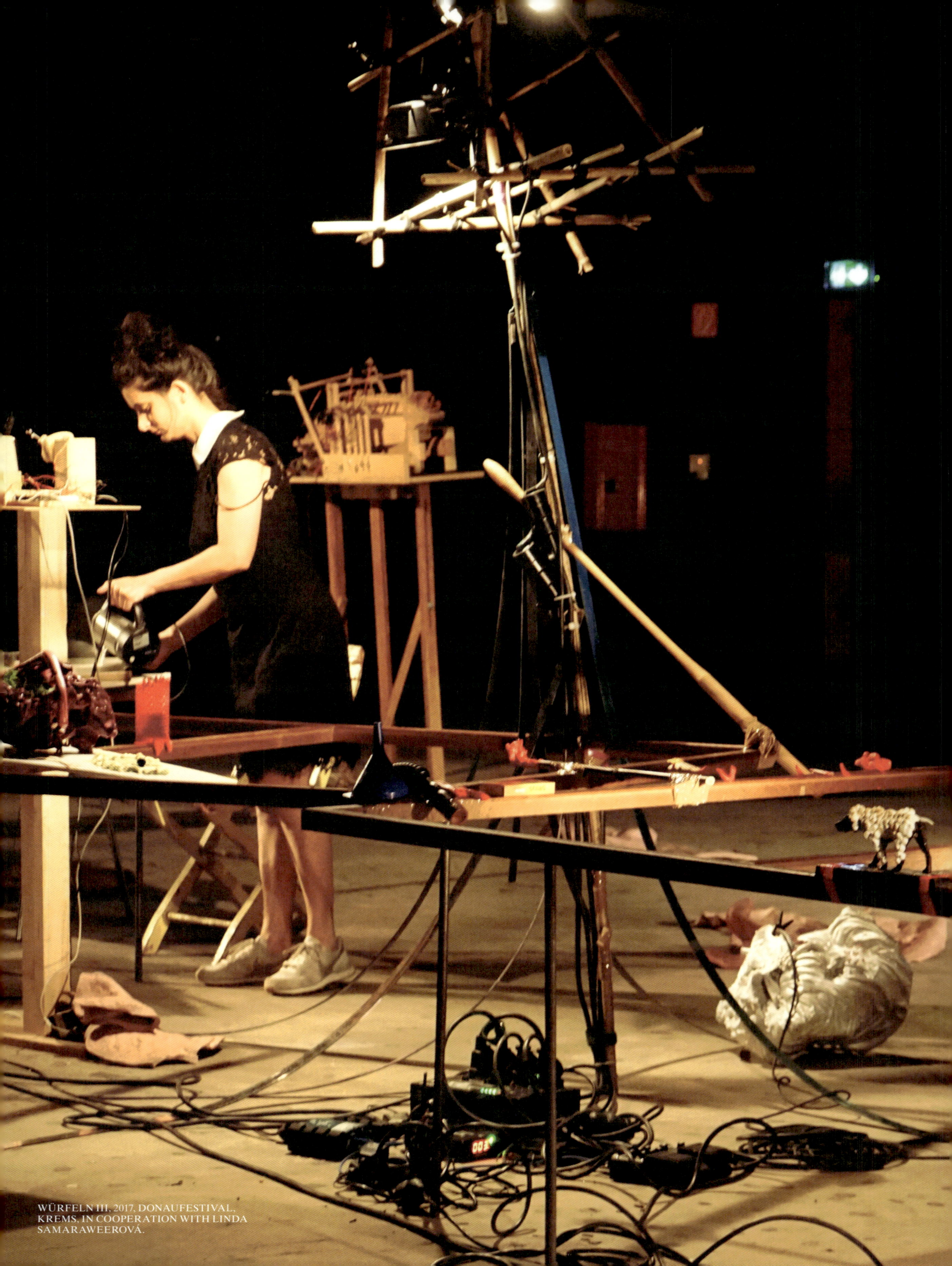

WÜRFELN III, 2017, DONAUFESTIVAL, KREMS, IN COOPERATION WITH LINDA SAMARAWEEROVÁ.

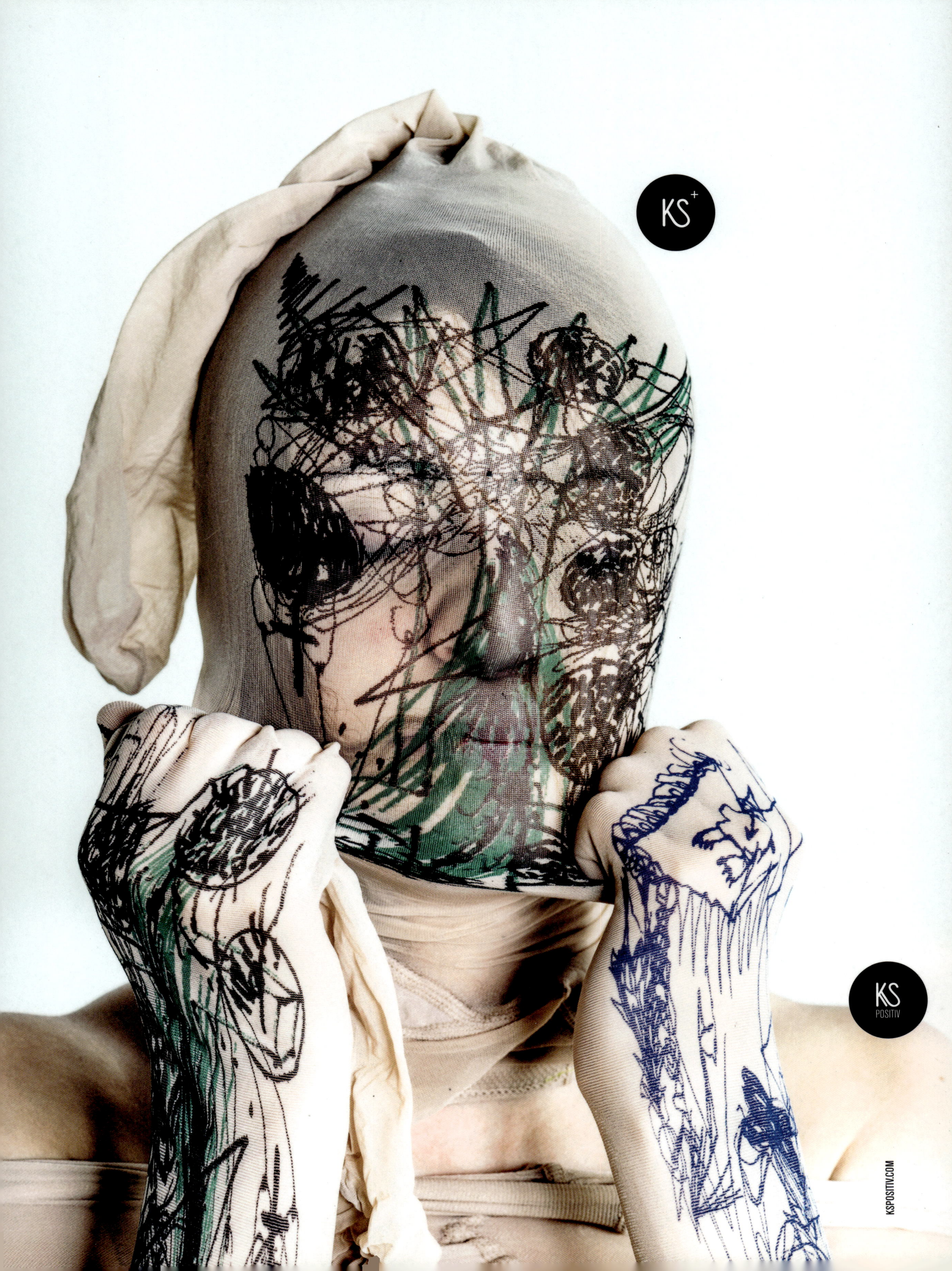
KS+
KS
POSITIV
KSPOSITIV.COM

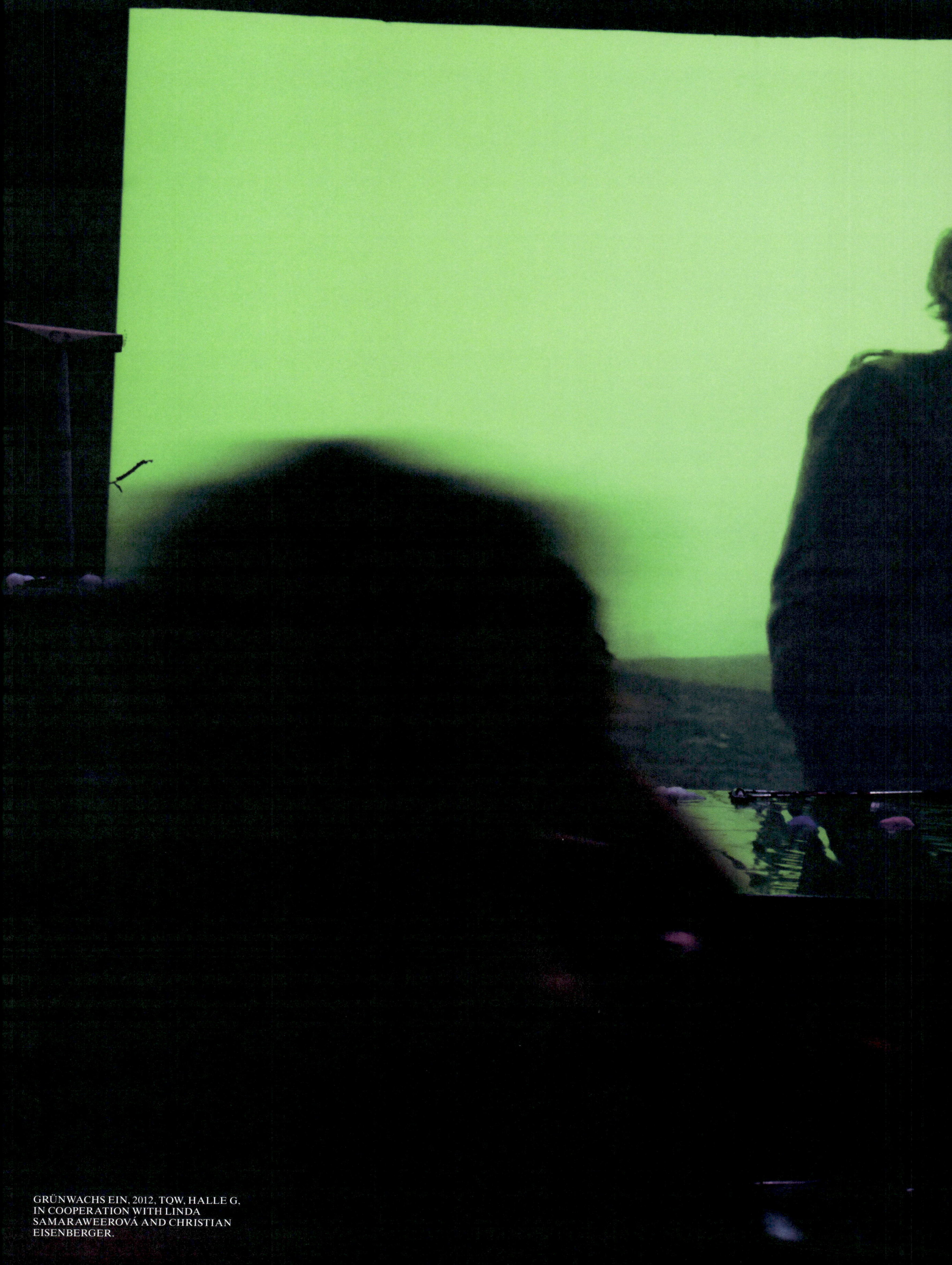

GRÜNWACHS EIN, 2012, TQW, HALLE G,
IN COOPERATION WITH LINDA
SAMARAWEEROVÁ AND CHRISTIAN
EISENBERGER.

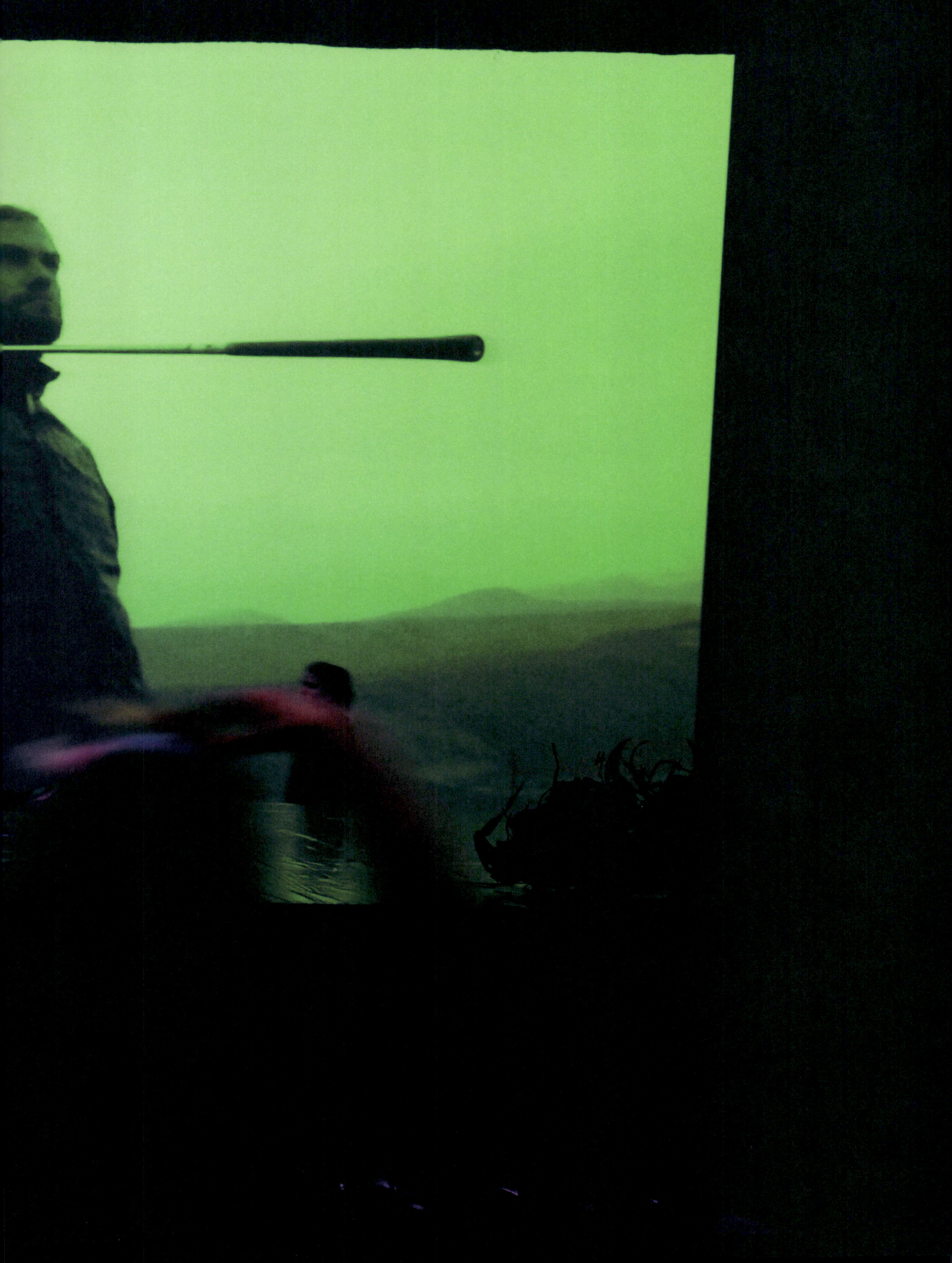

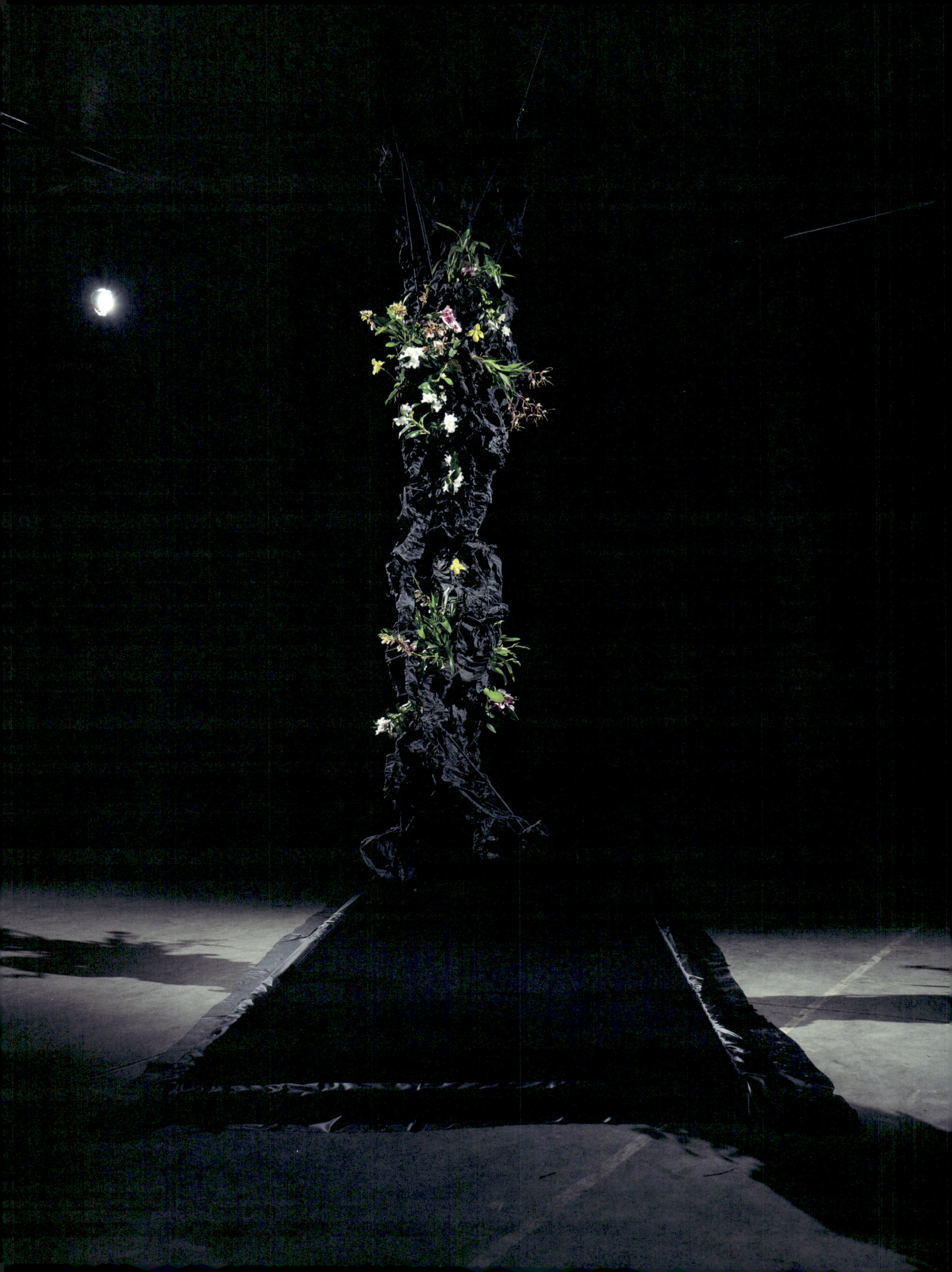

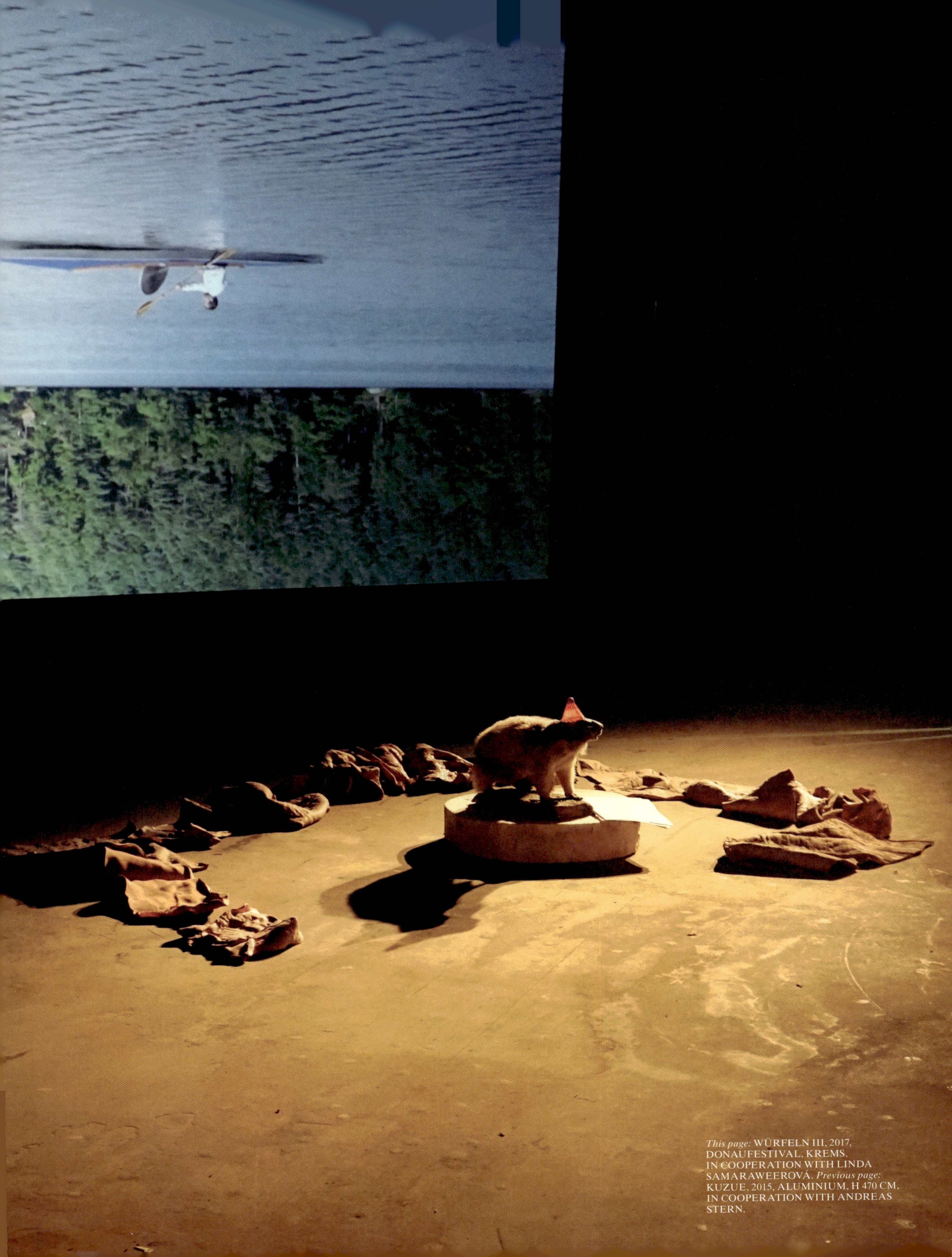

*This page:* WÜRFELN III, 2017, DONAUFESTIVAL, KREMS. IN COOPERATION WITH LINDA SAMARAWEEROVÁ. *Previous page:* KUZUE, 2015, ALUMINIUM, H 470 CM. IN COOPERATION WITH ANDREAS STERN.

*Published by*
VFMK VERLAG FÜR MODERNE KUNST GMBH
Salmgasse 4a
A-1030 Vienna
hello@vfmk.org
www.vfmk.org

ISBN 978-3-903153-91-2

Printed in Austria

*Distribution*
EUROPE: LKG, www.lkg-va.de
CH: AVA, www.ava.ch
UK: CORNERHOUSE PUBLICATIONS, www.cornerhousepublications.org
USA: D.A.P., www.artbook.com

*Bibliographic information published by Die Deutsche Nationalbibliothek*
Die Deutsche Bibliothek lists this publication in the Deutsche Nationalbibliografie; detailed bibliographic data is available in the Internet at http://dnb.ddb.de.

*Editor*
KARL KARNER

*Editing*
SOFIA GOSCINSKI

*Concept*
MARTIN FAISS, SOFIA GOSCINSKI, KARL KARNER

*Graphic design*
MARTIN FAISS

*Lithography*
PAUL GASSER

*Printing*
HOLZHAUSEN

*Print Run*
1.000

*Graphic design Ads KSpositiv*
NINA MARKART, STELLA PLAPP

*Photographers*
OSKAR SCHMIDT (exhibition views sculptures and details HÖLLENTOR, Gallery Lisa Kandlhofer, 2016)
ANNA PAUL (exhibition views NUDE PROGRAM, ABContemporary, Zürich, 2016)
KILIAN A. FLITSCH (installation views SKKT, KUZUE, Die Halle, Feldbach 2017)
KLAUS PICHLER (Ads KSpositiv)
KARL SCHROTTER (sculptures AUS SAMTKASTEN, 2410 PUNKTEN AUS ALAN GREENSPAN)

*Performances*
GRÜNWACHS EIN (2012, TQW, Halle G, Vienna)
In cooperation with: LINDA SAMARAWEEROVÁ and CHRISTIAN EISENBERGER and GUESTS
Photos: PETER KASPERAK

WHITE FOR (2013, TQW Studio, Vienna)
In cooperation with: LINDA SAMARAWEEROVÁ
Guests: ANGELIKA LODERER, ROSI REHFORMEN, ROYL CULBERTSON
Photos: LAURA SAMARAWEEROVÁ

WÜRFELN (2015, TQW-Halle G, Vienna)
In cooperation with: LINDA SAMARAWEEROVÁ
Guests: NATALIA DNES, TANIA PASHYNSKA, ANIA PASHYNSKA, ROSI REHFORMEN, SCHROTTY, IRENA TAVPASH
Stage Design by: ANDREAS STERN
Music composed by: SIR TRALALA
Text by: BRUNO BATINIC, SUSANNE SCHUDA
Photos: JUDITH STEHLIK

WÜRFELN FELL MIT BALL (2016, Künstlerhaus, Halle für Kunst & Medien, Graz)
In cooperation with: LINDA SAMARAWEEROVÁ
In the frame of the exhibition: 'YES, BUT IS IT PERFORMABLE? UNTERSUCHUNGEN DES PERFORMATIVEN PARADOXES', 2016
Music composed by: ROBERT JÍŠA
Photos: MARKUS KROTTENDORFER and JUDITH STEHLIK

WÜRFELN III (2017, Donaufestival, Krems)
In cooperation with: LINDA SAMARAWEEROVÁ
Guests: ALFRED LENZ, RÉKA KUTAS
Music composed by: ROBERT JÍŠA
Photos: JUDITH STEHLIK, DAVID VISNJIC and KK

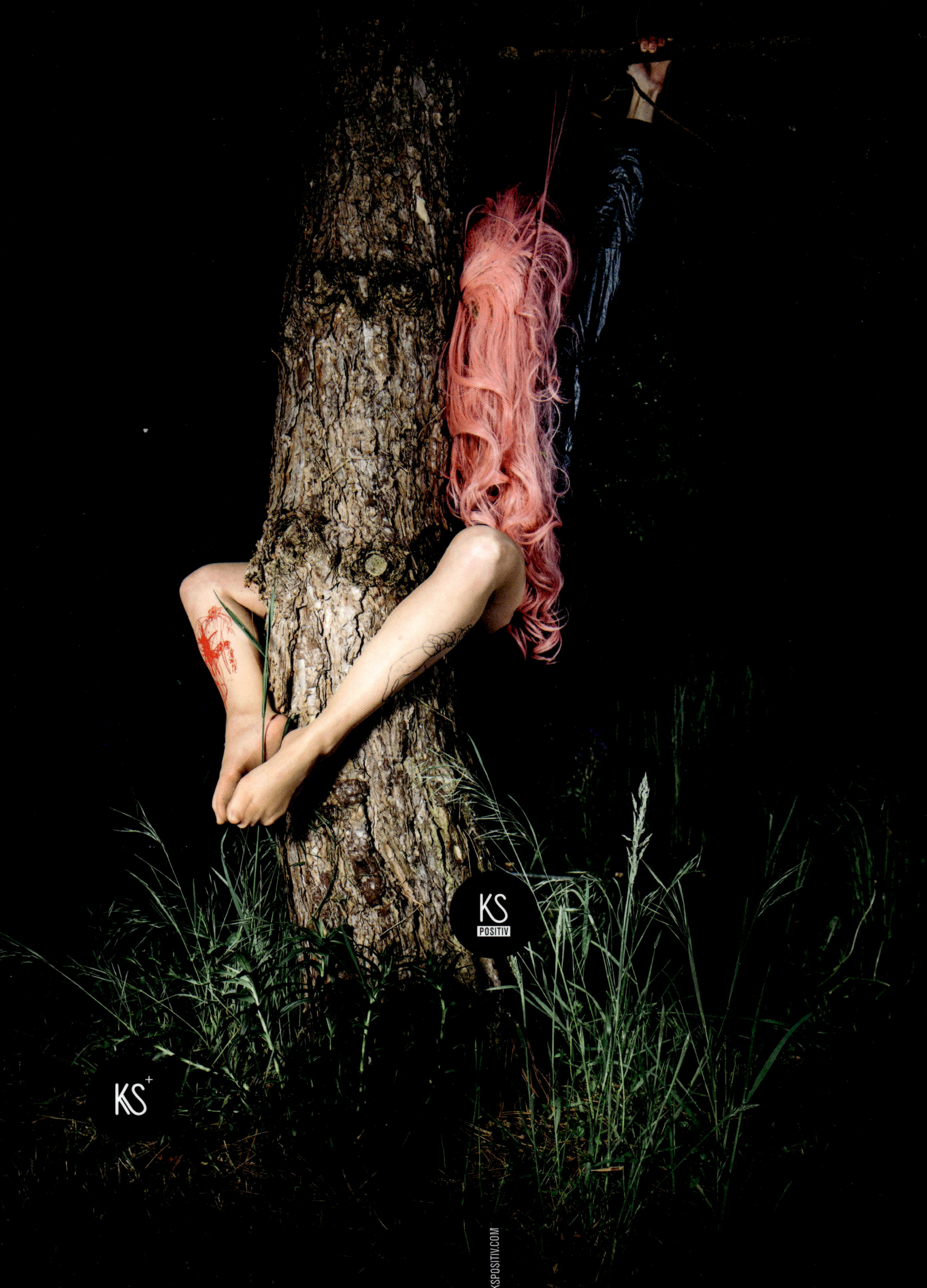
KS
POSITIV
KS+
KSPOSITIV.COM

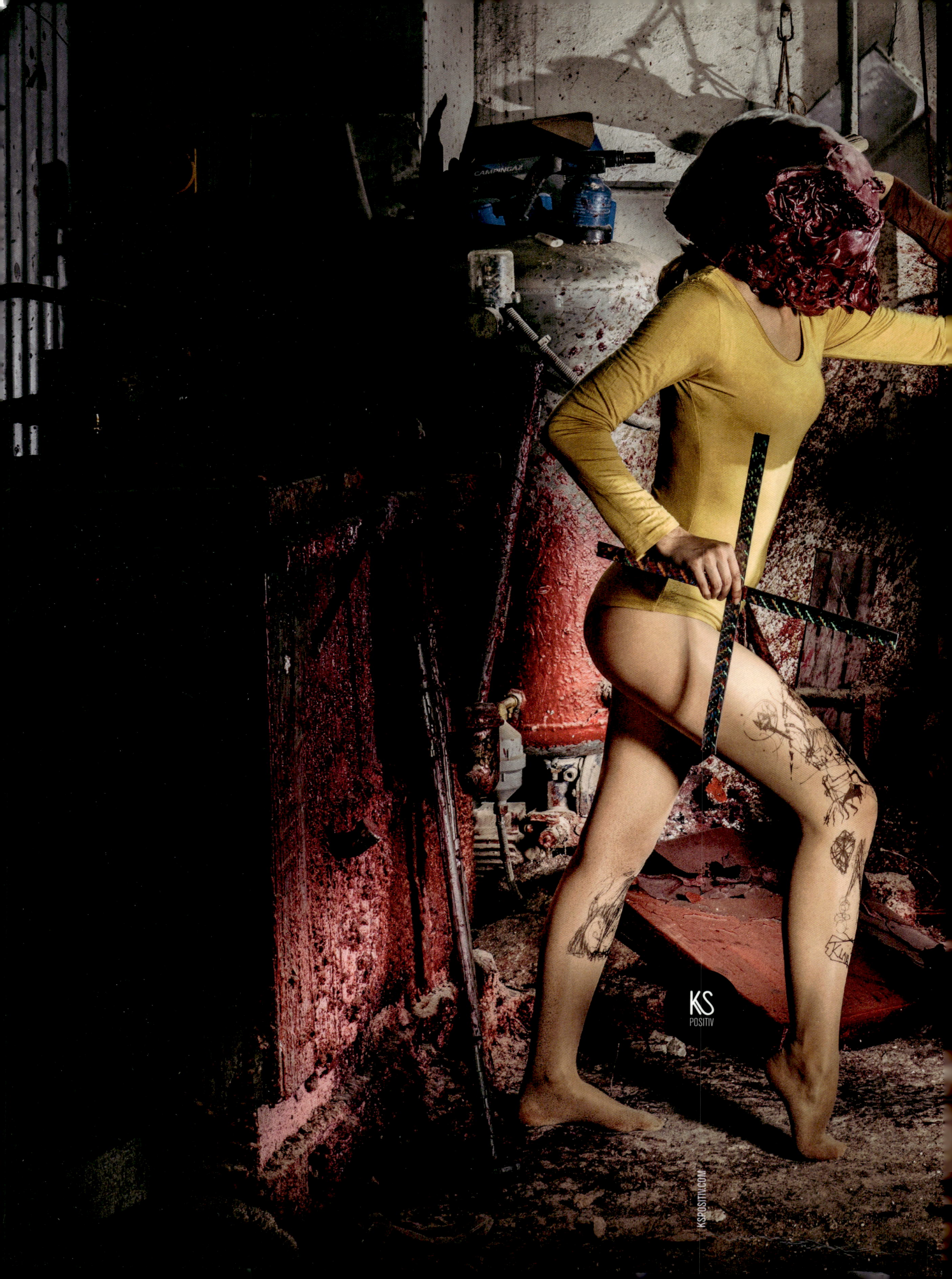
CAMPINGAZ
KS
POSITIV
KSPOSITIV.COM